The Kelowna Story

THE KELOWNA STORY

AN OKANAGAN HISTORY

Sharron J. Simpson

HARBOUR PUBLISHING

Harbour Publishing Co. Ltd.
P.O. Box 219, Madeira Park, BC, V0N 2H0
www.harbourpublishing.com

DUST JACKET IMAGES BASED ON PHOTOGRAPHS COURTESY OF KELOWNA PUBLIC ARCHIVES—FRONT COVER: postcard of Bernard Avenue, circa 1930, #5228; BACK COVER: the first apple trees planted in the Okanagan, #2223; FRONT FLAP PHOTO: the SS *Sicamous* under construction at the Okanagan Landing shipyard, circa 1914, #6196; AUTHOR PHOTO: Stuart Kernaghan, xyphotos.ca.

FRONTMATTER PHOTOGRAPHS COURTESY OF KELOWNA PUBLIC ARCHIVES—PAGE II: panorama of the city of Kelowna from Dilworth Mountain, 1909, #3047; OPPOSITE THIS PAGE: an elegant day of boating on Okanagan Lake with Knox Mountain in the background, 1910, #1355; PAGE VI: tall, heavy wooden ladders were required to pick apples from the early varieties of large trees planted in the valley, #3074; PAGE VIII: cars waiting to take delegates from the Western Irrigation Convention of 1912 on a sightseeing tour of Kelowna, #2196.

EDITED BY—Pam Robertson
DUST JACKET, COVER AND TEXT DESIGN BY—Five Seventeen
INDEX BY—Ellen Hawman

Printed on FSC certified paper with 10% recycled stock and soy-based ink
Printed and bound in Canada

Harbour Publishing acknowledges financial support from the Government of Canada through the Canada Book Fund and the Canada Council for the Arts, and from the Province of British Columbia through the BC Arts Council and the Book Publishing Tax Credit.

LIBRARY AND ARCHIVES CANADA CATALOGUING IN PUBLICATION

Simpson, Sharron J., 1938–
    The Kelowna story : an Okanagan history / Sharron J. Simpson.

Includes bibliographical references and index.
ISBN 978-1-55017-539-4

    1. Kelowna (B.C.)—History. I. Title.

FC3849.K36S56 2011   971.1′5   C2011-904634-2

For Payton and James—

With hopes that someday they will add
their stories about growing up in Kelowna to
the stories in this book

Contents

INTRODUCTION:

Kelowna's Stories

Kelowna has changed profoundly over the past few years. People arrive from far-off places knowing they want to live here. Others choose to live here though they work elsewhere. The population has mushroomed as orchards have become townhouses, and wilderness mountaintops are suddenly laced with streets that deer comfortably saunter down in the middle of the day. Motley collections of shops become smart shopping districts, world-renowned artists tell audiences that they've heard Kelowna is a cool place to play and the new university adds intellectual pizzazz to the sunshine.

The transformation sometimes becomes furious when parkland is challenged by development. Or when high-rise proponents argue with those who value history and want to honour the community's roots. Or when established residential areas struggle to retain their character as densification becomes the latest mantra. For newcomer and old-timer alike, it is a challenge to know what is right, or wise, or how to best preserve that elusive quality that makes us all want to live here. For those of us who call Kelowna home, perhaps a look back will offer the insights and the context we need to make decisions about the future with confidence and wisdom.

I think part of the turmoil is caused by Kelowna no longer having a collective memory. Those choosing to move here often arrive without knowing the why or the how, the who and the when, of the city they now live in. History has a way of providing context. Why is there a sawmill on prime lakeshore land? Why is Bernard Avenue so wide and still lined with low brick buildings? Who was Bernard? Why are Okanagan Mission, Rutland and Glenmore the unique communities they are? I'm hopeful these stories of Kelowna's past will provide some of the missing links and serve as a bridge between those who have lived here awhile and those who have recently arrived.

I'm also a great proponent of the notion that history is best told through the stories of ordinary people. While we've had the occasional lord and lady settle here, most of the stories in this book are about ordinary people who lived ordinary lives. Our notion of "ordinary," however, has changed over time. Few today would think it "ordinary" to walk over mountain ranges to collect mail or buy supplies. Most of us couldn't imagine climbing into a narrow pipe to scrape the rust off the inside as an "ordinary" job. Rowing freight from one end of the lake to the other is no longer "ordinary." Even building our own road, in the face of government indifference, isn't "ordinary." In their time, those who did these truly extraordinary things were simply doing what needed to be done to get ahead. And their stories tell of the remarkable investment early settlers made in this community.

I am also abundantly aware of the pitfalls of writing a narrative history. There are many knowledgeable people in Kelowna who don't necessarily call themselves historians but know about or were part of many of the stories in this book. I know too that some will remember things differently than I have. I apologize to those readers. Try as I did to check my facts, it was sometimes hard to find out if the Lake View Hotel had twenty-three rooms or twenty-five, or whether Bernard Lequime left Kelowna in 1901 or 1902. Or whether the date recorded was when a decision was made to build a boat or when the boat was launched. Sometimes my only source of information was the memories of other people, and they may not have remembered too well either. I hope those who disagree with how my stories unfold will be generous if they remember otherwise.

In writing this book, I've realized that early days are much more fun to read about than more recent times. Sometimes it is the sheer audaciousness of what was being attempted, or language that now sounds quaint, or the sense of unlimited possibility that pervaded so many early adventures. Time also changes our perceptions, and the discrimination that was once commonplace reminds us that we have, fortunately, moved on. The later chapters of this book tell of more recent years, and felt more like reportage than storytelling. Perhaps in fifty or so years, another writer will come along and find more humour and awe in today's ordinary.

I have chosen the stories in this book not only because I think they tell of the significant events that shaped Kelowna, but because there was something a bit quirky, or unusual or funny in many of them. The choice of this story and not that was solely mine. There are many stories still left to tell, and another writer or another volume will eventually record those too. The errors in telling, if there are any, are mine.

The writing of this book has truly been a labour of love. Five generations of my family have now lived in and grown up in Kelowna and our roots are deeply embedded in the community. I have revelled in the opportunity to learn more about those who lived here before me and greatly enjoyed looking back at some of the events I've lived through. I hope those who pick up this history will have fun reading it—and then take a minute to consider their good fortune to live in or visit such a beautiful city… with such a colourful past.

Sharron J. Simpson
Kelowna, BC
2011

A small, white, red-roofed replica of Father Pandosy's second church stands in a cornfield just west of the restored Mission. It marks Father Pandosy's gravesite. As the Mission site and the fence surrounding the original graveyard deteriorated, the location of the priest's grave became a mystery. It was not until 1983, during an archaeological dig in the area, that James Baker, a professor at Okanagan College, discovered Father Pandosy's grave. Two other priests had been buried alongside him. The grave was on land owned by the pioneer Rampone family. Two years later, the family built a replica of Father Pandosy's sawn wood church and transferred the gravesite and half an acre of land to the Bishop of Nelson. It is visible from the surrounding roads. | STUART KERNAGHAN, XYPHOTOS.CA

CHAPTER ONE:
Before Kelowna

THE FIRST PEOPLES

Long before there was a Kelowna, indigenous peoples known as the S-Ookanhkchinx, the Syilx speakers, were a group of the Interior Salish peoples who lived along the shores of the lakes and rivers that flowed into the great Columbia River. These resourceful people followed the seasons as they gathered the roots and berries that grew on the valley floor; hunted elk, deer and small game that flourished in the surrounding hillsides; and traded with neighbouring tribes. Each fall, families would gather for the great harvest of kokanee (land-locked salmon) and smoke their abundant catch before settling in their villages for winter. Theirs was a peaceful, loosely structured society where family took priority.

Horses arrived in North America with the Spaniards in the 1500s when the conquistadores conquered the lands of Mexico and Central America. Large herds of mustangs flourished during the following years as nomadic Mexicans and Native Americans travelled the southwest. The offspring of the original Spanish horses made their way northward by the 1700s and transformed the methods of travel and trade patterns of the aboriginal residents of the Okanagan Valley region. Yet when winters were severe, the horses became an emergency source of food, so herds never became large. When the fur brigades began passing through the Okanagan in the early 1800s, they bought or traded for the Natives' horses.

In these early years, the word "Okanagan" appeared in many forms. Its origins seem to be in the Syilx language: "S-Ookanhkchinx" means "transport toward the head or top end." The earliest inhabitants of the valley travelled northward from the great Columbia River basin, along its tributary, the Okanogan River, and continued past the chain of lakes that dot the valley floor. Once they reached the south end of Okanagan Lake, they continued northward to the head of the lake. These lakes and rivers defined the traditional territories and transportation routes of the Syilx people. In 1811, David Thompson wrote of the Oachenawaw people; the following year he referred to the Ookenaw-kane. Other early records note about thirty-five variations of the name, including the Oakinnackin, the O'kanies-kanies, the Oukinegans and the O-kan-a-kan.

The local people also worked as guides and sometimes traded pelts with passing traders, though the valley was never a primary source of furs. Relations between the Interior Salish and the Europeans were friendly in the early days, as colonial Governor James Douglas promised the rights of the Native people would be equal to those of the new settlers. The indigenous tribes' traditional nomadic lives gradually transformed into more permanent settlements as they began cultivating the land, though they continued to fish their historic streams and graze their cattle on traditional ranges.

The federal and provincial government established Indian Reserves in the Okanagan during the late 1800s and early 1900s, though they were subsequently reduced in size by a 1916 Royal Commission. The Okanagan Nation reserves at the time included lands from the north end of Okanagan Lake, near Vernon, through the Central Okanagan. In spite of being adjacent to the lakeshore, the reserves near the present-day West Kelowna were seen to have little value as they lacked a source of water.

As more settlers arrived, reserve lands were increasingly encroached upon and the indigenous people gradually lost access to their traditional water sources and the newly designated Crown grazing lands. Land use became even more insecure with the enactment of the federal Indian Act in 1876. The government's policy of assimilation, the arrival of foreign religions and the residential school system soon diminished and marginalized the once-proud and self-sufficient Okanagans.

WESTERN EXPLORATION

Early exploration in northern and western North America mostly occurred as a result of the Hudson's Bay Company and the North West Company (the Nor'Westers) trying to outdo each other in finding a Pacific port, in order to ship their furs to the Orient and Europe more quickly. Alexander Mackenzie, a Nor'Wester, went in search of the Pacific Ocean in 1789, only to end up on the shores of the Arctic Ocean. After returning to Britain to sharpen his skills, Mackenzie came back in 1792 and this time followed the Peace River to the soon-to-be-named Fraser River. Hearing its downstream waters were unnavigable, he diverted westward to a Native trading route over the Coast Mountains, where he was halted by the hostile Heiltsuk people at Bella Coola on an inlet along the Pacific Coast. He soon realized it wasn't a viable port, though he did achieve the distinction of making the first recorded crossing of the North American continent, north of Mexico.

Mackenzie and Captain George Vancouver missed each other by a mere two months, as the captain and his crew had recently arrived at the inlet as part of their survey of the west coast. Mackenzie's failure to find a Pacific port left the earlier shipping routes unchanged: the Hudson's Bay Company shipped from York Factory on Hudson Bay and the North West Company shipped from Montreal. Both routes were lengthy, arduous and fraught with enormous challenges.

The Rocky Mountains remained a formidable barrier to the Pacific Ocean and most of the early exploration of Canada's western territories was made along its north–south flowing rivers. Simon Fraser, another Nor'Wester, picked up where Mackenzie left off when he was sent to take charge of the area west of the Rockies in 1805. In spite of the aboriginal tribes in the area warning that the river was impassible and the portages worse, Fraser set off southward in 1808 along what he was sure was the Columbia River. Thirteen days later the canoes were abandoned, and Fraser and his crew proceeded on foot along the treacherous river until eventually reaching the Strait of Georgia. They were driven back inland by hostile Natives and Fraser soon realized the river that would later bear his name was not the Columbia. The journey also revealed the river's largest tributary, the Thompson River, which Fraser named after his friend and colleague, David Thompson. This new discovery provided access inland—and to the area that was soon to be known as the Okanagan Valley.

The Okanagan Fur Brigade Trail. Furs from northern Canada began their journey to the Pacific by canoe on the Fraser River. At Fort Alexandria they were transferred to pack horses for the journey south. The fur brigade continued through the Okanagan Valley to Fort Okanogan. There, the furs were transferred back into canoes and paddled down the Columbia River to Fort Vancouver, where ships were waiting to carry the furs to lucrative European markets. | NEIL THACKER

DISCOVERING A PACIFIC PORT

In the late 1700s, American businessman John Jacob Astor and his Pacific Fur Company joined with the North West Company, and together they became a formidable competitor of the Hudson's Bay Company. The elusive Pacific port was everyone's priority. Scotsman David Stuart, a Nor'Wester, boarded the *Tonquin*, an American merchant ship owned by Astor, in New York harbour in September 1810, heading for the west coast of North America via the Falkland Islands and Cape Horn, off the tip of South America. The ship arrived at the mouth of the Columbia River six months later, and fought its way upstream through fifteen miles of sandbars to where the crew would build Fort Astoria (named after John Jacob Astor). Two months later, another Scot, David Thompson, also a Nor'Wester who had been charged with finding an overland route to a Pacific port, arrived at the partly constructed fort.

Later in the summer of 1811, Stuart and Thompson left Fort Astoria by canoe and travelled up the Columbia River until they reached the mouth of the Okanogan River. Stuart and his small party headed a half mile upstream, where they built Fort Okanogan, as Thompson continued along the Columbia, eventually arriving back in Montreal in 1812.

The Okanagan Valley is unique in the annals of Canadian exploration as it was discovered from the south, by Scottish explorers employed by an American. David Stuart proceeded up the Okanogan River, along the aboriginal trails skirting the Okanagan lakes, and continued northward until he reached Cumloops. He overwintered there before returning to Fort Okanogan the following year. Cumloops, soon to become Fort Kamloops, was built at the confluence of the North and South Thompson Rivers. It was David Stuart's journey north from Fort Astoria that finally revealed the elusive connection between Canada's north and the Pacific Ocean. The route was soon to become a vital link in the lucrative North American fur trade.

FOR THE SAKE OF A HAT: THE OKANAGAN FUR BRIGADE TRAIL

It took a few years to sort out whether the Okanagan Valley really did provide a better route for getting northern furs to market and vital supplies to the remote forts. Some years the fur brigades travelled through the Okanagan Valley to Fort Astoria, while in other years the furs were shipped overland and took months to reach the eastern ports. Competition was fierce, and in 1821 the Hudson's Bay Company absorbed the North West Company, and the governor of the combined company, Sir George Simpson, came west to look over the company's shipping options. The logic of the southern route quickly became apparent, and from 1826 until 1847 fur brigades regularly travelled the Okanagan Trail.

The North American fur trade was driven by European fashion and the desire for beaver-felt hats and exotic furs. Beavers were close to extinction in Europe and the New World became another source for pelts—as well as new colonies and untapped riches. | HAT: KELOWNA MUSEUMS COLLECTION CA 969-020-001. PHOTO: SHARRON SIMPSON COLLECTION

Westbank Fur Brigade Cairn

The first brigade cairn was unveiled in Westbank in 1949. It read: "Okanagan Brigade Trail—A link in the fur-trading route from New Caledonia (North Central British Columbia) to the Columbia River. First explored by the Astorians in 1811, the trail was used by the North West Company and from 1821 by the Hudson's Bay Company. The fur brigades from New Caledonia journeyed overland by this route from Kamloops to Fort Okanagan until 1848. The gold seekers of 1858 coming through the Okanagan Valley followed the old trail, which also in the early 1860's became a second road to Cariboo."

The original cairn and plaque were subsequently replaced with inscriptions in English, French and Sylix. The English inscription reads: "This historic trail was developed from a network of travel and trade routes used by Aboriginal people for centuries. David Stuart of the Pacific Fur Company explored the trail from Fort Okanogan to Kamloops in 1811, and it was used in turn by fur brigades of the North West Company and the Hudson's Bay Company. Until the mid-century, fur traders passed by here to exchange goods for furs with the Okanagan and Shuswap Nations and others further north. Surviving sections of the trail along Lake Okanagan are a testimony to these former trading partnerships and the rich heritage of the region." | SHARRON SIMPSON COLLECTION

Furs were collected from the various forts on the northern tributaries of the Fraser River and transported by canoe to Fort Alexandria, near present-day Quesnel. Since the Fraser was not navigable south of the fort, the furs were transferred to pack horses and successive brigades of two or three hundred horses headed south. Fresh pack horses were picked up halfway along the route at Fort Kamloops, and the brigades continued on through the Okanagan Valley and along the Okanagan River to Fort Okanogan. Once they arrived, the furs were again loaded into canoes for their journey to Fort Vancouver (near present-day Vancouver, Washington), the new outpost established by Simpson in 1824 a few miles upriver from Fort Astoria, on the Columbia's more accessible northern bank. There they would be loaded on ships bound for Europe. The distance from Fort Vancouver to Fort St. James, the brigades' northern terminus, was approximately 1,200 miles and the journey would take about two months to complete. The brigades would usually spend a month in Fort Okanogan collecting supplies and trade goods before returning north.

Bagpipes reverberated across the hillsides as the brigade travelled the length of the Okanagan Valley. It must have been quite a sight: a long line of pack horses and their handlers, led by the distinguished-looking chief factor, or head trader, in his high beaver hat, a stiff white collar that reached to his ears and a finely tailored black jacket. Ceremony was essential and bagpipes set the stage for the gunfire salutes that marked entering and departing from forts or campsites. The day's routine rarely varied: the campfires were lit at the first morning light and breakfast, usually dried salmon, was prepared for all. The scouts departed first to find the next night's campsite, while the brigade horses were rounded up and each reloaded with two eighty-four-pound packs of furs and camp supplies. The brigade broke camp about nine a.m. and by four that afternoon, having travelled about twenty miles, they would arrive at the new campsite. The factor's tent was always the first to be erected, set apart from the others, and his fire was the first to be lit.

The agreement signed between Britain and the United States in 1846 establishing the forty-ninth parallel as the international boundary restricted the brigade's access to Fort Vancouver, and brought an end to the Okanagan Fur Brigade Trail. Governor Simpson had foreseen the possibility of Fort Vancouver being lost to the British and had already established Fort Langley, on the south side of the Fraser River, as an alternative port. The Hudson's Bay Company and the fur trade remained part of the west for another twenty-five years, although the demand for pelts decreased as fashionable Europeans lost interest in fur, and aboriginal communities became less nomadic as they turned to farming and raising cattle.

Today, a map showing remnants of the Okanagan Brigade Trail is available to the curious who want to search it out along Westside Road, across Okanagan Lake from Kelowna. Part of the trail is on private land—some has been built on or planted—while other sections have vanished. Occasionally a marker will appear on a tree, identifying the "H.B.C. Fur Brigade Trail." In West Kelowna, at the intersection of Highway 97 and Old Okanagan Highway, a cairn marks the high point of land were the local indigenous peoples and the brigade traders carried on their business. Otherwise, there is little evidence of the Okanagan's short-lived involvement in Canada's fur industry.

GOD FOLLOWED

By the time the last of the fur brigades passed through the Okanagan in 1847, Protestant missionaries were already well established in the Oregon territories. The Catholic Church needed a presence in the new land but was so short of priests that it had to appeal to France for assistance. Twenty-four-year-old Charles John Felix Adolph Pandosy

Father Pandosy's first building was a log chapel with living quarters above. The larger building beside it was a root cellar with walls of parallel logs built four inches apart and packed with earth to insulate the fruits and vegetables stored for the winter. | KELOWNA PUBLIC ARCHIVES 7075

MR. CASORSO'S ONIONS ON THE GROUND (30 TONS TO THE ACRE.) ROMAN CATHOLIC CHURCH IN THE BACKGROUND. KELOWNA, B.C.

Father Pandosy's second building, the Church of the Immaculate Conception, was built of sawn lumber and had a bell tower and Gothic arched windows. The Casorso onion fields are in the foreground. | KELOWNA PUBLIC ARCHIVES 4642

was part of a small group of Oblates who left their motherhouse near Marseilles in 1847 and sailed to the New World.

Pandosy was from a prosperous landowning family in Provence, yet took vows of poverty and devotion when he joined the Oblates of Mary Immaculate (OMI). An unlikely candidate for mission work, the young man had excelled in Latin and French literature and was recognized for his beautiful singing voice. Pandosy, however, wanted more than a cloistered life and welcomed the opportunity to venture off to an unknown world. Once in New York, the small party of Oblates joined a wagon train and travelled across the sparsely populated continent to Fort Walla Walla, in present-day Washington state.

Pandosy was soon ordained and became known as Father Charles Marie Pandosy OMI. The young priest worked and lived among the Yakama tribe, where he learned their language and taught them to plant and harvest, and then baptized them into his church. He could not have anticipated such a life: there were few comforts, he lived with loneliness and isolation, and he persevered through immense hardship. It wasn't long before hostilities escalated as settlers thought he was siding with the Yakamas and the Yakamas thought he was aiding and abetting the settlers. Militias were sent in to protect the newcomers and soon local wars escalated into massacres as both sides fought to the death. It became impossible for Father Pandosy and his colleagues to remain in the American territories.

The Washington missionaries were called to Esquimalt on Vancouver Island in the summer of 1858. Pandosy stayed for the winter and began planning to start anew in the colony of British Columbia. The young priest briefly returned to Colville, just across the American border, in the spring to gather supplies and find settlers who were willing to join him in establishing a new mission in the Okanagan Valley. Cyprienne and Theodor Laurence, French Canadian brothers who had been involved in the fur trade, and Cyprienne's wife, Therese, from the Flathead Indian Reservation, agreed to accompany him, as did an unnamed Flathead man who was so devoted to Father Pandosy that he and his wife decided to follow the priest to the new land. William Peon (or Pion), a Sandwich (Hawaiian) Islander, one of many who made their way to the west coast on the sailing ships that reprovisioned on the islands, agreed to pack the small party into the Okanagan Valley.

Following the Okanagan Fur Brigade Trail across the new international border, Pandosy and his party made their way northward until they reached the Native village at the south end of Okanagan Lake. Once there, Therese was called upon to convince her uncle, Chief Capot Blanc, and the other chiefs from the area that the priest and her husband intended to help improve the Natives' condition and should be allowed to settle their valley. The Hudson's Bay Company had rarely encouraged settlement, and the traders and trappers who had previously passed through the valley hadn't created a problem for local aboriginal groups. Settlers, however, were another matter, and those who had arrived earlier with the idea of staying had been threatened by the chiefs and ordered to move on. Therese, perhaps as an enticement, added that if the chiefs did not agree to her request or harmed her companions, her uncle, Capot Blanc, would have to accept responsibility for her care. It took a few days, but she prevailed.

Instead of following the established trail, the party chose to travel along the rocky, mountainous east side of Okanagan Lake. The route took them through the "Grand Canyon"—likely Wild Horse Canyon—and onward to the south end of Duck Lake (near Winfield today). Father Pandosy and his party arrived in the fall of 1859 and declared they had at last reached the site of his new mission. The winter was bitterly cold and the snow was uncommonly deep. Game was scarce, and with no time to build shelter or gather provisions, the party lived in tents, slaughtered their horses for food and survived on the diet of the local peoples: berries and roots, baked mosses and native teas.

When spring arrived, the area proved too marshy and the group moved to higher ground for the summer and scouted around for a more suitable permanent site. They eventually discovered a broad sweep of flat land a few miles south, near a creek that would soon be known as Mission Creek, and quickly determined that the surrounding land would better meet their needs. Not wanting to spend another winter in tents, the men quickly built a small log house with a church on the ground floor and sleeping quarters above. The Mission of the Immaculate Conception became a reality on the site they called L'Anse au Sable, or Sandy Cove.

Father Pandosy's Mission of the Immaculate Conception

When Father Pandosy's Mission of the Immaculate Conception was finally closed in 1902, the land was purchased by the Kelowna Land and Orchard Company, then subdivided and sold as potential orchard sites. Two years later, fifteen acres of the Mission's ranch were purchased by Dr. Paul dePfyffer, a Swiss lawyer who had come to the valley to farm. The property was again sold in 1947 and the dilapidated buildings were slated for demolition. A group of concerned people, including the Bishop of Vancouver and the Father Pandosy branch of the Knights of Columbus, rescued and restored the three original buildings. Father Pandosy's sawn wood church was sold to a local Seventh Day Adventist congregation, who dismantled it and moved it to their property in Rutland. It was subsequently destroyed by fire.

In 1954, the Oblates of Mary Immaculate repurchased the two acres of land containing the original buildings. Four years later they re-dedicated the site as part of celebrations recognizing their one hundred years in British Columbia. The Oblates transferred the land to the Roman Catholic Diocese of Nelson in 1967, and it was subsequently designated as a BC Heritage Site in 1983.

The Father Pandosy Mission has since grown by another two acres and other historic buildings have been added to the grounds. A celebration of the 150th anniversary of Father Pandosy's Mission was held in August 2010. Representatives from the Catholic Church, the Oblate Order and the Westbank First Nation gathered to acknowledge the remarkable priests whose early arrival transformed the Okanagan Valley. The Mission is located on Benvoulin Road. | STUART KERNAGHAN, XYPHOTOS.CA

The wider area became known as the Mission Valley, after Father Pandosy's Mission at L'Anse au Sable—though many thought "Sandy Cove" referred to the mouth of Mission Creek, not the Mission itself. The settlement had been established at about the midpoint of Okanagan Lake, and the settlers soon noticed that the tillable land surrounding the Mission, and to the north and south, was immense. In a letter to his superiors in France, Father Pandosy wrote that this was the largest valley that could be cultivated in the surrounding countryside, saying, "All who know it, praise it." By the early 1900s, the area became known as the Okanagan Valley.

Soon after Father Pandosy settled, Father Pierre Richard (1826–1907), who had also been in Esquimalt, arrived in the valley for the first of what became a succession of visits. He stayed for varying periods of time and was known as the more practical of the two priests: Father Pandosy taught the Natives to speak French, play musical instruments and sing their Latin masses with such beauty they rivalled the choirs of the great cathedrals of France. Father Richard taught them to build fences, plant fruit trees and a vineyard, and grow the ground crops that would sustain them. In November 1860, Father Richard filed a rural pre-emption claim for the Mission on the Great Lake, noting that the river of L'Anse au Sable was to the south.

The missionaries soon had considerable success converting and ministering to their flock: in just the two years after the Mission was founded, they baptized 121 persons. Father Pandosy worked in the fields, devised ways to irrigate his crops and built a root cellar to store their harvest. A brothers' house was added to the site in 1865 to house the succession of priests who stayed at the Mission, along with those travelling through the area. The following year, a log barn was added to the site. In 1882 a new sawn lumber church was built, which featured five Gothic-inspired windows on each side of the nave and a bell tower.

During these years, Father Pandosy was sent to various other missions around the province, sometimes for two or three years at a time, but he always returned to his home at Okanagan Mission. In February 1891, Pandosy was called to Keremeos to give final rites to a dying parishioner. It was fiercely cold but he was undeterred as he walked through the drifting snow—he had travelled the route several times before, though he was now sixty-seven years old and in somewhat tentative health. After leaving Keremeos, he made it back as far as Penticton, where he was taken in by Chief Francoise of the Penticton Indian Band, as he had become seriously ill. Recognizing the priest's perilous condition, the chief sent for

Mrs. Ellis—the wife of Tom Ellis, one of the area's cattle barons—who was known for her nursing skills. Little could be done and Father Charles Pandosy died on February 6, 1891. He was returned to his Mission on the steamer *Penticton* and buried across the road from his church.

While the Okanagan Mission benefitted from the presence of many priests during its forty-two-year existence, none have been identified as strongly with the place and its history as Father Pandosy. Most of those who served were devout and passionate men who felt they were called by their God to go forth to save, educate and minister to the New World's indigenous peoples. They were true pioneers who suffered privations beyond our present-day comprehension: they were frequently close to starvation, often isolated and lonely, and knew few creature comforts. Clothing, blankets and seeds were hard to come by, and most went barefoot and bare-headed in the summer and used pelts and hides to survive the winters. They worked constantly, walking to their destinations, which were often over the next mountain range or two. Though their physical and mental well-being concerned their superiors, most priests were on their own to make the best of whatever was available. Their abiding faith carried them when little else was available.

The Mission and the community around it continued to flourish after Pandosy's death. The farm grew to about 2,450 acres, and the Mission became the Catholic Church's headquarters for the area from the international border in the south to Fort Kamloops in the north, the Similkameen Valley in the east to the Nicola Valley and Merritt in the west. When the Canadian Pacific Railway completed its transcontinental line in 1885, however, Kamloops became the nearest rail connection. The Oblates moved their headquarters to the St. Louis Mission in Kamloops in 1895. The Okanagan Mission and all related properties were sold to Father Eumelin and other members of his family in 1896. Though Eumelin was not an Oblate, he continued to run the Mission as its priest until 1902, when the original Mission of the Immaculate Conception was officially closed. The land was purchased by the Kelowna Land and Orchard Company in 1906, then subdivided and sold as prime orchard sites.

GOLD EVERYWHERE

The Hudson's Bay Company had been buying gold from the Okanagans for many years, though David Douglas was the first to record its discovery in 1833. Douglas, a Scottish botanist, was collecting specimens for the Royal Horticultural Society while travelling through the area with one of the company's fur brigades. The Hudson's Bay Company was in the fur business and wasn't interested in having its lucrative trade disrupted by an influx of unruly miners: it kept Douglas's discoveries to itself for many years.

Gold was discovered in California in 1848. Over the next seven years the hopeful, the delusional, the skilled and the ill-equipped converged from all over the world to pan the rivers, creeks and gullies for the magical metal. As it became harder to find and mining became more technical and more costly, word of gold discoveries in British Columbia drifted south and enticed miners to leave for the British territory. First there was gold in the creeks near Kamloops, then Bear Creek on the west side of Okanagan Lake, and then Mission Creek, Rock Creek and the Fraser River. By 1858, amid turmoil and lawlessness, over thirty thousand miners had moved into British territory—and they fought with the Natives and each other to stake their claims.

The chaos also brought opportunity as the newcomers needed to be fed and supplied. An uneasy truce was negotiated that same year with various Washington tribes, which allowed the Palmer and Miller wagon train to leave Oregon and make its way through the Okanagan Valley to the Cariboo goldfields. Miller, an adventurer, and Palmer, an experienced wagon captain and treaty negotiator, were accompanied by two hundred miners who were fearful the truce wouldn't hold and wanted the security of travelling in a convoy. Ox teams pulled nine wagons loaded with food, equipment and clothing to sell to miners. Once through the Washington Territory, they picked up the Okanagan Fur Brigade Trail and headed north. One wagon loaded with sugar overturned crossing the Columbia River, and another was lost farther along the trail, but the remaining seven crossed the international boundary and continued along the old brigade trail to Deep Creek, near present-day Peachland, on the west side of Okanagan Lake.

Stalled by the rough shoreline and the ravines that ran down to the lake, the group had to find another way to continue northward. Undaunted, they felled trees and lashed them together into rafts—some reports say fifty logs were needed for each one. The wagons were dismantled and loaded onto the rafts, piece by piece, along with all the goods they were carrying, and paddled across the lake to the flat eastern shore. After they landed the wagons were reassembled and reloaded, and then everyone waited for the cattle and horses that had backtracked to the south end of

Okanagan Lake to be rerouted down the eastern shore. Once they were all back together, the wagon train continued on to Fort Kamloops.

This was challenging travel. Each wagon carried about three thousand pounds of provisions and merchandise for sale to miners, and when the terrain became too rough, the wagons were once again disassembled and the goods transferred onto the horses and oxen. As the countryside flattened out, the wagons were again reassembled and reloaded and the journey continued. When the group finally arrived in Kamloops, the wagon masters heard the terrain to the north was even more challenging and it made little sense to continue on. The Cariboo was still a long way off, but Palmer and Miller and the other wagoneers found a needy and hungry market at the fort and were able to sell everything for a great profit, including their oxen, which were soon seen roasting over open fires. Normally sustained by the wild meat they shot or trapped along the trail, the hungry miners were overwhelmed by the prospect of so much tame meat: they devoured the animals without giving much thought to what other uses the beasts might have been put to. So great was the impression created by this first wagon train that tales of its size and its troubles were told and retold in Native villages for many years.

Cattlemen from Washington and Oregon used the Okanagan as a supply route to the Fraser River and the Cariboo goldfields for a few more years, but settlement didn't come quickly to the Okanagan, as the valley was still isolated and access was difficult. However, the new colonial government in Victoria was becoming increasingly alarmed by the number of Americans crossing the international boundary and making their way into the southern and eastern parts of the province. Gold was being discovered, mines were being built and the new government needed the revenue and soon established its own tax collectors in the area. The Fraser River sternwheelers carried government agents, settlers and supplies as far inland as Hope, but only a narrow foot trail continued on to the Southern Interior.

By 1860, Edgar Dewdney, a British engineer, was commissioned to build a wagon road from Hope through to the goldfields in the Kootenays. The existing footpath was converted into a four-foot-wide trail, wide enough for a pack train, and cut through to Vermillion Forks (Princeton). Then the contract ended and nothing happened for four years. Finally, Dewdney was commissioned to pick up where he had left off and continue the trail along the Similkameen River to Keremeos, and over what would become Richter Pass, to Osoyoos. The trail, soon known as the Dewdney

Trail, continued on for another three hundred miles and eventually reached Fernie and the coal fields awaiting the arrival of the Canadian Pacific's transcontinental trains.

The Dewdney Trail, or Hope Trail, also provided access from the Lower Mainland to the Mission Valley. Pack trains carried the ordinary and the extraordinary, settlers rode and walked, and Father Pandosy travelled back and forth many times as the Okanagan's first pianos and billiard tables were hauled over the pack trail. Riders on horseback strapped mail pouches to their saddles, prospectors followed the latest rumours of gold discoveries and cattle barons drove their herds from the Interior over the trail to the port of New Westminster. The famous also used the trail: American General William Tecumseh Sherman travelled from Osoyoos to Hope in 1883 with a military escort of sixty men, and Archduke Franz Ferdinand of Austria travelled over the trail to the Similkameen in search of bighorn sheep before his 1914 assassination, the event that triggered World War I. The remarkable engineering of the Dewdney Trail established the first route into the Okanagan from the Lower Mainland of BC.

FEEDING THE INFLUX

There were more cattle in Oregon than buyers and Palmer and Miller's expedition encouraged ranchers to look north to sell their stock. Soon a succession of cattle drives followed the old brigade trail through the Okanagan and continued on to the Cariboo goldfields. Attempting to collect all the revenue due them, the colonial government levied taxes of a dollar a head at Kamloops, or drovers could pay a one-time fee to cover them for a six-month period. Yet the government was aware there were too few cattle in the British territory to feed the miners. Not wanting to deal with a food shortage, government representatives were known to turn a blind eye to those who slipped past the forts. It wasn't long before cattle began overwintering on the abundant bunch grass ranges along the Thompson River, near the fort at Kamloops, waiting to be driven to the Cariboo when the trail re-opened in the spring.

Old Hudson's Bay men and drovers who knew the land began pre-empting the ranges along the Thompson River in the early 1860s, and settling in the area. About the same time, the Vernon brothers arrived from Ireland in search of gold, and a man named Cornelius O'Keefe decided he could make more money raising cattle instead of driving them from Oregon. All pre-empted large acreages in the North Okanagan. As mines developed in the Boundary and Kootenay areas, Thomas Ellis, another Irishman, and J.C. Haynes, a customs officer who took payment in cattle when the drovers didn't have the cash, accumulated even larger acreages in the South Okanagan. The settlement around Father Pandosy's Mission was at the midpoint of the valley, and farther from the gold discoveries and the mining boom; it received little benefit from the activity going on to the north and to the south. Most of those who settled around the Mission were subsistence farmers, though some also ran herds of cattle on the bunch grass hillsides and sold their stock to miners passing through the area.

When the Cariboo's gold was mined out, the number of men working claims also diminished, and the demand for beef and other provisions disappeared. Those settlers who retained remnants of their once-large herds took great interest in discussions about the colony of British Columbia becoming part of the Canadian Confederation. Of even greater interest was the promise of a railway that would join British Columbia with Eastern Canada. Construction was rumoured to be starting within two years. In addition to feeding the construction crews, ranchers could use the rail line to deliver cattle to the Cariboo and the Kootenays. On the strength of the promised railway, British Columbia joined Canada in 1871.

In the meantime, the once-abundant bunch grass ranges of the Okanagan were over-grazed, and many ranchers had little choice but to become subsistence farmers, though the entrepreneurs among them opened trading posts, became postmasters or started up sawmills or grist mills. Those with connections ran for public office or were appointed to government positions. Few had any cash to buy additional land, even at a dollar an acre, and those with cattle used nearby Crown ranges as their herds began to grow. The winter of 1879–80 was unusually severe, and when thousands of cattle starved to death, ranchers realized they needed to grow hay to prevent such catastrophes from happening in the future. It wasn't long before the valley's bottomlands were transformed from range to hayfields.

The long-awaited construction of the Canadian Pacific Railway finally got underway in early 1880. The chosen route through the Kicking Horse Pass and Kamloops set the stage for a dramatic turnaround in the Okanagan cattle business. Five thousand men constructed the line between Yale and Savona (about 175 miles) and the demand for beef was so great that even the large syndicates—the Douglas Lake Cattle

Company in the Nicola Valley and the British Columbia Cattle Company in the South Okanagan—couldn't meet the railway's demand for beef. Cattle sales provided the ranchers with the cash needed to buy land; the large O'Keefe and Coldstream ranches in the North Okanagan and the Lequime, Knox and Postill ranches in the Mission Valley grew to many thousands of acres. The railway also brought settlers to the Prairies, and then took BC cattle eastward to feed them. Some Okanagan ranchers saw an opportunity closer to home and opened their own butcher shops in the Lower Mainland to provide for the growing number of settlers heading west. The Okanagan was transformed into wide-open rangeland where large herds of cattle thrived on the luxurious bunch grass that covered the valley's hillsides and bottomlands.

AND, FINALLY, SETTLERS

The Americans always coveted Southern BC. Even after the international boundary was established in 1846, many maintained that the British part of the Columbia District—the land between Oregon and Alaska—was still rightfully part of their Oregon Territory. It didn't take long for those in BC's colonial government to realize they needed settlers in the Okanagan and the Kootenays. To ensure the land stayed in British hands, British citizens could pre-empt 160 acres of land by 1860. Some registered their land, stayed to work their property and quietly became part of the growing community. Others claimed land but moved on, and those who followed claimed the same property. Some just squatted on the land or made minor improvements, then moved on and left little or no trace of their presence.

Many of those passing through the Mission Valley commented on the poverty of those trying to eke out a living there. With few exceptions, the houses were small and poorly constructed—one leather-hinged door and two small windows, perhaps filled in with glass brought by pack train, or just thinly scraped hides. There was little opportunity to sell what was grown, so most settlers only grew or raised what their family needed. Yet with Father Pandosy as the founding force behind the new Mission and his French Oblate order supporting his endeavours, French-speaking settlers from both Quebec and France were drawn to the Mission Valley. French was the language of instruction at the school as well. Many details of these early settlers have been lost to time but names such as Laurence, Christien, Boucherie and Bouvette continue to resonate locally. Others left a more substantial record.

First, the Lequimes

Eli Lequime and his wife, Marie Louise, were among the first to settle near Father Pandosy's Mission. Eventually, Eli would become known as "King of the Mission Valley." He cleared the land and created a substantial and productive farm: his cattle herds grew and he built the area's first trading post, hotel and saloon, sawmill and grist mill. The Lequime homestead served as the social and economic heart of the Mission community for many years.

Eli was born in France and ran away to sea in 1825, when he was fourteen years old. He travelled the world for nearly three decades and then arrived in San Francisco in 1852, when so many of the hopeful from around the world were flocking to California to search for gold. Eli staked his claims and persevered for a couple of years, but finally gave up and returned to join the French forces on the Russian front during the Crimean War. Returning to France from the battlefield, Eli met Marie Louise Altabagoethe, the woman who would eventually become his wife. Eli left France again soon after and by 1856 was back in San Francisco running the city's first French hand laundry. Marie Louise followed, and they married and moved to Marysville, California, a declining gold town, where they ran a successful saloon for the next three years. As gold was becoming harder to find, rumours began filtering south about new discoveries in British Columbia.

Eli, Marie Louise and their two-year-old son Bernard boarded a Spanish ship in San Francisco and travelled for five days before disembarking in Victoria. They caught another boat to the mainland, joined a pack train and travelled to Fort Hope, where their second son, Gaston, was born. They stayed at Hope and panned for gold for the next two years. Then gold was discovered in Rock Creek on the Kettle River, west of Osoyoos near the US border, and it didn't take long for the Lequime family to decamp and move on. With their two young children tied in panniers on the back of an ox, the couple walked 175 miles to the new hotspot. Deciding there was more money to be made catering to the miners than panning for the elusive mineral, the couple opened a trading post and saloon.

Within a year, that boom also went bust. The family packed up, yet again, and began walking to the Cariboo, 300 miles away. Rock Creek had been a tumultuous time for the family: Gaston, at two years of age, had fallen into a miner's sluice box and drowned; Bernard had been kidnapped by a curious Native, though he was returned home after a couple of days; and another son, also named Gaston, was born. Father Pandosy discovered the family on the trail: the parents were walking, their belongings tied onto their horse, and the children rode the family's cow. Always looking for more settlers, Pandosy convinced the Lequimes to settle in the Okanagan instead of continuing on to the Cariboo.

In 1861, Eli registered a land claim northeast of the Mission; the site was noted to have good soil, ample water and many trees. After building their first house, a fourteen-by-twenty-foot log cabin with a dirt floor and roof, Eli opened a trading post next door. Marie Louise was known for her firm hand and sympathetic heart and ran the store for many years. She was a big woman and seemed undaunted by the rough, wild and unforgiving country that surrounded her. With few other women nearby for company, she raised her children, ran the store and doctored lonely souls stricken with smallpox, mountain fever, broken bones, broken hearts or fallout from the latest barroom brawl.

Their nearest competitor was a trading post in Fort Kamloops, 110 miles away, and the Lequimes' business thrived. Eli's merchandise came by wagon train from Walla Walla, Washington, crossing the international boundary near Yahk, in the Kootenays, and travelling on to the Okanagan. As the trails improved and Hope was only eight travelling days away, Lequime's thirty- to forty-horse pack trains would travel to Hope four or five times a year to stock up on goods for his store. Once a year, Eli would continue on to Victoria to buy fancy goods and replenish his own library.

The Lequime trading post became the business and social hub of the Mission Valley. Trappers traded furs and Eli kept a well-calibrated scale on his office desk for the miners who wanted to exchange gold dust for food and supplies. While some things were in short supply, whisky wasn't one of them, and a still is known to have been on the site from the mid-1860s on. Try as they might, the priests couldn't convince those attending Mass in the morning that there was an alternative to the gambling, horse races and drinking that filled the rest of their day. By sundown, the morning's congregants were often roaring drunk and many would have gambled away their most precious possessions.

The Lequimes had two more children while they lived near the Mission: a daughter, Aminade, in 1866 and another son, Leon, in 1870. Eli and Marie Louise were among the most worldly of the French settlers in the area, and looked forward to the monthly arrival of the mail, including the newspaper *Le Courier*, from San Francisco. Bernard was sent to school in New Westminster at the age of twelve and then on to Victoria to learn carpentry before returning to the valley. The Lequime family ran over 1,300 head of cattle on two thousand acres of valley bottom land and used an additional six thousand acres of rangeland on the upper benches. Their hotel was the first in the area and the only stopping-off place for many years. When the Okanagan Mission post office opened in 1872, Eli was appointed its first postmaster and remained in that position until he left the valley. Bernard, his son, succeeded him.

Eli had lived in the Mission Valley for twenty-seven years when he decided, at seventy years of age, that it was time to return to civilization. He had begun with almost nothing, and amassed a fortune far greater than anyone else in the area. He had created jobs for others and financed many who needed money to get started. Life in the Mission Valley wasn't easy and many moved on, but Eli and Marie Louise had stayed, worked hard and created an empire. They sold it to their sons, Bernard, Gaston and Leon. Eli moved to San Francisco in 1888, along with his daughter, Aminade, and Gaston's two-year-old daughter Dorothy. (Gaston had married Marie Louise Gillard, niece of another pioneer, but he died in 1889 as a result of an unfortunate encounter with a steer during a cattle drive.) Eli's wife, Marie Louise, left the Okanagan a year or two later and joined Eli, her daughter and her granddaughter in San Francisco. She died there in 1908, ten years after Eli passed away. The two remaining brothers continued to run the Lequime family businesses: Bernard was the operational and financial partner, while Leon looked after the family's cattle business.

Gillard and Blondeaux: An Unruly Pair

Auguste Gillard and his mining partner, Jules Blondeaux, met Father Pandosy in Hope in 1862 when the priest was collecting his mail and supplies. He convinced the pair to join his Mission community. The two were among the many who had left France in the 1850s in search of gold, and had panned the creeks and gravel beds of California. When they heard rumours about the discovery of gold in British Columbia, they boarded a Spanish ship in San Francisco and arrived in New Westminster a few days later. From there, they headed to Boston Bar, where they dug ditches and built sluice boxes, but then Gillard got into a fight with a local Native, and the two decided they'd better get out of town before word got around that the man was dead.

Once they arrived in the Mission Valley, each man pre-empted 320 acres, with Gillard's acreage extending from the foot of Knox

Mountain in the north to Mill Creek in the south, and Richter Street in the east to the lakeshore in the west. Some years later, this pre-emption would become the Kelowna townsite. Blondeaux's pre-emption encircled his partner's, extending to the north and east, and would also be incorporated into the early Kelowna townsite some years later.

Blondeaux soon sold out and returned to France, yet Gillard remained in the area. He never married, and in spite of the missionaries' efforts he spent much of his time betting on the horses, drinking too much and gambling away his possessions—the last of which was his land, which he sold to Bernard Lequime in 1890. Letters addressed to his sweetheart in France, assuring her of his impending return, were found on his deathbed in 1898. He died poor, and alone, and still in the Mission Valley.

A.B. Knox, the Cattleman

Arthur Booth Knox was either a vengeful arsonist or the victim of a serious miscarriage of justice, depending on whose side you were on. Knox was a Scot who arrived in the Mission Valley in 1874 from the Cariboo goldfields. He bought the land once owned by Jules Blondeaux and expanded it to include the lakeshore property that became known as Manhattan Beach. There he built a driving shed, a warehouse capable of storing the many tons of wheat grown on his farm, and a wharf—where, in time, the wheat would be picked up by sternwheeler for shipment out of the valley.

At some point, Knox increased his holdings to include the mountain that now bears his name and a substantial part of the Glenmore Valley, which ran north to what is now Okanagan Centre and parts of Winfield. He farmed his land for over twenty years, and ran over 1,700 head of cattle and 50 horses. When the Kelowna townsite was laid out, he built a fence along its eastern boundary to keep his cattle from wandering onto Bernard Avenue, the town's main street.

The Mission Valley was becoming over-grazed by the 1890s, and the abundant bunch grass that had supported the earlier cattle drives was being replaced by hayfields. About this time, Tom Ellis, the biggest cattle baron in the South Okanagan, arrived in the Mission Valley and bought one of the financially troubled pioneer ranches. The locals were suspicious of this interloper and his motives, and what other farms he was going to take over. Ellis's new ranch had three stacks of premium and scarce timothy hay in the yard awaiting the arrival of his cattle from Penticton: they were being brought in to overwinter. A second herd arrived in early

January 1891, and when the farm manager wandered out to the yard shortly after their arrival, two stacks of the hay had already burned to the ground and the third was well on its way. The flames were seen all over the valley, and while there were various suspects, Arthur Booth Knox was charged with arson. A battle of the cattle barons ensued. Ellis owned huge amounts of land, was an influential man with a forceful personality and, as a magistrate, was well known throughout the province. Knox also owned a lot of land, but he was a quiet, unassuming loner who was only known by his friends and neighbours.

The ensuing court case was heard in a Vernon schoolhouse and it became a legendary battle. Ellis posted a $250 reward—huge for the time—for the conviction of the arsonist. Witnesses were bought and bought off by both sides. Henry Bloom, one of Knox's employees, claimed the reward saying Knox had offered him money to either burn the hay or dissolve strychnine and drench the stacks in order to poison the cattle. Bloom couldn't quite remember the actual amount he was paid: $50 or maybe it was $150 or $250... it had a fifty in there somewhere. Others claimed Knox had tried to bribe them to change their testimony. Ellis's witnesses were unsavoury characters, though, and it was highly unlikely they would tell the truth.

Knox was found guilty in spite of a vigorous defence. He was sentenced to three years' hard labour. Nine months later, Ellis sued Knox, who was still in jail, to recover the value of the hay—$4,000—plus $500 for the weight his cattle lost, plus the $250 reward he had paid to get the evidence against Knox, plus another $500 for loss of time in hiring an extra watchman and a boat to check out another suspect. Knox's lawyer said his client wasn't guilty in the first place and certainly not responsible for these costs. The same cast of unreliable characters was called in again to give evidence. The judge declared the previous trial had no bearing on the new trial and unless reliable evidence was introduced to prove that Knox actually burned the hay, he could not be held liable. The jury found in favour of Knox, and Ellis had to pay the trial costs. By this time, Knox had served most of his three-year sentence.

The *Vernon News* subsequently noted that A.B. Knox, "who had been absent for some time," was warmly welcomed back by his many friends and had again taken charge of his large ranch. Two years later, Knox donated a lot on the southeast corner of Richter Street to the Presbyterians and added a further $250 toward the construction of their church. Five years later, Knox was elected president of the influential

Agricultural & Trades Association of the Okanagan Mission, which had, on its board of directors, a number of the community's leading citizens. This curious episode in the Okanagan Valley's history was made even more so when Knox retired and sold his ranch and all his cattle to his adversary, Tom Ellis.

The Ill-fated Postills

After living in Ontario for several years, the Postill family, originally from England, arrived in the Okanagan in 1872. Edward, Mary, their three sons—Alfred, the eldest at twenty, William and Edward Jr.—and daughter, Lucy, had travelled to Yale by steamer and then overland to Kamloops, where Edward became ill. Not wanting to delay their journey, the family placed Edward on a makeshift stretcher, attached to their stagecoach, and continued toward their destination. Edward died near Priest's Valley (near Vernon), and his body was carried to the family's new home and buried in the meadow of the ranch he had never seen. He was fifty-two years old.

The Postill family went on to build a "commodious" house with a long, winding lane—visitors could be seen approaching long before they reached the door. The ranch flourished as Alfred took over the business end of farming while William looked after the cattle. The family holdings soon grew to five thousand acres, with an additional two thousand acres of grazing range a few miles away. They had the largest herd of cattle in the Mission Valley and bred some very fine horses. Sheep and pigs were added to the ranch, and the Postills also ran the sawmill that had been left behind by a previous owner.

Always on the lookout for a new opportunity, Alfred was one of the first in the valley to plant an apple orchard and a berry patch. The dry benchlands became productive when the family planted the first alfalfa grown in the area and their prize peanuts took awards at the 1896 Vernon Agricultural Fair. Alfred was a man ahead of his time: in 1891, and at the cost of fifty-five dollars a mile, he had the first telephone in the valley installed between his ranch house and that of his brother, William. The line was then extended to Thomas Wood, Alfred's neighbour five miles to the north along the wagon road linking Priest's Valley to Okanagan Mission.

The fruit industry was also taking hold elsewhere in the province and orchards in the Fraser Valley, on Saltspring Island and in Lytton began producing more apples than their local markets could absorb.

Seeking to develop marketing opportunities elsewhere, the first meeting of the BC Fruit Marketing Board was held in Vancouver in 1889. Alfred Postill attended as the only Okanagan member of the organization. The board represented a diversity of interests, including those of George Grant MacKay, a well-known and successful land promoter from Vancouver. MacKay was sixty-two years old when he arrive in Vancouver to check out Western Canada and decide if it was a suitable place for his son to settle. He was so impressed with what he found that he sent for his wife, daughter and son to join him. Alfred Postill's advocacy of his valley's fruit-growing potential likely caught the attention of MacKay. It was a fortuitous encounter, as G.G. MacKay would soon play a very significant role in the transformation of the Okanagan.

The Postill house was the social centre of the northern part of the Mission Valley and people would rarely travel the wagon road without stopping off for a visit. Alfred became a Justice of the Peace and presided over the court proceedings when Knox and Ellis argued their hay-burning case. Lord and Lady Aberdeen, who arrived in the valley in 1891, were frequent visitors at the Postill home. Unfortunately Alfred, despite his enormous zest for life, followed the path of his father and died in 1897, when he was only forty-five years old. The ranch was sold in 1903 to Price Ellison, the area's Conservative member of the provincial legislature.

Today the original Postill ranchland wraps around Kelowna International Airport. It has had a succession of owners, including Countess Bubna of Austria, who named it the Eldorado Ranch; Austin C. Taylor, the Vancouver horse-racing magnate and entrepreneur, who doubled the size of the ranch and made some attempt to raise purebred cattle, though he used the land mostly for hunting pheasant; and the Bennett family, who bought the ranch in 1969. It remains a cattle ranch, though some areas of it have been leased out for growing echinacea and ginseng. The graves of Edward, Alfred and William Postill remain within an enclosure on the meadow.

The Italians Followed

The Catholic Church also enticed a number of Italian immigrants to settle in the Mission Valley. A fortuitous encounter between a bewildered Giovanni Casorzo, his friend Paulo Guaschetti and Father Caccola, an Oblate priest, encouraged the two men to join the other settlers at the Mission. Caccola, who had recently returned from Corsica and understood the Italian dialect spoken by the two men, overheard them talking about how much they disliked cutting logs in the nearby forests and wondering what else they could do.

Casorzo had left the political turmoil of Italy in 1883 to make his way in the New World. The thirty-four-year-old father of three landed in New York City but found no contentment in the turmoil of the concrete city: he longed for an opportunity to follow in his father's footsteps and work the land. Casorzo made his way to San Francisco, caught a ship north to Nanaimo and crossed to the mainland, where he and his newly acquired friend encountered Father Caccola in the mid 1880s.

Father Pandosy soon offered the men a job at the Mission and said that if they would stay for the next six years, the missionaries would help them establish a homestead. Their job would be to do whatever needed to be done: act as cook, ranch hand, cowboy, carpenter, Native agent, teamster or packer. Giovanni Casorzo planned to save his money and send for his wife, Rosa, and his children: Caroline, Tony and the as-yet-unseen Carlo Enrico, soon to be known as Charles.

Giovanni had stayed in touch with his family and sent small amounts of money to them from New York. When he got to the Okanagan he realized the only international currency available to him was gold dust, so he sent small amounts of the precious metal to Italy, though he was never certain it would arrive. Rosa must have received the funds, or perhaps someone in the Oblate order stepped in to help, because passage was booked for Rosa and her children on a windjammer leaving Genoa, Italy, for San Francisco, via Cape Horn, in 1884. Rosa packed food for the journey, and six weeks after leaving her homeland, she and her young children were dropped on the dock in San Francisco. Rosa spoke no English and the only indication that her journey hadn't ended was a small piece of paper she clutched in her hand. It read "Father Pandosy, Okanagan Mission." By a stroke of luck—or perhaps divine intervention—someone noticed a large crate that had been left at the shipping office. A label identified the contents as a church bell that was to be sent to Father Pandosy at Okanagan Mission. The bell, a gift for the Oblate's church, had been ordered by Joseph Christien, one of the valley's early settlers. It had been cast in France and shipped to Okanagan Mission via San Francisco, and was subsequently named "MaryAnn" in honour of Christien's wife.

Rosa Casorzo did not let the bell out of her sight as she and her children boarded another boat to New Westminster. Giovanni had asked friends to watch for his family and when the bell was finally loaded onto one of the Fraser River sternwheelers, Rosa and her children followed.

It took two weeks for the bell and the Casorzos to get to Yale and then to Kamloops. There, a stagecoach was waiting for the family—and the bell—to take them on the final leg of their amazing journey.

Giovanni was out in the hills when his family arrived but they were welcomed by the priests and taken to their new home. Before long, Rosa became the mission's cook and her salary of $7.50 a month added to the family's income. Later that year, Giovanni registered his pre-emption, though there was a shortage of surveyors and the land wasn't officially surveyed until 1889. The swampy acres on the south side of Mission Creek were thick with underbrush, alders and scrawny birch, and needed to be cleared. Giovanni made a deal with the missionaries to buy two sows on instalment, and then borrowed money from Eli Lequime after Marie Louise convinced her husband the Italian would be a good risk. The land was fenced with the help of their Native neighbours and then drained by lining the ditches with long poles to create channels that would carry the water away from the site.

Rosa Casorzo became an independent, resourceful woman. She worked alongside Giovanni as they both learned to speak French and the Native dialect. They also relied on the knowledge and skills of the indigenous people and were able to survive poor harvests and medical emergencies by adopting their wilderness cures. These served the family well, as the nine children eventually born to the couple all survived, when many others didn't. Rosa also became very resourceful and used her needle and thread to stitch up the wounds of her children, as well as those of others who sought her help.

The spelling of the family's name changed from Casorzo to Casorso when the children started at the Mission school, and when the priests called Giovanni "Jean" (soon anglicized to John) everyone was far too busy with survival to make a fuss, and the changes remained.

One day a stranger arrived at Casorzo's farm offering to swap a bull and a few heifers for enough vegetables and supplies to get him out of the valley. Giovanni agreed, then discovered the cattle were across the lake and he would have to go and get them. He had two choices: one was a long arduous journey around the south end of the lake and up the west side to find the cattle and a return trip home the same way. The second and much shorter option would be to borrow a canoe to cross the lake and hire the McDougall family's old scow to carry the cattle back across. Giovanni chose the second option and had his horse swim over behind the canoe. Once he had rounded up the cattle and loaded them all onto the scow, he grabbed the oars and headed out. Just as they were about to land, the wind blew up and the animals panicked. The horse leapt off and headed to the eastern shore; the cattle bolted and swam for the western shore. Giovanni tossed the canoe overboard, jumped in, and abandoned the scow. It took awhile but he eventually rounded up the cattle and his horse and herded them to his side of the lake. The scow soon drifted to shore, so Giovanni rowed it back across the lake with his canoe on board, and returned it to the McDougalls. They were unimpressed with his tale… said it happened all the time.

Giovanni worked for the Mission for many years while his family and his farm grew and diversified. As his children left home, they purchased other properties nearby. The family's original log house can still be seen south of Father Pandosy's Mission, across the Casorso Road Bridge. The Casorzos were the first Italians to settle in the area. Others, including the Rampone, Turri, Capozzi and Ghezzi families, followed.

THE FIRST SETTLEMENT

During the 1880s, there was little change in the lives of the Mission Valley settlers. Their world was defined by their farms, and most didn't move far beyond the Okanagan, even as the next wave of gold seekers headed east to Grand Forks or farther south to Fairview, near Oliver. While those growing areas could have been markets for the Mission Valley's produce and cattle, transportation was a formidable challenge and most farmers continued to rely on those living nearby or passing through to sustain them.

By the final decades of the nineteenth century, a small community had begun to develop around Father Pandosy's Mission. Most settlers avoided the lakeshore, where the land was marshy and often flooded, and instead established their farms inland. Frontier life became less harrowing as the settlers grew what they needed to sustain themselves and sometimes enough to sell to those passing through. A wagon road eased travel to the north and the Dewdney Trail provided access to Hope for mail and supplies. Father Pandosy's original trail along the east side of the lake remained challenging: it was used when there was little choice, but it didn't encourage travel southward.

Still, survival itself was often remarkable, and while some thrived, others didn't make it. Many of those arriving in the Okanagan at this time were adrift in the world without the ties of family, church or community. Even those who found a place for themselves were often faced with near starvation, contaminated water, diseased milk, broken bones, measles or fevers, and were provided with only the most rudimentary of medical care, if any at all. Cheap alcohol was always available; time hung heavily during the long winters and gambling could be a ruinous diversion. Spousal and child abuse were prevalent, and discrimination against the aboriginal population was growing as more settlers arrived in the area. Hardy women made do with little and their children took on responsibilities beyond their years. Survival itself was often remarkable, and while some thrived, many didn't make it.

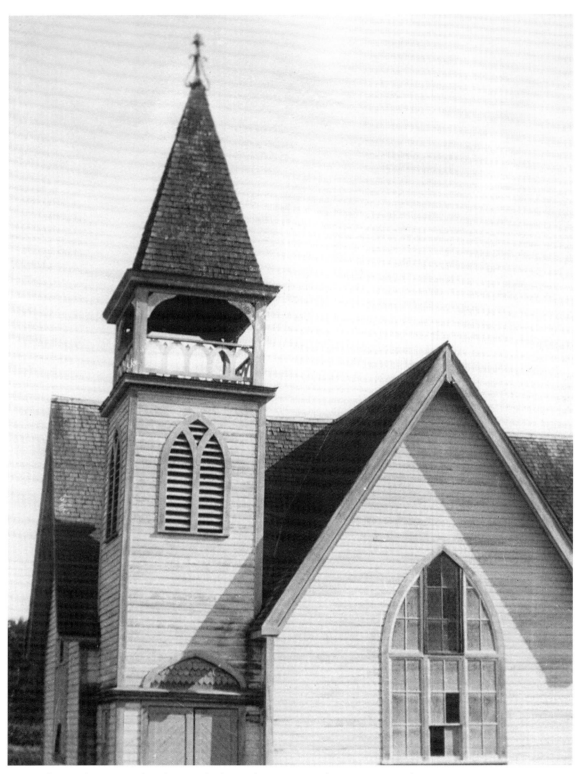

Benvoulin Presbyterian Church was dedicated in 1892 at the new Benvoulin townsite. | KELOWNA PUBLIC ARCHIVES

5606

CHAPTER TWO

Discovering the Okanagan

The wave of change that followed the completion of the CPR's transcontinental railway was being felt in the Okanagan by 1890. Rumours of a branch line through the valley encouraged investors to buy acreage along the railway's most likely routing. BC's mountainous terrain dictated that wagon roads and railroads generally ran east-west, while north-south travel could take advantage of the area's abundant river systems and lakes. Sternwheelers had been running freight and passengers on the Fraser River since the mid-1850s, and steam had been introduced to the Kootenay Lakes by the mid-1880s, so it wasn't long before boat traffic began to increase on Okanagan Lake. Settlers had been rowing themselves and their supplies up and down the lake for years, but steam would soon replace muscle. The Okanagan Valley was once again about to undergo a major transformation.

THE REAL ESTATE BOOM

Rumours and speculation flooded the region in the early 1890s with talk of new railroads, larger boats and new towns. It wasn't long before the valley's first real estate boom became a reality. The British and several of the Anglo-Irish aristocracy were discovering Canada's west and many, including the Vernon brothers, came with capital to invest, influential contacts through which to attract more and a lifestyle they intended to preserve. Change started at the northern end of the valley in about 1887, when the townsites of Centreville and Priest's Valley were collectively renamed Vernon, after Forbes George Vernon, owner of the nearby Coldstream Ranch. Vernon was a man to be reckoned with, as he was also a member of the provincial legislature and chief commissioner of lands and works.

The Shuswap & Okanagan Railway was incorporated in 1886 with a mandate to connect the CPR mainline at Sicamous with Vernon, and then continue on to Okanagan Lake at Okanagan Landing. The CPR was its dominant shareholder and while construction took some time to get underway, the track was complete enough by 1892 that a slow train was able to reach Vernon. In that same year, the Okanagan Land Development Company laid out the new townsite, built the Coldstream and Kalamalka hotels, installed a water system and published the *Vernon News*. Two of that company's principal investors were Forbes George Vernon and George Grant MacKay, the well-connected Vancouver land promoter who knew of the valley's fruit-growing potential from his fellow director at the BC Fruit Marketing Board, Alfred Postill.

The Okanagan Land and Development Company placed an advertisement in its newspaper at the end of 1891 touting Vernon as the gateway to the Okanagan, Nicola and Similkameen Valleys, as well as the mining camps of Rock Creek and Keremeos. Rumours were rampant that a Vernon & Okanagan Railway would soon be built through the Mission Valley to Penticton and connect the CPR with the Great Northern Railway in the US. Vernon was sure to become the area's natural marketplace and supply headquarters as settlers arrived to take advantage of the abundant fruit growing, ranching and mining opportunities. Prospective land purchasers were invited to come in person, meet with the company's local representatives and be introduced to the community's unlimited potential.

With Vernon established, G.G. MacKay was certain the rumoured railway running through the centre of the valley would be the next best development opportunity. It wasn't long before he laid out a new Benvoulin townsite. It was at the intersection of the wagon roads between the Catholic Mission and Vernon, and the westerly road to Knox's wharf at the base of the mountain (today's intersection of Benvoulin and Byrns Roads). MacKay signalled the settlers he hoped to attract by donating land for a Presbyterian church, which would be the first Protestant church in the Mission Valley. (The one on Richter Street would not be built until 1898.) The new townsite soon grew to include a blacksmith shop, a Chinese laundry, a general store and a ten-room hotel painted yellow with a mixture of oil and the ochre found in Mission Creek. MacKay called his new town Benvoulin because of a similar valley view near Oban, in his native Scotland.

ROYALTY DISCOVERS THE OKANAGAN

Among the well-connected Scottish aristocrats interested in Canada were Lord and Lady Aberdeen, who arrived in Vancouver in 1890 as part of their cross-Canada rail tour. John Campbell Hamilton Gordon, the Seventh Earl of Aberdeen (and later First Marquess of Aberdeen and Temair), had succeeded to his title after the untimely death of a brother. His wife, Ishbel Maria Marjoribanks (pronounced Marshbanks), was the daughter of the first Lord Tweedsmouth. They were both from prominent families and part of Queen Victoria's colonial administration: the earl had been appointed Lord Lieutenant of Ireland before serving as Canada's Governor General from 1893 to 1898.

Their trip had been designed to give Ishbel a rest from her demanding commitments to various social and political causes at home, and the recurring bouts of nervous exhaustion that plagued her for much of her life. Never one to let an opportunity pass, Ishbel also wanted to check up on some of the British girls who had been sent to the colony by one of her charitable organizations; such emigrations were seen as a good way to deal with the social problems plaguing industrial Britain, as well as to ensure the colony was populated with the "right" sort of people. The Aberdeens had already decided to purchase a holiday retreat in Western Canada and with Lady Aberdeen's brother, Coutts, in need of a job, he would be available to manage it for them.

Shortly after their arrival, the viceregal couple re-established contact with George Grant MacKay, who had been the engineer in charge of building roads at Lady Aberdeen's ancestral home in Inverness-shire. MacKay had been in Vancouver about three years by the time the Aberdeens arrived and was well established in the real estate business. The viceregal couple had little time to look at property during their short stay but decided MacKay's first suggestion of the Fraser Valley, at fifty to sixty dollars an acre, was too expensive.

MacKay's next suggestion, a little farther away, was the Okanagan Valley. He knew the area not only because of its fruit-growing potential, but because he had already bought three thousand acres of land along the rumoured railway's most likely route. These lands included many of the originally pre-empted acres, whose owners were both aging and weary of the struggles of the past decades; they were also likely surprised anyone wanted to buy their land. This suggestion was more to the Aberdeens' liking, and before the viceregal couple left Vancouver they had engaged MacKay to act on their behalf and purchase property. The 480-acre

McDougall homestead half a mile or so from Father Pandosy's mission had already been purchased by MacKay; he resold to the Aberdeens for ten thousand dollars. A rough though functional house was already on the property and the sale included seventy head of cattle, horses and other livestock, plus wheat and farm implements. MacKay's assurances that a new railway would soon be built through the area, and increase property values at least tenfold, further enticed the couple to purchase the property, sight unseen.

The farm was a perfect opportunity for Ishbel's brother, the Honourable Coutts Marjoribanks. Coutts was a remittance man—one of those young English men, often the second or third sons of British nobility, who didn't inherit the ancestral property, didn't seem much attracted to the church or the army and for whom a career in business was simply unsuitable. Many of these young men were sent off to the colonies to earn their keep or, at the very least, not embarrass the family. Each Marjoribanks son was sent to the New World and given a cattle ranch: Archibald the 200,000-acre Rocking Chair Ranch in Texas, and Coutts the 960-acre Horse-Shoe Ranch in North Dakota. They also each received remittances of four hundred pounds a year. Neither son knew much about raising cattle or running a business, though both were genial and popular—especially in the neighbouring saloons, when their money arrived. It wasn't long before both ranches were up for sale.

It didn't take Coutts and his friend and new ranch manager, Eustace Smith, long to vacate their old ranch and head north for a new adventure. The old farmhouse was far too primitive for the Aberdeens so the pair had a new elegant clapboard ranch house built, patterned on the style of an East Indian cottage and complete with gold Japanese wallpaper, seven chimneys and a wraparound veranda. The ranch was soon called Guisachan, after the Marjoribanks' ancestral home in Scotland. Once the house was finished, the two men felt their job was done and set about enjoying valley life, filling their days with hunting expeditions and visits to the various saloons.

The Aberdeens returned to British Columbia in the fall of 1891 and made their first visit to the Okanagan. The Shuswap & Okanagan Railway was still a work in progress and the Aberdeens had to pay seventy-five dollars (later negotiated to half by his lordship) to hire an engine to pull their passenger car; two luggage cars loaded with a motley collection of men, dogs, parcels, trunks and agricultural machinery; and a caboose. The train moved so slowly that the party was able to clamber off and walk alongside the engine; other times they had to climb on board as the train crossed bridges still being worked on by large gangs of men.

The party finally arrived in Vernon, where they were met by Coutts, who had been enjoying himself for a week as he waited for the couple: old-timers remember Coutts riding his horse up the stairs of the Kalamalka Hotel and into the commodious bar for a drink. The Honourable Mr. Forbes Vernon had been scheduled to greet the couple and open the Vernon Agricultural Fair, but had been detained in Victoria. Lord Aberdeen took his place and was delighted to declare the Vernon Fair officially open. It was a grand occasion for the Aberdeens: they met many important people from all over the Okanagan and renewed their acquaintance with George MacKay, who was in town to buy more of the old Mission ranches. He had already begun to subdivide them into forty- to sixty-acre lots to sell to the settlers he was hoping to attract to the valley.

The viceregal party dallied so long at the fair that the small steamer that was to carry them down the lake to their Guisachan property had already departed by the time they were ready to go. The crews of other boats had all decamped for the ball and festivities in Vernon, so the party was left to accept Leon Lequime's offer to take them south. His little boat was not equipped to carry passengers but the party appeared undeterred as they crowded into its makeshift cabin and sang their way through much of the four-hour moonlit trip down the lake.

The Aberdeens and their party landed near the Mission wharf very early in the morning, walked the two miles to Guisachan House and startled the ranch manager: not expecting anyone, he opened the door with shotgun in hand. While Foo, the Chinese cook, prepared a meal, the family admired the bachelor manager's handiwork: stag horns and deer heads were mounted on the gold wallpaper, the large sitting and dining rooms were well furnished, as were the six bedrooms, and the kitchen and office were separated by the veranda that encircled the house.

This was the first time the Aberdeens had visited their new property and their arrival in the dark of night did nothing to dispel their expectation of flat plains and bare hills. They were delighted when the morning light revealed that their property looked more like Scotland than they could have imagined. Woods surrounded the house, the lake was off in the distance and pine trees covered the nearby hillsides. The autumn-gold poplars and cottonwoods along the banks of Mission Creek added to the charming vista.

The Kelowna Story: An Okanagan History

Discovering the Okanagan

Guisachan House in Okanagan Mission

Lord and Lady Aberdeen's original Indian colonial style bungalow was built in 1891 and given the name of Lady Aberdeen's ancestral Scottish home. Guisachan means "place of the firs." The above photo shows the family gathered with neighbours for a bear hunt during their short stay, but no bear was found, so the hunters had to make do with prairie chickens. | KELOWNA PUBLIC ARCHIVES 3412

PREVIOUS PAGES: Guisachan House has undergone several renovations and restorations in the intervening years, and is currently a restaurant. The two and a half acres of Edwardian gardens surrounding the building were first planted by Elaine Cameron, who, with her husband Paddy, purchased the property from the Aberdeens. Mrs. Cameron kept meticulous journals and photographs of her plantings, which were used to reconstruct the garden. The main entrance to the house was originally through the avenue of cedars to the north. It has been said that on a clear moonlit night, the clip-clop of the horse carriages that long ago visited the house can still be heard. The square-cut log house on the property originally belonged to John McDougall, and was built in 1886; it was moved onto the site in the 1980s. The Guisachan buildings and garden are off Cameron Avenue. | STUART KERNAGHAN, XYPHOTOS.CA

The Aberdeens stayed for a full and busy week. They went on a bear hunt with a group of locals (though only shot prairie chickens), they donated four hundred dollars to help build the new Benvoulin Presbyterian Church, enjoyed a picnic at Long Lake (Kalamalka Lake) and visited Alfred Postill and his mother for tea. They also hosted a social—an unusual event in this unsophisticated community—where guests performed songs and recitations and the Aberdeens' daughter, Lady Marjorie, sang three French songs to much acclaim. Tea was then served and Lady Aberdeen brought the event to a close with two readings. A few days later, the family held an informal church service in their living room and were surprised by the arrival of the Mission priests, who seemed much pleased with Lord Aberdeen's words.

The Aberdeens were soon convinced that the Okanagan showed great promise as a fruit-growing centre. Hoping to attract a good class of settler, Lady Aberdeen noted that orcharding would be a "delightful occupation" for those with capital to invest who could also provide the good influences and high moral tone so needed in the area. They led by example and soon had two hundred acres of their property planted with apples, pears, plums, cherries and peaches. Strawberries, raspberries and blackberries were set between the trees to provide a more immediate cash crop. Lady Aberdeen also mused that a jam factory would be a great addition to their farm as it could surely produce jams to rival those produced by Crosse and Blackwell, her favourite English brand. (Hers would be sold as "The Premier Preserves manufactured from the celebrated Okanagan Orchards.")

It was a whirlwind visit and the Aberdeens were on their way back to Scotland a few days later, on October 24, 1891. But the lord and lady were so enchanted with their time at Guisachan they instructed George MacKay to find them additional property. MacKay and Forbes Vernon were still partners in the land development company, and MacKay knew Vernon was interested in selling his thirteen-thousand-acre Coldstream Ranch. It was an obvious choice for the Aberdeens. They wasted no time and a week after departing from their first visit to Guisachan the Aberdeens had purchased the larger property, plus two thousand head of cattle, seventy horses, farm implements, hogs, hay and furniture. Coutts soon moved north to manage the new ranch. A second home was built for the family on the Coldstream property and the Aberdeens rarely visited Guisachan again, and never stayed at the house.

Lord and Lady Aberdeen in their viceregal finery in front of their Coldstream Ranch jam factory. No jam was ever made but it was a fine location for parties. | KELOWNA PUBLIC ARCHIVES 3409

It was three years before the Aberdeens were able to visit their new property. By then, Lord Aberdeen had already been Canada's Governor General for a year. Lady Aberdeen's jam factory was built at the Coldstream Ranch. No jam was ever produced, but the building became the perfect setting for the couple's grand balls. The Aberdeens owned Guisachan until 1903, when it was sold to the Cameron family. They last visited the Coldstream Ranch in the winter of 1915–16; Lord Woolavington, who had joined the Aberdeens as a business partner, assumed ownership of the property in 1921.

Discovering the Okanagan

Among Lady Aberdeen's many attributes was that she was a prolific journalist. *Through Canada with a Kodak*, published in 1893, the same year Lord Aberdeen became Governor General of Canada, told the story of the couple's first train trip across Canada. The Kodak camera had recently been invented and Ishbel included a number of photographs, along with several of her own sketches, in the book. With her well-developed social conscience, formidable organizing talents and political astuteness, she was also a force to be reckoned with. Lady Aberdeen established the National Council of Women (including a chapter in Vernon), the Victorian Order of Nurses and the May Court Club (Canada's oldest women's service organization) during the brief time she was in Canada; in fact, she sometimes overshadowed her quiet husband and is known in some circles as Canada's Governess General.

Though the Aberdeens' agricultural endeavours were never a financial success, the couple's willingness to visit, to invest in the land, to build homes and to encourage others to join them put the Okanagan on the British Empire's map. In particular, their belief in the valley's fruit-growing potential attracted immigrants and it wasn't long before the Okanagan became one of the most sought-after destinations in the empire. The Aberdeens' appeal to British settlers set the stage for most future immigration to the valley, though a few settlers of other nationalities, already homesteading on the Prairies, were also drawn to the area's benign climate. The romantic notion of planting orchards and then sitting back and reaping the benefits was certainly attractive, though many who bought into the Aberdeens' vision soon realized that much more effort was required.

EARLIEST KELOWNA

G.G. MacKay's arrival in the Mission Valley seemed to roust the old-timers from their lethargy. The two remaining Lequime brothers, Bernard and Leon, were among the few early settlers who had enough money to expand their holdings. They bought Auguste Gillard's original pre-emption in 1890. It was a logical choice as the property shared a common boundary with theirs as well, and Gillard's included a workable slice of Okanagan lakeshore.

The Lequime sawmill had been packing lumber to settlers up and down the valley for a number of years, but with increased traffic on Okanagan Lake the advantage of having ready access to the waterway was becoming more apparent. In 1891 the brothers dismantled their mill on

Kelowna in 1894 was described as a "crude and unpromising little place," with the Lequime Bros. & Company store, a farm implement warehouse, a livery barn and not much else. One of the rare signs of life in the settlement was when the whistle blew to announce the arrival of the SS *Aberdeen*, the valley's first sternwheeler. Everyone within hearing distance would rush to the dock to see who was arriving and who was departing. | KELOWNA PUBLIC ARCHIVES 7973

the bench above their Mission property, packed up what was salvageable and reconstructed it on the lakeshore of their new property. The main building was a ninety-two-foot-long sawmill, the second a forty-five-foot-long planing mill, and there was a dry kiln housed in a separate building. Just north of the sawmill, a sixteen-by-forty-foot boarding house was built for men working at the mill. Over time it became known as the Grand Pacific Hotel and also began welcoming travellers passing through town. A Chinese cook prepared meals in a nearby lean-to cookhouse and a painted sign inviting people to "Eat and Flop" remained visible on the side of the building for many years.

When the Lequimes purchased Gillard's property, a townsite plan had already been prepared but not registered; Bernard saw to this in August 1892. Earlier that year Bernard had commissioned J.A. Coryell, C.E. and Company, surveyors from Vernon, to lay out the approximately three-hundred-acre townsite, and placed an advertisement in the *Vernon News* to say that the new town would be called Kelowna. There are a number of versions of the story about how Kelowna got its name, but it is generally agreed that on one cold winter day, Auguste Gillard, the original owner of the land who lived beside the creek at the south end of today's Ellis Street, was seen climbing up the ladder of his kekuli (or kickwillie), an

Indian pit house built half below the ground and half above, with a rough timber roof and an access ladder extending up through the smoke hole. A passing group of Natives heard a great commotion coming from inside the dwelling and stopped to stare as a large hairy creature backed up the ladder. It being winter, Gillard had cut neither his hair nor his beard, and the Natives, thinking he was a bear, called out *Kemxtu´h, Kemxtu´h*—or "Kim-ach-touch, Kim-ach-touch"—meaning "brown bear, brown bear." The name stuck with Gillard for many years. Some of the old-timers thought "Kimachtouch" would be a great name for the new town, but Lequime wasn't convinced—he thought it might be awkward for those not familiar with the Native language. However, when "Kelowna," the Native word for grizzly bear, was suggested as an alternative, Lequime was more agreeable and undeterred by the fact that Natives traditionally did not name places after animals.

In addition to announcing the townsite and its new name, Bernard Lequime placed another advertisement in the same issue of the *Vernon News*, offering lots for sale in "The Garden Town of B.C. and the natural shipping and distributing point for the fertile Okanagan Mission Valley." The rivalry between Vernon and Kelowna had begun. Lequime seemed naively optimistic that his Kelowna townsite would prevail over Benvoulin.

George MacKay returned to the Mission Valley late in 1892, still certain that construction of the new rail line was imminent. It would be his last visit, as the Okanagan's first great real estate promoter passed away at his home in Vancouver a few weeks later, at the age of sixty-seven. MacKay had only been in Canada five years and had already made a profound impact: in Vancouver he was known as the "Laird of Capilano" for constructing the first suspension bridge across that canyon. He had arrived in the Okanagan and instigated the break-up of the valley's large cattle ranches into orchard-sized properties. His introduction of the Aberdeens to the Mission Valley was a timely stroke of genius: they became his most enthusiastic and influential ambassadors and spread word of the Okanagan around the British Empire as few others could have done.

Bernard Lequime was among the few who didn't buy into MacKay's sales pitch and remained convinced that Okanagan Lake would be the preferred travel route in the future. Lequime built a wharf and a freight shed in the nearby bay (now the north-facing beach in City Park) and soon became the sole owner of the lakeside sawmill. Not long after, he was plagued by a series of fires: the dry kiln caught fire three times in the first year of operation; another fire soon destroyed the sawmill, planing mill and nearby piles of lumber. Only the great efforts of a bucket brigade saved another 200,000 feet of lumber piled a bit farther away from the plant. Insurance wasn't an option, and Lequime financed the reconstruction himself. The business was likely profitable, however, even though it operated only during the warmer months of the year and usually only employed about twenty men.

Though Leon Lequime left the sawmill business, he joined Bernard to create the Lequime Bros. General Store which opened across the dirt road from their sawmill. The new store, built by newcomer David Lloyd-Jones and measuring twenty-six by forty-five feet, catered to the lake trade. (The brothers also continued to operate their family's Mission store, which Eli, their father, had opened thirty years earlier.) A few months later, the store became Lequime Bros. & Company when Clinton Atwood and Edwin Weddell became partners in the business. They advertised in the *Vernon News*, stating that Lequime Bros. & Co. of Kelowna carried "the best stock in the country" and assuring the people of the district that their prices compared "with any in the Valley." The stock consisted of dry goods, boots and shoes, crockery, glassware and groceries, all new and well bought.

DEALING WITH OGOPOGO

As settlers began to travel Okanagan Lake, the Ogopogo became a fearsome reality in their lives. The creature began life in the legends of the Okanagan people as N´ha-a-itk (or Naitaka), a lake monster that was both revered and feared. The monster was said to be the embodiment of an evil wanderer who murdered a kindly old man and was cursed with having to spend eternity near the scene of the crime. Pictographs of the creature were found on the rock bluffs above the lake, and early stories tell of the need to appease the monster by offering small animal sacrifices. Those who ignored the warning or didn't show the proper reverence would all too often be caught in a wild and unexpected storm. Among N´ha-a-itk's victims was the young Chief Timbasket, who scoffed at the stories, paddled too close to the monster's home in the caves around Squally Point (across the lake from present-day Peachland) and was suddenly sucked under in a great swirl of angry waves. He and his family members vanished. Some time later his canoe was found far up the mountainside, farther than any wave might have thrown it... had N´ha-a-itk devoured the chief and flung his canoe away in anger?

Early settlers knew to respect the turbulent, unpredictable lake, but also knew the Native legends. They told stories of paddling across the lake with their horses tied behind canoes, when the horses would inexplicably be drawn down and down by some strange force from below. The once-sacred monster turned into a demon as early settlers patrolled the lakeshore, musket in hand, to protect their families. Other times, great slabs of meat were stuck on large iron hooks and set out in the lake to trap the creature.

Descriptions vary, though most of those reporting sightings agree that the monster is a curious aquatic species. Its appearance hasn't changed much over time—the eyes are bulging, and it is dark green or shiny black—though its early snake-like head has evolved into something more horse- or sheep-like. Its early upright ears have also become tiny horns. Perhaps there is a forked tail. Its long slim body, usually between thirty and seventy feet in length, is seen as two or three or more humps above the water. The creature has been seen moving against the wind, though it is most often sighted as a swell in a calm lake when no boat or debris is in sight. It moves too fast to be a swimmer and leaves a wake that washes up on the beach a few minutes later.

THE ADMIRAL OF THE OKANAGAN

The wave of change created by the completion of the Canadian Pacific's transcontinental railway slowly found its way into the Okanagan. By this time, the Shuswap & Okanagan Railway carried passengers from the transcontinental train through Vernon and onto the lakeshore at Okanagan Landing. Rumours of the next likely branch line were rampant as various companies were laying tracks across the international border, over mountain ranges and into mine sites. Everyone was certain the Mission Valley line was inevitable. Yet the geographic reality of the east side of Okanagan Lake, with its deep canyons and steep mountainsides, conspired against any such plans: no rail line would ever materialize. Although the idea never entirely disappeared, the arrival of the lake steamers soon pushed talk of it aside.

Captain Thomas Dolman Shorts was the first of many enterprising individuals to travel the length of Okanagan Lake by boat. He whipsawed lumber, built a twenty-two-foot-long rowboat, calling it the *Ruth Shorts*, after his mother. The boat could carry two and a half tons of cargo, accommodate a few passengers and hoist a sail if wind and weather permitted. There was nothing scheduled or ordinary about travelling with the captain. Shorts didn't like to be tied down so he departed when he felt like it, or when there was enough business to warrant the effort.

He rowed during the day and would pull up to a beach at dusk, where he and his passengers would sleep under the trees for the night. If the weather took a turn for the worse he would head for land. Even the most fragile governess travelling to join a new family at the south end of the lake had little alternative but to join the captain and camp out until the weather improved. If Shorts travelled in a straight line, the trip between Okanagan Landing and Penticton was about sixty-five miles and took about nine days of rowing—if the weather was fine. If the weather was bad, it took as long as it took.

Shorts soon moved on to steam power and built the thirty-five-foot *Mary Victoria Greenhow* in about 1884. He could now carry five tons of freight and several passengers, and he used kerosene as fuel. The maiden voyage wasn't a great success as the captain had underestimated the amount of fuel he would need and was forced to resort to his oars several times, begging or borrowing more kerosene along the way. His arrival in Penticton was celebrated with a twenty-one-shotgun salute—no cannons were available. After acknowledging the tribute, Shorts refuelled and headed back north. The Lequime store at Okanagan Mission was his next supply point: he beached the boat and walked across the fields to the store. On his return, Shorts discovered that fire had destroyed most of his boat, though fortunately not enough to prevent him from returning to Okanagan Landing.

Shorts wanted to change the engine to burn wood, so he removed it, made revisions and, in 1887, installed the converted engine into the hull of the new thirty-foot-long *Jubilee*. Named in honour of Queen Victoria's fifty years on Britain's throne, this boat could tow a barge—which was a bonus, as the volume of freight heading to Penticton for the nearby mines had increased significantly. The engine continued to have an insatiable appetite, however, and Shorts had to arrange for cord wood to be stacked along the shoreline on both sides of the lake. Even these reserves were often not enough, and Shorts continued to run out of fuel regularly; on one trip he was forced to feed his cargo of cedar shakes into the boiler so he could reach his destination. The *Jubilee* lasted for two years: the winter of 1889 was particularly cold and when the ice finally thawed around its berth at Okanagan Landing, the boat promptly sank.

Not having the funds to improve or expand his fleet of one, the ambitious Shorts convinced pioneer South Okanagan rancher Tom Ellis to invest in his next venture. The new boat would be his largest yet, but it would take some time to build. Shorts couldn't afford to be sidelined during its construction, however, so he salvaged the engine from the *Jubilee*, attached it to a scow and called the result the *City of Vernon*. No one had a kind word to say about the aberration but it kept him in business. When the new boat was finally ready, Shorts christened it the *Penticton*. Though it was intended to carry passengers as well as freight, Shorts still wasn't into luxury: the *Penticton's* cabin could hold twenty-five people, but it contained only one chair—first come, first seated. And there was still no semblance of a schedule—the good captain sailed when he felt like it. The *City of Vernon* was sold and renamed the *Mud Hen* because it spent more time at the bottom of the lake than on the surface. Remarkably, the engine was again salvaged and installed in the *Wanderer*, later known as the *Violet*. Today, the engine is on display at the Vernon Museum.

Leon Lequime bought the *Penticton* from Shorts and Ellis in 1892. He paid the hefty sum of five thousand dollars for the boat and then negotiated a contract with the CPR to meet the Shuswap & Okanagan Railway at Okanagan Landing and deliver passengers and mail to their various destinations. Since Okanagan Lake froze over again that winter, the 1892–93 boating season was short. The CPR had also begun to build its first sternwheeler, the SS *Aberdeen*, at Okanagan Landing. Leon continued to operate the *Penticton* for a number of years, including during the winters when the *Aberdeen* was removed from service. The boat was later converted to tow logs for the Kelowna Saw Mill. When that was no longer viable, the *Penticton* was dismantled and abandoned on the beach near the mill. A few years later, the boat mysteriously burned to the waterline.

The feisty Captain Shorts, who became known as the "Admiral of the Okanagan," wasn't intimidated by the "grasping octopus of the CPR." He bought another old hulk, named it *Lucy*, and took out an advertisement in the *Vernon News* to announce: "The opposition is here to stay, and so am I." In spite of the bravado, Shorts couldn't compete with the luxury, the schedule or the freight capacity of the newly launched *Aberdeen*. It wasn't long before he left the Okanagan and headed off to strike it rich in the Klondike goldfields.

A NEW ERA OF LAKE TRAVEL

Sternwheelers have a long and storied history in British Columbia. Though often associated with the Mississippi River, the boats were used more extensively throughout this province than anywhere else in North

America: they paddled up and down the stormy Pacific coastline, through rock-strewn rivers, and along the abundant lakes nestled between the mountain ranges. Some of these vessels were elegant and stately, finished with exotic teak and mahogany and outfitted with brass spittoons, ladies' lounges and potted palms. Others were more like makeshift packing crates, built to carry men and supplies into the wild and otherwise inaccessible parts of the province.

The SS *Aberdeen* was named after Lord Aberdeen, who bought land in the Okanagan and encouraged settlers to come to the valley. This was first of the CPR's fleet of sternwheelers, which brought a new era of luxury travel to the Okanagan. |

Steam travel was slow in coming to the Okanagan. While paddlewheelers had been used on the Fraser River since the 1850s, most people coming to the valley either walked or rode, taking the original Okanagan Fur Brigade Trail along the west side of the lake, the Dewdney Trail from Hope and Father Pandosy's trail down the east side of Okanagan Lake. The new boats, which arrived in the early 1890s, were flat-bottomed, made mostly of wood and had paddlewheels that only needed inches of water to generate enough thrust to propel them through shallow water or over river sandbars. On the lakes, the boats could nose up to a beach if no wharf was available—the paddlewheel would be left in deeper water, so it could reverse and get underway again.

Okanagan Landing, the terminus of the Shuswap & Okanagan Railway, was the location of a two-stall roundhouse, a freight warehouse and a hundred-foot-long wharf. At the time it was just a sleepy village with an old hotel, a general store, a red schoolhouse and a few summer shacks along the beach. Yet Okanagan Landing became the shipbuilding yard for the CPR: everything—the steel hull, the engines, the boilers and the fittings—arrived by train for assembly at the yard. The company's master carpenters added the wooden decks while local sash and door factories supplied interior fittings. The Okanagan sternwheelers were launched sideways and since there was no dry dock, hull repairs required several teams of horses to haul the boats back up the stringers to be worked on.

The keel of the lake's first paddlewheeler was laid in the fall of 1891 and the boat was launched on May 22, 1893. The SS *Aberdeen* was named after Lord Aberdeen, owner of the nearby Coldstream Ranch and Canada's seventh Governor General. Given their experience with the colourful Captain Shorts and his boats, travellers were awestruck. The *Aberdeen*'s wooden keel was 146 feet long, and the paddlewheel added

Winters were particularly challenging for lake travel, so barges were added in an attempt to break the ice. When that didn't work, men came with their saws, hoping to open a channel. | KELOWNA PUBLIC ARCHIVES 6225

another 19 feet. The grand sternwheeler had two decks and a pilot house. As Captain Shorts had cared little for comfort, the furnishings of the *Aberdeen* were also remarkable. There was an observation lounge with plush seats and curtains on the windows, fine meals were served by stewards in a dining room fitted with fine silver and white linen, and passengers could request that the well-stocked bar be opened between ports. Though a trip down the lake rarely exceeded six hours, the *Aberdeen* had eleven comfortable staterooms for rent, each of which was fitted with screens to keep out the summer's pesky mosquitoes. The CPR would advertise a package including rail travel from Vancouver to Okanagan Landing and travel aboard the SS *Aberdeen* to Penticton for thirty dollars per person.

The Shuswap & Okanagan Railway met the CPR mainline at Sicamous each Monday, Wednesday and Friday and delivered passengers and freight to Okanagan Landing by about 10:30. As soon as the people and cargo were transferred on board, the *Aberdeen* would depart and head south, zigzagging down the lake from the east side to the west side until it reached Penticton in the early evening. Since any settler could fly a white flag to signal the boat ashore, or light two fires on the beach at night, travel times varied. The *Aberdeen* returned north each Tuesday, Thursday and Saturday, departing Penticton about noon, arriving in Kelowna about three and then travelling onward to Okanagan Landing in time to connect with the waiting train to Sicamous. The sound of the ship's whistle would announce the *Aberdeen*'s imminent arrival, and though its time at each wharf was brief, everyone within hearing distance would gather to see who was coming and going, and to pick up the latest news—or gossip.

The Lequime Bros. & Company store across the street from the wharf soon developed a brisk lake trade: the boat would pick up orders from settlers along the lakeshore and deliver them to the general store or the butcher shop when they reached port. The filled orders would be picked up on the return trip, and dropped off at the respective homes.

Reliable and regularly scheduled boat service had a profound impact on the Okanagan as increasing numbers of settlers arrived in the valley to buy orchard-sized lots that had once been part of large cattle ranches. Advertising campaigns lured often innocent settlers to come, plant fruit trees and then enjoy the genteel lifestyle as they waited for their trees to bear fruit. New communities such as Peachland and Naramata came into being while others—including Kelowna, once thought to be too inaccessible to attract settlers—grew. People travelled with greater confidence and took comfort in the regular passenger and freight service. The *Aberdeen* could carry two hundred tons of freight and was sometimes so overloaded that crew had to walk along the outside rubbing boards to get around. The more established settlements flourished, as did the new communities that were springing up along the lakeshore.

1892: A PIVOTAL YEAR

As sometimes happens when a number of otherwise random events converge, 1892 became the year that the Mission Valley—and Kelowna, in particular—began to flourish. The Shuswap & Okanagan Railway, the SS *Aberdeen*, newly available land, ambitious British settlers and the Aberdeens: it was a unique combination. Newcomers were mostly young and energetic, well-educated and worldly, physically fit and looking for adventure. Several had money of their own or knew how to access it.

The Lake View Hotel was built in 1892. With its fine dining room and facilities for receptions and balls, it catered to both those passing through and those staying longer. Tommy, the resident card shark, ran the poker tables in the back rooms. |

Though Benvoulin was slated to become the valley's premier townsite, its existence was still dependent on the much-rumoured new rail line.

Bernard Lequime had created his own momentum: his sawmill was beside the wharf he had built at the end of the Kelowna townsite's only street, to replace the original wharf farther along the bay. Then he named the street Bernard, after himself. Lequime's general store was well established, and Archie McDonald had built the Lake View Hotel around the corner, next door. The hotel was the first in the new town and offered both travellers and those needing short-term room and board the additional benefits of a fine dining room and a well-stocked bar. With a veranda along the front of the building, a gallery along the second floor and twenty-five well-appointed rooms, McDonald's hotel hosted many banquets, bachelor balls and receptions over the next few years. The backroom poker game was run by Tommy, the resident card shark, who was prepared to take on anyone, regardless of the time or the day. Later the same year, Messrs. Riley and Donald built a forty-by-sixty-foot farm equipment warehouse just east of Lequime's store and then held a gala

Footloose bachelors pitched their tents in what would soon become City Park. The carefree lifestyle was a marked contrast to the stuffy British drawing rooms many were accustomed to. | KELOWNA PUBLIC ARCHIVES 762

ball in the building before their stock arrived. A blacksmith shop opened and Thomas Spence ran the town's first real estate business in the small cottage wedged in between Lequime's store and McDonald's hotel.

More settlers arrived and while some went into business, others bought land and planted orchards. Another general store was built and a few substantial three- and four-room family homes were built nearby. Single men built one-room shacks on the many empty lots around town, though in the summer they pitched tents amid the brush in what would shortly become City Park. Most of these men were unfamiliar with keeping a house or even cooking: many subsisted on bacon and eggs, learned to live with dust and used the lake for bathing, if they felt the need. It was, at least initially, a wonderfully unencumbered way to live.

With their Mission store as a prototype, the Lequimes' Kelowna store soon became the trading and social centre for the new community. The outside stairway and second-floor room were available to any group in town who needed space to meet or celebrate. That space became the first schoolroom in Kelowna and supported what would become the remarkably vibrant social life of the frontier community. The first of an endless number of public concerts was held there on December 8, 1892, and featured Miss Thomson, who recited "Mary Queen of Scots"; Miss Blackburn and D.W. Crowely, who sang a duet; and Reverend Mr. Langill, who gave a recitation. Unnamed participants concluded the evening program with a reading of "The Society of the Declectable Les Miserables" before everyone joined in with rousing renditions of "The Maple Leaf Forever" and "God Save the Queen." The settlers had to raise the funds for any service they wanted—a school, a church or a hospital, a band or a cricket club—and held concerts, balls and musical productions to entice people to contribute. These events soon became a regular feature of community life.

In fact, any excuse (or no excuse at all) seemed to give rise to an astounding array of social gatherings. Hard physical work and long distances rarely deterred residents from attending events in settlers' homes or in the various hotels dotted around the countryside. A bachelors' lunch at the Lake View Hotel might be followed that night by a dinner and dance at the Benvoulin Hotel; a cricket match would conclude with a banquet, a concert and then a ball. A thirty-mile trip by sleigh, wagon or horseback through a moonlit night to attend a gathering usually included the whole family, especially during the boredom of long winters. A frozen Okanagan Lake was no deterrent as horses and sleighs carried both people and freight across the icy surface.

THERE WAS ALWAYS TIME TO PLAY

Many of those arriving in the Okanagan Valley at the time came out of the English public school system, where sports and the arts were ingrained parts of daily life, and they were determined not to change their ways. Cricket, long jump and foot races were on the same programs as horse races and lacrosse competitions. When the games were finished, competitors would turn their talents to the stage and mount expansive productions of most of what Gilbert and Sullivan had to offer. Celebrating Queen Victoria's seventy-fifth birthday in 1894, local cricketers overwhelmed the Trout Creek (Summerland) team and then carried on to a splendid concert in the CPR warehouse. The building had been transformed with flags, bunting and evergreens and lit by as many lanterns as could be borrowed from around town. A large crowd from Vernon boarded the *Aberdeen* and travelled down the lake for the concert and then stayed on for the ball. There were undoubtedly many toasts to good Queen Victoria before they departed for home around three in the morning.

The next year, Vernon's cricket team travelled to Kelowna on the steamer *Fairview* while a large group of merrymakers followed on the *Aberdeen*. The Kelowna team again proved to be invincible. The concert that followed featured songs by many local residents, a banjo solo by Mr. Dan Gallagher and a farce, *Slasher and Dasher*, where "the fun was fast and furious, and the audience convulsed with laughter." A pattern was soon established: sometimes the visiting team would be from Vernon; other times, from Trout Creek. They might have been celebrating Dominion Day or raising money for the school, and the competition might start with baseball or lacrosse, then move on to the long jump, the high jump, the hundred-yard dash and a wheelbarrow race. Or it might involve a caber toss or the shot put, and finish up with a sack race. At other times, horse races would start the day. Before the town had a designated racetrack, Ellis Street, between Gaston and Bernard Avenues, served that purpose in spite of an abundance of mud, potholes and inevitable tumbles.

These sporting events would be followed by a banquet and a concert that might feature the black-faced Kelowna Minstrels or a farce where gentlemen played most of the roles, before everyone moved on to a ball. The Kelowna Brass Band was formed in 1894 and added their considerable talents to every community event. "The Maple Leaf Forever" preceded all goings-on while "God Save the Queen" concluded them. At a time when Kelowna's population was less than one hundred, it was not uncommon for more than five hundred people to gather for these celebrations.

The season was irrelevant: Christmas offered many opportunities to gather, as did the many frozen ponds around the community. Married couples took on the singles in outdoor curling competitions, ice skaters donned masks "novel, beautiful and ludicrous," and prizes were awarded to ladies for "fancy skating"... they were "the personification of fairy gracefulness." Men also competed in fancy skating events and won prizes for being the best-dressed "gent masker"—where an otherwise ordinary man transformed himself into a Highland chief. In the summer, swimming, canoeing and sailing races were added to the list of organized activities and became the genesis of Kelowna's legendary Regattas.

Other towns throughout the valley reciprocated with their own invitations. Shared social and sporting events strengthened the communities and enabled newcomers to replicate the lives they had left behind. As the bonds of community strengthened, friendships evolved into business relationships, and what might have been social or class barriers at home had no relevance in this new world. Kelowna was known from the beginning as having a spirit of friendliness between all sorts and conditions of people and a sense of social equality seemed to prevail. Vernon had the advantages of a railroad and government offices, while residents of Kelowna were forced to rally themselves to ensure their success. The early towns competed with each other over just about everything… and those early rivalries have never quite vanished.

A NEW KIND OF SETTLER

Okanagan Mission had officially appeared on a map when its post office was established in 1872. However, as more newcomers congregated around the Kelowna townsite, it was discovered that three quarters of the mail delivered to the Mission was actually destined for Kelowna. The town finally got its own post office in 1893, tucked into a corner of the real estate office directly across from the CPR wharf—which was handy, since the company had the contract to deliver Canada's mail.

The newcomers arriving in the Okanagan Valley in the 1890s had a different agenda to those who had come before them. The earliest settlers, with few exceptions, had struggled to survive in the remote countryside and had grown crops and kept livestock to feed their families and the few other people who travelled through the area. The next wave of settlers arrived with a more worldly view and tackled their new life with optimism. They intended to earn a good living and enjoy comfortable lives, and took the initiative to make sure that happened.

A substantial amount of small fruit was being produced by this time, along with a great variety of vegetables, hay and oats. It was more that the locals could consume, which led to the formation of the Agriculture & Trades Association of the Okanagan Mission: membership, fifty cents. The group lobbied the CPR for better freight rates and tried to guide members to plant crops that they knew they could find markets for. A succession of Kelowna Agricultural Fairs were held in the centre of town to showcase locally grown quinces, prunes, peaches, mangolds (a root vegetable used for feeding livestock), pumpkins, citrons, melons, onions and apples. Residents' handiwork—including handmade shirts, embroidery, painting on silk, watercolours, some very fine oils, sketches and pencil drawings—was also featured, as was homemade bread, jam and cheese. It didn't take long for the fall fair to outgrow the available space and land was bought for an exhibition hall. A half-mile horse racing track was nearby with space on its infield for lacrosse, football, and baseball.

Marketing the area's produce remained a problem, though everyone was aware the Kootenay mines were flourishing. When about one hundred people lived in Kelowna, over five thousand lived in Sandon, in the Slocan Valley, where rich silver-bearing lead ore deposits attracted the optimistic and hopeful. Kelowna had its muddy main street, a couple of stores and a single hotel, but Sandon had twenty-nine hotels, twenty-eight saloons and one of the largest red light districts in the west. Of course, the young Kelowna was not planning to become *that* kind of a community, though the locals did consider the mines around

Lequime Bros. & Company general store and the Kelowna Shippers' Union (KSU) at the foot of Bernard Avenue. The Kelowna Saw Mill, across the street, is adjacent to the wharf where the SS *Aberdeen* docked. | KELOWNA PUBLIC ARCHIVES 77

Sandon as a potential marketplace. Alfred Postill and his friends saw the opportunity and formed the Kelowna Shippers' Union (KSU) in 1893. At a meeting held in the Benvoulin Schoolhouse, $160 was collected to send a delegation of four plus a shipment of produce and hay to Sandon to see if it would sell.

The foursome left Okanagan Mission with their cargo, and travelled by boat to Okanagan Landing, caught the Shuswap & Okanagan Railway to Sicamous and the CPR to Revelstoke. Once there, their produce was loaded onto one of the Arrow Lakes sternwheelers, transferred over to Slocan Lake and carried on to Sandon. Though the CPR hadn't yet completed its rail line into the community, the company had staked out a station and a freight shed. With the CPR siding on one side and the road to the mines on the other, the delegation traded their vegetables and hay for lumber, then dug a twenty-by-sixty-foot cellar, covered it and opened for business. Leaving Bob Hall, one of their delegation, in charge, the others returned home to organize more shipments of fruit, vegetables, hay and oats.

Before long, the KSU built a warehouse near the CPR wharf in Kelowna. Two years later, the original co-op disappeared and shares were sold in the new KSU, under new ownership. The names of the new shareholders would become synonymous with both the fruit industry and Kelowna's development: Stirling, Hobson, Weddell, B. Lequime and Pridham.

Okanagan Tobacco Crop

When railroad construction was over, many Chinese men settled in Kelowna and found employment in the tobacco and lumber industries. They also grew vegetables, which they sold door to door from baskets balanced on poles across their shoulders. The top left photo shows the planting of new tobacco plants.

Green tobacco leaves were hung on stakes and collected in the field, and then secured to horse-drawn drying racks as shown in the top right photo. Tobacco leaves dried in the barns that dotted the landscape while small plants were grown under muslin (in the foreground, bottom left photo) to protect them from intense sunshine.

Tobacco was once one of the Okanagan's most promising crops. Cigars rolled and packaged in Kelowna (bottom right photo) and sold as "Kelowna Specials" or "Flor de Kelowna," along with cut tobacco, were sent to miners working the flourishing Kootenay mines. In the hope of developing a wider market, samples were featured at agricultural exhibitions overseas. It has been suggested that more people lost money investing in the Okanagan tobacco crop than through any other agricultural venture. | KELOWNA PUBLIC ARCHIVES 5746, 1365, 2170, 122

Today, the original British North America Tobacco Company building houses a nightclub (above photo). Once cigars were no longer being made in the building, it became the Occidental Canning Company. When Macdonalds Consolidated of Winnipeg took the entire cannery's production, the company expanded, used the three-storey building as a warehouse, and then added on to both the south side and the north of the building. In 1929, Occidental was bought out by Canadian Canners Ltd. of Hamilton, Ontario, who sold the Aylmer and Del Monte labels. The cannery at this site closed in 1960. It was one of the last of the forty or so canneries in the valley to cease operations. The building is located on Ellis Street. One of the few remaining tobacco-drying barns in the valley can still be seen near the corner of Benvoulin and KLO roads (overleaf photo). | STUART KERNAGHAN, XYPHOTOS.CA

The Kelowna Story: An Okanagan History

Discovering the Okanagan

The new organization flourished with an imposing building on the waterfront and a new wharf adjacent to the CPR wharf. Two years after its first foray into the Slocan, the KSU shipped seventeen railcars of vegetables and other farm produce. The venture was a greater success than expected, as orchardists realized their future depended on markets beyond the Mission Valley. They took the initiative and were soon sending wagonloads of apples and plums to Vernon, and later to the Prairies.

New opportunities spawned new products and services. A thriving hog business had developed in the Mission Valley but the unco-operative animals refused to be herded to market. A "pigaloo" was built just north of Lequime's sawmill, with a slaughterhouse on the lakeshore, complete with a scalding trough and heavy tables for cleaning the hogs. The carcasses were taken to the smokehouse behind the KSU on Bernard Avenue, and instead of live pigs the resulting hams, bacon and lard were then shipped out of the valley.

Louis Holman, a Wisconsin tobacco man, arrived in the Okanagan about 1893 and soon pronounced the valley's soil most suitable for tobacco production. With capital from John Collins, newly arrived from England, the first crop was planted in the Mission across the road from the Lequimes' blacksmith shop. The following year, C.S. Smith arrived from the West Indies and made some suggestions to further refine production. Several tobacco barns were built around the Mission, where the green leaves harvested in September were hung to dry until the usual January thaw, when the leaves were stripped off the stems.

The KSU added a cigar factory in a small building beside its packing operation where "Kelowna Pride," its cut tobacco, was produced, along with hand-rolled cigars made of a blend of Havana and domestic tobacco. Attractive boxes of fifty were sent off to the miners in the Kootenay and Boundary areas, and for awhile it looked like tobacco would soon become the valley's major crop. More acres were planted, more drying sheds were built, and when the Kelowna Shippers' Union sent tobacco to the New Westminster Fall Fair in 1898 it won the second prize of one hundred dollars. With Okanagan tobacco making a name for itself beyond the valley, the future looked promising. As a news story in the *Toronto World* newspaper stated on October 12, 1914:

Fine Tobacco Grown In British Columbia Okanagan Valley Promises to become Famous for Its Cigars

OTTAWA, OCT. 11 -- A trade report from London states that Canadian tobacco grown in the Okanagan Valley of British Columbia is second only in quality to the Havana and Sumatra leaves. It is expected that in time this tobacco will be equal to the best foreign grown leaf. Cigars made from the Okanagan tobacco have already a large sale.

KELOWNA GROWS AS A TOWN

Many of those arriving in Western Canada in these early years were transient, following the latest mining boom or a rumoured job. They stayed in one place long enough to make some money before moving on, often repeating this several times before finding a community to settle in. Some towns only lasted as long as the local vein of ore held out while others developed a reputation as being a pleasant place to live with an active, congenial lifestyle. Kelowna belonged in the latter category.

Kelowna saw significant development in the 1890s. The townsite, laid out in 1892, grew around the lakeshore and along Bernard Avenue, its main street. The Kelowna Saw Mill defined the industrial area immediately north of Bernard Avenue and because land to the south often flooded, residents built their homes, schools and churches eastward.

Dr. Benjamin De Furlong Boyce, the town's first resident doctor, arrived from Fairview, the mining town near Oliver, in 1894. For many years he was the only doctor between Vernon and the US border, and on numerous occasions he and his wife, Molly, turned their home into a makeshift hospital. When contagious diseases such as diphtheria were diagnosed, patients were treated in the town's new two-room jail. By this time, the temporary school above the Lequime Bros. & Company store had been replaced by a second school, a new one-room schoolhouse accommodating sixty pupils. D.W. Sutherland, who would eventually become both mayor and a local businessman, was sent by the provincial Department of Education to take charge.

Six-foot-wide wooden sidewalks were built along Bernard Avenue. Elsewhere, people had to make do with wooden planks laid end to end to avoid being mired in mud or blocked by massive puddles. Rain turned streets into quagmires and when Okanagan Lake flooded each spring, life almost came to a standstill. Sometimes the water was level with the wharves; the inundated sawmill would be forced to close, and rowboats replaced horses.

A few Chinese men settled near Mill Creek just south of the Lake View Hotel, and worked as cooks, lumber stackers and market gardeners. Kelowna's Chinatown soon became significant, and on New Year's Eve the street near the men's shacks would be lit with thousands of firecrackers. The men worked hard and usually in mundane and relentless jobs that few others would do. Many still wore their hair in a queue (a braid) and were single, relying on each other to survive their hard lives. Arrests—for illegal mah-jong games and, reportedly, opium dens—were part of their daily lives.

Within a few years, however, the boom that propelled Kelowna's early growth began to slow: by 1897, the area was hit by another economic downturn. The KSU was losing money on its meat-packing business and closed that down. Many orchards that had been planted five or so years earlier were bearing fruit, but sales were so slow that they couldn't cover the costs of production. The promise of tobacco soon vanished as the mines closed and the valley's best market disappeared with them. Efforts to revive the industry continued for several more years as various promoters tried to convince farmers to plant, but poor financial management, an inconsistent product and a challenging marketplace eventually caused the demise of Kelowna's tobacco industry. New settlers continued to arrive but some of the old-timers had had enough and went looking for better opportunities elsewhere.

Bernard Lequime had been through slow times before and didn't want to wait to see if things would pick up. He sold the Kelowna Saw Mill to his manager, David Lloyd-Jones, in 1901 and the still-empty lots he owned around town to Dr. Boyce. Lequime and his family then left for Grand Forks, sure that the Boundary country mines held more promise than the Mission Valley. Bernard hadn't entirely given up on Kelowna, however, and kept his interest in Lequime Bros. & Company. The family's original trading post in Okanagan Mission remained open until 1906, when the goods were transferred to the Kelowna store and the landmark business was closed. It wasn't long before Archie McDonald sold the Lake View Hotel and left town as well.

By this time another Scot, Lieutenant Commander Thomas W. Stirling, RN, had arrived in Kelowna. "T.W.," as he was soon known, had become a naval cadet at thirteen, served in Australia, India and South America, resigned his commission at the age of twenty-seven and travelled to British Columbia in 1894. He soon became one of the community's leading citizens and was involved in just about every significant organization and event during the next ten years. Arriving with substantial working capital, T.W. bought land from the MacKay estate, built a large house and called it Bankhead, planted a pear orchard and imported purebred cattle and hogs. Stirling also bought shares in the Kelowna Saw Mill, became involved with the KSU and bought a large amount of empty land in downtown Kelowna.

By 1900, the KSU didn't seem able to move beyond its Kootenay markets and since fewer people were employed in the mines and orchard production continued to increase, marketing became a problem... again. T.W. soon took the initiative and joined W.A. Pitcairn, an earlier manager of the Coldstream Ranch, to create Stirling and Pitcairn, to take over the crop marketing that had previously been done by the KSU. In 1901, they shipped their first boxes of apples to the Prairies: it took the *Aberdeen* about two weeks to collect the seven hundred boxes needed to fill a railcar from various orchardists around the lake. Stirling and Pitcairn shipped two railcar loads of apples to Glasgow, Scotland, two years later. One car carried apples that had been individually wrapped in a tissue-like paper; in the other car, apples had been directly packed into the boxes. It was an experiment to see which method delivered the best apples. The tissue-wrapped apples arrived in better shape and this became the standard method of shipping for many years.

Stirling was also at the forefront of the most significant change in the valley's land use since G.G. MacKay had swept through the area. Real estate agents Edward M. Carruthers and W.R. Pooley joined with Stirling to buy Bernard Lequime's 6,743 Mission Valley acres in March 1904. It cost them $65,000. In July of that same year, Stirling and Pooley formed the Kelowna Land and Orchard (KLO) Company and sold the land to the new company for $70,000. The following year, the original eighty-three-acre Eli Lequime homestead was added to the KLO holdings for an additional $12,000. The Kelowna Land and Orchard Company then built a bridge across Mill Creek, near Kelowna, and extended the road all the way to their new orchard lands on the East Kelowna benches. The area was being subdivided into lots ranging in size from one to forty acres, and a new ambitious irrigation system was installed. Untried orchardists flocked to the area. Everyone soon realized the best orchard sites were on the benches while hay, tobacco and onions were better crops for the valley floor.

The Central Okanagan Heritage Society rescued, restored and reopened the Benvoulin Church in 1986. Today it is a popular setting for many community events. Reid Hall was built adjacent to the original church in 1956, to serve as a Sunday school and meeting room. In 2000, the original hall was removed and replaced with a modern, complementary building. Benvoulin Church is located on Benvoulin Road. | STUART KERNAGHAN, XYPHOTOS.CA

AROUND THE TOWN

Okanagan Mission

When the Kelowna and Benvoulin townsites were settled, newcomers began to move southward, beyond Father Pandosy's Mission and across Mission Creek. Though a seventy-two-foot bridge had been built across the creek in 1879 and had made the trail to Penticton more accessible, it did little to encourage settlement. Giovanni Casorzo had crossed the creek and then gone uphill but others, initially undeterred by the lowland swamps, began to settle along the lakeshore and the hillsides above the lake. Crossing the swamps soon became impossible, however, and the settlers petitioned the government to build a road across the many marshes covering the area. Drainage ditches were dug, and a corduroy road with logs placed side by side was built. The logs soon sank and the road remained a sea of mud for most of the year. It was—and is still—called Swamp Road. A new Okanagan Mission school and post office were built beside the muddy road, and it wasn't until 1912 that an alternative road was built to connect Kelowna with Okanagan Mission.

As the French abandoned the area around Father Pandosy's Mission, the British moved in. Locations in the Mission still record the names of these early settlers who arrived around 1900 and created a vibrant community: Walker Road and Dorothea Walker School, Hobson Road and Crescent, Crawford Road and Falls, and Frost Road. A sense of permanence settled on the area when Gifford R. Thomson pre-empted land south of Mission Creek, near the lake. The family had arrived in the Mission Valley in 1892, purchased land from G.G. MacKay and built a house and planted an orchard, which didn't survive the high water table and the cold winters. Undeterred, Thomson took on the mail contract and drove the stage from Benvoulin to Vernon on Mondays, Wednesdays and Fridays, and returned on the intervening days, for which he was paid $600 a year. Thomson also planted hay and grain, ran cattle and eventually planted lettuce and celery. Today the property is a heritage farm and is still owned by the Thomson family.

Black Mountain and Rutland

Settlers from Missouri established a new settlement in 1893, at the foot of Black Mountain, about eight miles to the east of the Kelowna townsite. The families, most of whom were related, arrived in Penticton in their covered wagons and loaded their cattle, their wagons and themselves

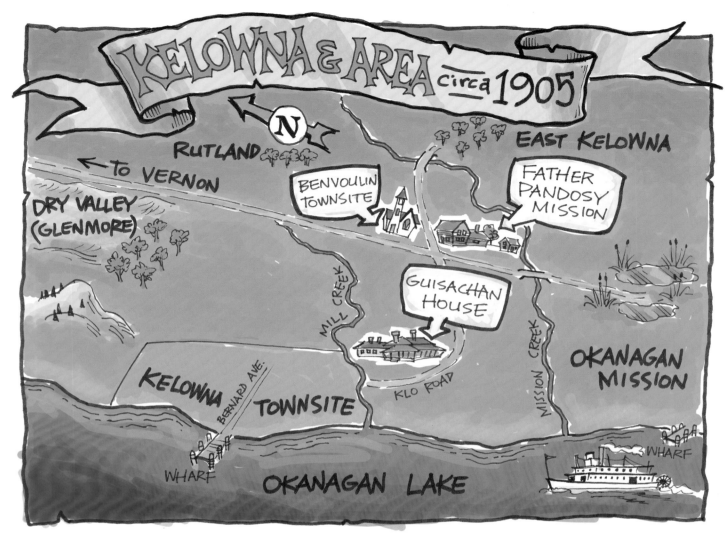

The Kelowna townsite and surrounding farming communities. | NEIL THACKER

onto the deck of the *Aberdeen* and headed to Kelowna. They pre-empted land along Mission Creek and into the Joe Rich Valley, and by 1896 had built their own fourteen-by-eighteen-foot log schoolhouse and hired their own teacher. Eight families enrolled their children, some of whom travelled several miles to attend, and the kids and their families returned on Saturdays to clean the room and scrub the floors. The group built a larger school two years later and was by then well-established enough to have the teacher's salary paid by the government. McClure and Prather Roads are named for two families of Black Mountain settlers.

A few years later, Australians John Matthew Rutland and his wife, Edith, were honeymooning in Canada and fell in love with the Okanagan. They went back home and sold everything they owned, then returned and bought the benches and flat land of what had previously been parts of the Brent, Simpson and Ellison ranches. John, called "Hope" by his wife (apparently because of his innate optimism), was familiar with horticulture and soon planted one hundred acres in apples. It wasn't long before he had the area's first substantial irrigation system underway, with several intakes along Mission Creek and a series of flumes and ditches snaking across his fields. Yet John Rutland was selling small parcels of his land to new settlers by 1904; it had been a demanding and expensive few years and the Rutlands had decided to move on. They sold the remainder of their holdings to the Okanagan Fruit and Lands Company, the same syndicate that had purchased much of A.B. Knox's ranch a year earlier and was fast becoming one of the area's major land developers. One of its principals was D.W. Sutherland, Kelowna's first schoolteacher.

The Rutland townsite was laid out in early 1905. By that time, the Rutlands had auctioned off their livestock, farm implements and nearly new dining room, kitchen and bedroom furnishings and left Canada for Santa Rosa, California. The couple apparently made enough money from the sale of their land and possessions to ensure their independence for the rest of their lives.

Starvation Flats/Dry Valley

The valley running between Rutland and Knox Mountain was named Starvation Flats for a reason: it was used as a shortcut between Wood Lake and Kelowna and wasn't good for much else. Riders passing through would be engulfed in a cloud of dust, as the earth had been left parched and barren by overgrazing. The flats had originally been settled by the optimistic and unknowing, and only dilapidated buildings and sagging fences were left to mark their forsaken dreams.

The name eventually evolved into Dry Valley, and it was clear that little would grow there until irrigation was available. The Morrisons, from Inverness-shire, Scotland, bought land on the west side of the valley and called it the Glenmore Ranch, after their family's ancestral home. Once their house was built and the well dug, an irrigation ditch was carved out of the hillside. Water from small upland lakes flowed onto their land and irrigated the Central Okanagan's first peach orchard. But for the most part Dry Valley remained dry for several more years, until developers arrived with money to finance irrigation schemes and advertising campaigns to attract buyers.

KELOWNA AS THE CENTURY TURNED

Prospectors and dreamers on the way to the Klondike's goldfields lifted the Okanagan Valley out of its early 1890s depression just as aggressive advertising campaigns enticed settlers to come and plant orchards. The land surrounding the Kelowna townsite was bought by a variety of development companies in a remarkably short period of time and subdivided, sold, irrigated and planted. Kelowna was not only a beautiful place to live but for relatively little money one could become an orchardist: life promised to be interesting and pleasant, and after the first year or so, easy. As a 1909 book on fruit ranching assured, orcharding "affords a satisfactory escape from the stress and strain of city life, and gives an added dignity and freedom to one's sense of individuality."

Stirling and Pitcairn were by now expanding their markets and shipping more and more apples out of the valley. Other enterprising newcomers arrived in Kelowna too, including F.R.E. (Frank) DeHart, who came to manage the Okanagan Fruit and Lands Company and then got involved in promoting the fruit industry. DeHart became one of the most successful fruit exhibitors in Canada as he introduced Okanagan fruit to surprised markets in Spokane, Washington, and then elsewhere in Canada, the US and Europe.

As more settlers arrived, so did the need for more classrooms and a large four-room school was built on the edge of town (it is now the Brigadier Angle Armoury). Several new battery-powered telephones connected homes to butcher shops, stables, the drugstore and the doctor's office. Mr. Millie assembled several of these lines in his watch-repair shop, hired Miss Mamie McCurdy as the telephone operator, and then turned the system over to the newly formed Okanagan Telephone Company.

Crossing the lake became easier when the provincial government paid Mr. Lysons one thousand dollars a year to operate a twice-daily ferry service, weather permitting. The *Skookum* was a thirty-foot gas-powered boat with an eighteen-by-forty-foot scow attached to one side to accommodate horses, wagons or cattle. Passengers were charged twenty-five cents each while animals cost a dollar a head—most were likely left to swim across. The Bank of Montreal felt that Kelowna was ready for its own branch by 1904. Previously, residents needing the services of a bank travelled to Vernon, though most made do with wads of bills wrapped in binder twine.

A community newspaper was a status symbol back then, and signalled a certain maturity. R.H. Spedding had edited newspapers in small Manitoba towns and, while looking for a more benign climate, he

The initially uninspiring town soon began to grow as new stores and a board sidewalk appeared along the south side of Bernard Avenue. A newspaper, a branch of the Bank of Montreal and a second hotel, the Palace, on the north side of the street, signalled better times to come. | KELOWNA PUBLIC ARCHIVES 3122

discovered Kelowna was without its own newspaper. He published the first issue of the *Kelowna Clarion* on August 14, 1904. Week-old news arrived, already printed, from Winnipeg with the inside pages empty and ready to be filled with local news and advertising. The following year the paper was purchased by George Rose, who changed its name to the *Kelowna Courier and Okanagan Orchardist*.

Fire was a constant concern to newcomers whose time, money and futures lay in the shops, offices and homes clustered in Kelowna's downtown. The sawmill's frequent fires were often caught by the wind sweeping across the lake, endangering the wooden stores and houses nearby. Gas lamps also lit every home and shop, concert and ball, and bales of hay and straw were everywhere. Only so much could be done with buckets and manpower, and the town's businessmen soon collected funds and bought the old Broderick fire engine from Vernon. The engine started its life in San Francisco in the 1850s and had been sold from one frontier town to the next until it ended up in Vernon. The old hand-pumped engine came with four hundred feet of hose at a cost of four hundred dollars, and arrived at the Kelowna wharf on the forward deck of the *Aberdeen*. It provided some protection… and some comfort.

By this time, Kelowna had grown dramatically. The south side of Bernard Avenue was lined with more-or-less substantial buildings that housed a variety of businesses: a bank, a newspaper, a drugstore, at least two general merchants, a furniture store, a post office, restaurants, two hotels and a CPR warehouse and billing office. The Anglican and Methodist churches were well established, as was the school. Two halls over the general stores remained available to the community or any fledgling organization wishing to raise money. The Kelowna Club, a private club for gentlemen, had been organized, and Masons congregated from other parts of the world and established St. George's Lodge No. 41.

Kelowna, it seems, was never destined to become a wild frontier town. From the outset, those who arrived in the community were educated, worldly, and looking to replicate a familiar lifestyle. They were happy, however, to leave the social constraints of the old country behind. Opportunities were unlimited for those who wanted to make the effort, though a bit of working capital also came in handy.

In 1904, 299 qualified business and professional men petitioned the Lieutenant Governor of British Columbia for Kelowna to be incorporated. The charter was granted on May 5, 1905, and soon after Mayor H. Raymer, a contractor, was elected along with aldermen David Lloyd-Jones, owner of the Kelowna Saw Mill; E.R. Bailey, the postmaster; C.S. Smith, who had been the manager of the KSU for a number of years; and D.W. Sutherland, schoolteacher and land developer. Fifty-three years after Father Pandosy walked into the Mission Valley, about a thousand people lived in Kelowna and the surrounding area, and the townsite had eclipsed the pioneer settlements of Benvoulin and Okanagan Mission.

CHAPTER THREE:

Kelowna Flourishes, 1905–1930

The first few decades of the twentieth century were golden years in the Okanagan. Vernon was the valley's leading city and the location of most government offices, including the recently completed and imposing red granite court house. A charter had just been granted for the Midway & Vernon Railway (M&V) to connect the mines in Greenwood and Rock Creek, through Vernon and along the Shuswap & Okanagan Railway, to the Pacific ports. Raising money to pay for the line was challenging, but just as a provincial subsidy was about to expire in the last days of 1903 a small survey crew climbed the hillsides south of Vernon and marked the proposed rail line along the west side of Kalamalka Lake.

Price Ellison, by this time the area's influential MLA, fired a blast of black powder off the rock face above the lake to launch the project and then headed to the Kalamalka Hotel for a gala dinner. Ongoing funding for what became known as the "Makeshift & Visionary" railway never materialized, however. The quarter mile of roadbed carved into the hillside above the lake's azure surface is all that remains of a pipe dream.

The excitement about the M&V was a momentary diversion from the real railway news at the south end of Okanagan Lake. Wagon trains were still supplying the mining areas east of Penticton as surveys were being completed for the Kettle Valley Railway (KVR). Both Canada and the CPR needed the ore and the territory of the Southern Interior to remain Canadian and saw this rail line as the best chance of ensuring that happened. Completed in 1915, the KVR was both an engineering marvel and one of the costliest railroads ever built anywhere. It ran from

Hope to Midway, connecting the mines of the Kootenays to the coast. Penticton was the railway's Okanagan headquarters and when the first engine pulled into Lakeshore Station in May of 1915, both the city and the South Okanagan were energized.

Though Kelowna had been promised its own rail connection by many politicians, over many years, nothing had materialized. Its residents were left to watch and wonder as the KVR's great steam locomotives were barged past their town on the way to Penticton. Though the rail line between Beaverdell and Penticton came tantalizingly close to the East Kelowna benches and stagecoaches delivered some passengers to the Myra station, this was not Kelowna's railway.

Yet newcomers still managed to find their way to the Central Okanagan. Many succumbed to the advertising campaigns extolling the valley's climate and the lifestyle opportunities inherent in orcharding. Some packed up their families and their belongings and moved here while others working their way across the country heard rumours of the area, came to have a look at Kelowna and chose to stay.

James B. Knowles left Windsor, Nova Scotia, in about 1905, after his family was decimated by illness and fire. He travelled by train to Vancouver and apprenticed with Birks Jewellers before scouting around for the best place to set up his own business. Jim wrote his fiancée, Lou, who was still in Nova Scotia, and told her about three possible locations, adding that Kelowna was on a lake. That was all Lou needed to know and it wasn't long before she climbed on the transcontinental train and crossed the country to Revelstoke. Jim was waiting, and they married before continuing on to Kelowna, where they were met by well-wishers who showered them with rice as they walked down the *Aberdeen*'s gangplank. The local paper reported that the Chinese men standing nearby thought it was a very strange way to waste perfectly good food.

The couple built a house on Bernard Avenue, at the edge of town just beyond the Presbyterian Church. Jim became the first jeweller in the area, helped organize the new Kelowna Regatta, served on the town council and became one of the first advocates for preserving the community's history. Lou was ahead of her time and spent many years working in the store alongside her husband.

Most of Kelowna's lakeshore near town flooded each spring and the water table was so high that other parts were covered with swamps, bulrushes and mosquitoes year-round: it wasn't the town's most sought-after real estate. A few of the hardier newcomers still wanted to live and play near the lake in spite of the conditions and sought out the higher parts of the shoreline. Cottages were built, each with its requisite screened-in porch. Camp Road, at the north end of town, was one of the first areas to attract summer residents, including Jim and Lou. They paid fifty dollars for their lot and lived in a tent until they could afford to build their camp. Lou thought "Camp Road" was much too common a name for their neighbourhood, though, and talked her fellow cottagers and the town council into upgrading the area's image. It was soon known as Manhattan Drive.

Those wanting to travel beyond downtown had to be prepared for the challenges: Jim and Lou Knowles and their neighbours put their boats in the water at the foot of Bernard Avenue and rowed north along the shoreline to reach their campsites. When the land dried out, a narrow trail was cut through the bulrushes and residents could walk or ride their bicycles. The trail was soon widened for cars but Brandt's Creek remained an obstacle until two large logs were laid across the channel. It helped if a second person stood nearby and shouted out directions to the driver.

The new town council enacted various bylaws and the lantern of the "honey wagon" could be seen swaying in the early morning as the horse-drawn wagon passed up and down the back lanes to empty galvanized privy buckets. Yet it was many years before the last of the outhouses disappeared, in spite of the high water table. The lines between country living and city life were none too clear at this time, and when cowboys crossed the new town's boundaries, their "furious riding" and lack of inhibitions about firing their guns sorely tried the patience of the city fathers.

Dr. Boyce had lived in Kelowna since 1894 and felt he needed to upgrade his skills. Not wanting to abandon his patients, he began looking about for someone to take over for the six months he would be in Montreal. Dr. W.J. (Billy) Knox (not related to the pioneer rancher, A.B. Knox) had just finished his medical training at Queen's University. Without the funds needed to intern or specialize, he had booked onto the SS *Empress of China* as the ship's doctor. While waiting in Vancouver for the ship's arrival, Knox heard about the short-term position in Kelowna, including the monthly salary of seventy-five dollars, and barely hesitated before accepting the job. When Boyce returned, Knox headed back to Vancouver to join the ship on its next sailing. Fate seemed to intervene again when there was another delay and Billy, impatient to get on with his life, decided to forgo the adventure and returned to Kelowna. He joined Dr. Boyce's practice for a few months before branching out on his own.

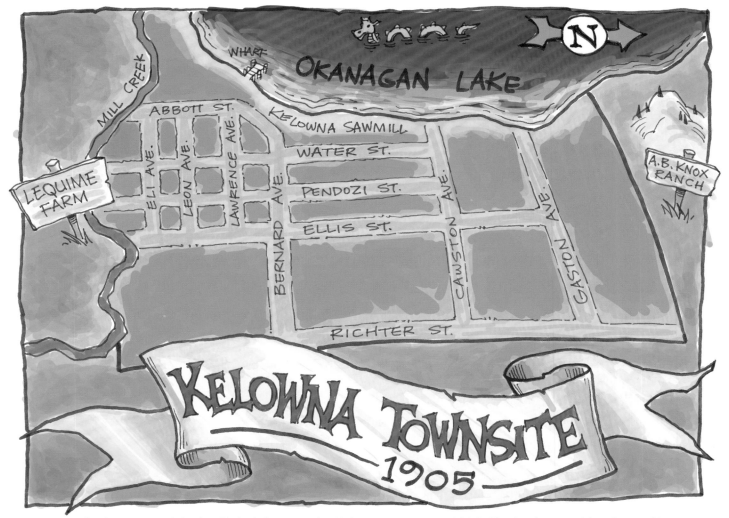

OKANAGAN LAKE

WHARF

MILL CREEK

LEQUIME FARM

ABBOTT ST.

KELOWNA SAWMILL

WATER ST.

PENDOZI ST.

ELLIS ST.

RICHTER ST.

ELI AVE.

LEON AVE.

LAWRENCE AVE.

BERNARD AVE.

CAWSTON AVE.

GASTON AVE.

A.B. KNOX RANCH

KELOWNA TOWNSITE 1905

Auguste Gillard pre-empted the land which became the Kelowna townsite in 1862. The land was sold to Bernard Lequime in 1890 and registered as the Kelowna townsite in 1892. | NEIL THACKER

Seeming to thrive on the challenges of frontier medicine, Dr. Knox travelled the valley in a cutter or sleigh, by horseback or by boat. His black medical bag was filled with the likes of mustard for the mustard plasters used to treat chest congestion, or laudanum (a mixture of alcohol and opium) to quieten a cough or a fretful child. Knox became a beloved and legendary presence in the community: he delivered over five thousand babies, looked after several generations of the same families and never forgot a name. During the sixty years he practised medicine, Dr. Knox became the embodiment of the healing power of devoted and loving care. Prime Minister Mackenzie King couldn't entice him into his cabinet, though he was subsequently awarded the Order of the British Empire (OBE) and an honorary LL.D. from Queen's University. Billy Knox passed away just before his ninetieth birthday; the Dr. Knox Middle School is named in his memory.

Citizens began lobbying for a local hospital soon after Kelowna was incorporated. A society was formed and set about raising the necessary five thousand dollars while the Ladies' Aid and Young Ladies' Aid promised to provide the linens and keep them in a good state of repair. The Kelowna Land and Orchard Company and T.W. Stirling donated twelve acres to the Hospital Society. The land was on a bit of a rise, running from Pendozi Street to the lake. Access to the new hospital was off Pendozi Street, down a winding dirt road cut through the brush and aspens. Sometimes a canoe could be paddled up to the building from the north when the spring floods inundated the lowlands between the hospital and town. (Today's much expanded Kelowna General Hospital occupies the same site minus Strathcona Park, which was gifted to the city in 1950.)

This was quite an achievement for a community of just over six hundred people, in the townsite proper. When Price Ellison, MLA, was called on to officiate at the opening in April 1908, he arrive late and then complained that he really didn't know why Kelowna needed its own hospital. Was it not entirely feasible for residents of this town and the Mission Valley to go to Vernon if they needed hospitalization? Ellison lived in Vernon and had been badgered by Kelowna Conservatives to share the provincial funds allocated for the Vernon hospital, and he wasn't happy about it. He then concluded his remarks by referring to the good-looking nurses (much to their embarrassment) and added his hopes that the Kelowna hospital would never be full.

The town ignored him and rejoiced in its accomplishment. The building's lower floor was made of cement blocks and left unfinished while the wood-clad upper floor was painted green to blend in with the natural setting. The roof was red and could easily be seen from a distance. The roughed-in basement housed the kitchen, the dining room, the nurses' quarters and the heating system. The upper floor housed two six-bed wards—one for men and the other for women. Two semi-private and three private rooms were also available for those who could afford to pay: daily rates were set at $1.50 in the wards, $2.00 for a semi-private room and $2.50 for a private room. Full linen and silver service was also available in the private rooms. Four bathrooms were roughed in but funds were only available to finish two. Large windows in the operating room ensured maximum light and most of the equipment was supplied by Mr.

The Kelowna hospital with its first addition, the maternity wing. Prior to the addition of the new building, expectant mothers were asked to have their babies at home as they were taking up too many of the hospital's beds. | KELOWNA PUBLIC ARCHIVES 2211

Stirling, while Dr. Boyce paid for the heating system. A septic tank had been installed to deal with the building's sanitation needs but it didn't take long for the system to be destroyed by the disinfectants being used in the hospital. Bedpans then had to be taken out back and emptied into the bush, and the sites covered with liberal doses of lime to kill the germs.

When they began taking up a disproportionate number of beds, pregnant women were told to have their babies at home. A ten-bed maternity wing became the hospital's first addition and was quietly opened in 1914, a month after World War I was declared. Sometimes it seemed like Ellison's opinion that Kelowna didn't really need its own hospital might be true: paying the bills and keeping the doors open was often a challenge. Hospital Society directors pleaded with citizens to help in any way they could: a call for food for the patients resulted in the arrival of fruit salad and lemonade, canned peaches, sacks of potatoes, loaves of bread, grape juice, pickles, chickens and wild game. Other times the hospital asked for firewood and coal but gratefully accepted whatever was dropped off. The nursing staff (two), the cook and the caretaker cheerfully agreed to cuts in pay so the hospital could keep running, while local merchants were asked to extend their credit terms. With rigorous management, the hospital's directors reduced their 1916 deficit to $32.32.

Elsewhere, Kelowna was taking on the appearance of a more substantial community. Elegant houses were appearing along Bernard Avenue, where circular driveways met columned porches and gracious gardens. The Stirling family moved to town from their Bankhead orchard and built Cadder House near the hospital. It has gone through many incarnations since 1911 but is one of the few early houses still in existence. The hospital included accommodation for nurses but when those rooms were needed for patients, Cadder House served as the nurses' residence. When it became too difficult to work around and over patients during a renovation, they were moved, many on stretchers, to Cadder House until the construction was finished. The house was subsequently converted into a group home until being rescued in 2004, when it was restored and made into condos.

Presbyterians, not wanting to have to travel to Benvoulin to attend church, built their first Kelowna church in 1898 and named it after A.B.

Knox, who had donated the land upon his return from jail. The original building was replaced by the current red brick building in 1909. With the amalgamation of the Congregationalists, Methodists and some of the Presbyterians, this became the First United Church. The Anglicans had established their own church in the town centre in 1894, but when their congregation grew they were torn between adding on to the original building or beginning again. The decision was made to move to higher ground and farther out of town. The cornerstone for a new St. Michael and All Angels Anglican Church was laid in 1911, southeast of the main townsite. Built of local stone and trimmed with granite from a quarry near Okanagan Landing, the "ecclesiastical Gothic" design took two years to complete.

First United Church (top photo) was established in the mid-1920s and was originally built on the site in 1909, as Knox Presbyterian Church (lower photo). It was named for A.B. Knox, a rancher and convicted arsonist who donated the land soon after he got out of jail. Located on the corner of Bernard Avenue and Richter Street, it marked the eastern boundary of the Kelowna townsite at the time. | STUART KERNAGHAN, XYPHOTOS.CA / COURTESY OF SYLVIA KNOWLES

Many of the original settlers and their descendants, the parishioners of Father Pandosy's Church of Mary Immaculate, had moved or died by 1902, when the Mission church closed its doors. It has been a church for forty-four years and while the property was sold, the original buildings were left on site. The Catholic community was so small by this time that priests came from Vernon for services for the next few years. By 1908, the congregation had replenished itself and needed its own priest. Land was purchased in Kelowna, cleared of brush and pine trees, and the new Church of the Immaculate Conception opened three years later. This was the third Catholic building in the Central Okanagan, though only the second church, as Father Pandosy's original Mission building was a chapel. The bell that Rosa Casorzo had followed from San Francisco was hung in the new bell tower and statues donated by the Lequime family were moved to the new church. All were subsequently moved again to the third and present Immaculate Conception Church in 1962.

St. Michael and All Angels Anglican Church was built of granite from a quarry near Okanagan Centre. As Kelowna outgrew its first Anglican church, the cornerstone for this new church (left photo) was laid in 1911. Except for the addition of a portico and some of the stained glass windows (above photo), the building remains much as it was when it opened in 1913. It is located on the corner of Sutherland Avenue and Richter Street. | KELOWNA PUBLIC ARCHIVES 1492 / STUART KERNAGHAN, XYPHOTOS.CA

Father Pandosy's sawn-board church in Okanagan Mission was the first Catholic church and housed Joseph Christien's bell and the statues given to Father Pandosy by the Lequime family. All were moved to the second Immaculate Conception Church, built in Kelowna in 1911 (above photo). The third and newest Immaculate Conception Catholic Church (right photo) was built in 1962, alongside the second church, both of which are located on Sutherland Avenue. The bell Rosa Casorzo and her children followed as she made her way to Okanagan Mission in 1884 to meet Giovanni, her husband who had left Italy some years before her, hangs over the front doors. The Lequime statues are inside, beside the altar.

| KELOWNA PUBLIC ARCHIVES 2242 / STUART KERNAGHAN, XYPHOTOS.CA

Kelowna quickly outgrew its one-room schoolhouse, just as it had the little tables and benches of the school above Lequime's store. A wood-frame four-room Board School was built in 1903, just behind the Knox Church. Irrigation ditches flowed along two sides of the building. It subsequently became the School of Manual Training and Domestic Science, before being transformed into today's Brigadier Angle Armoury. Students wanting to continue their studies beyond elementary school initially went to Vernon or Grand Forks. Kelowna's first high school was built across the street from the Board School in 1909, though senior students had no sooner moved in when they were forced out to make room for the ever-increasing number of younger students. Senior students were subsequently relegated to vacant rooms above the downtown stores until the 1913 completion of the new Kelowna Public School.

Now known as Central School, this imposing, classically designed ten-room red brick building could not be officially opened until the Honourable Mr. Ellison came to town. Featuring the latest designs, each room had no less than 280 square feet of windows with desks arranged so light would fall from the back and left hand of each student—at the time, left-handed students were "encouraged" to write with their right hand. The cloakroom attached to each classroom contained a "sanitary bubbling drinking fountain in which no cup is used, nor do the lips come in contact with anything but the stream of water which bubbles up at the drinker's touch." Teachers entered through the side doors while students lined up on either side of the huge woodpile in the playground at the back, and entered through the rear doors. At a recent reunion these same students were invited to enter the school through the main Richter Street doors. They were aghast—none had ever entered the school that way before, and most didn't recall ever seeing anyone use the front doors. Kelowna's citizens placed a high value on education and as the town continued to grow, bylaws were passed that added the cost of building more schools onto their taxes. During the 1920s, a four-room primary school was added behind the Kelowna Public School and the red brick Kelowna Junior High School, one of the first in Canada, was built on the other side of Richter Street.

The Kelowna Board School was a four-room school built in 1903 with footbridges across the irrigation ditches that flowed along two sides of the building (above photo). It subsequently became the School of Manual Training and Domestic Science. The Department of National Defence took over the building in 1935 and renamed it the Brigadier Angle Armoury in 1980 (right photo), in memory of Harry Angle, who settled in the Okanagan Mission in the 1930s and went on to have a distinguished military career in World War II. Angle died in 1950 while serving with the United Nations in India. A Sherman tank from World War II is among the armaments on display in front of the building, which is located at the corner of Lawrence Avenue and Richter Street. | KELOWNA PUBLIC ARCHIVES 8037 / STUART KERNAGHAN, XYPHOTOS.CA

The first Kelowna High School (above photo) was built in 1909 and then transformed into a hospital during the 1918 Spanish influenza epidemic. It later became the Glenn Avenue Elementary School, when the street in front was called Glenn Avenue. Today, the Kelowna Boys and Girls Club operate a variety of programs out of the building (left photo), which is located across from the Brigadier Angle Armoury, at the corner of Lawrence Avenue and Richter Street. | KELOWNA PUBLIC ARCHIVES 8027 / STUART KERNAGHAN, XYPHOTOS.CA

The Kelowna Public School was the pride of the community when it was built in 1913 (above photo). Citizens placed a high value on education and its construction was quite a remarkable achievement for a city of less than 2,000 people. The school, located on Richter Street, continues to be used for special classes today. It is known as the Central School, and houses a 1950s heritage classroom (right photo). | KELOWNA PUBLIC ARCHIVES 8029 / STUART KERNAGHAN, XYPHOTOS.CA

Elaborate productions of several Gilbert and Sullivan operettas were held at the Kelowna Opera House. This presentation of *The Mikado* was complete with an orchestra. | KELOWNA PUBLIC ARCHIVES 3061

Downtown also began to change as permanent-looking buildings replaced the clapboard stores lining Bernard Avenue. Lequime Bros. & Company moved across the lane into a stone building with large plate-glass windows to better display their merchandise. The Royal Bank and the Canadian Bank of Commerce soon joined the Bank of Montreal and built substantial and appropriately imposing buildings along the north side of Bernard Avenue. They were within a block of each other. The grandly named Kelowna Opera House opened—it was really the upper floor of the Raymer Building where the Raymer family lived. The Masons and Oddfellows had their respective halls in the same building, with the Thomas Lawson General Store and the Mason and Risch piano showroom on the ground floor.

The Kelowna Opera House was the centre of the community's social life and with its fine stage and sloping floor, it offered an array of entertainment. Amateur productions of *The Mikado* and *The Pirates of Penzance* were among the Gilbert and Sullivan favourites, with costumes and sets designed by people who had worked in the best British theatres. Hortense Nielson, "America's greatest emotional actress," toured with Norval MacGregor, the world-renowned Shakespearean actor. High-brow culture was interspersed with the more common; this was a time of travelling wrestlers and moving pictures with titles like as *How Rastus Got His Pork Chop* (tickets were fifteen or twenty-five cents).

An early morning fire was discovered in the rear of the opera house on October 31, 1916: it "obtained a great hold on all the rear and upper part of the building" before being discovered. Roaring flames were fanned by strong winds and it took the fire department over five hours to contain the blaze. By that time, only a few brick walls were left standing and the loss was over $135,000—only some of which was covered by insurance. Kelowna's only opera house vanished into history.

CITY PARK: A VISIONARY BUY

High water levels and frequent flooding were such a problem in the new town that the adjacent forty-one acres of bush and pine were never included in the original townsite plan. The lakeshore was a lovely place to be once the floods receded, and the town's bachelors would quickly pitch their tents along the beach for the summer. Bernard Lequime's original wharf and warehouse were abandoned when a new wharf was built at the foot of Bernard Avenue and the campers had all the amenities they needed. A diving board was added onto the end of the old wharf and a wall was built along the east side to ensure their privacy—no women and no bathing costumes!

The opera house was destroyed by fire in 1916 and never rebuilt. | KELOWNA PUBLIC ARCHIVES 821

Before he left town, Archie McDonald, the owner of the Lake View Hotel, had built a bandstand across from his hotel and cleared enough bush to create a playing field, but they were also only accessible and usable when the floods subsided. The locals were annoyed with the high water and in 1908 complained to the government in Victoria about the inconvenience. Public Works in Penticton was ordered to clear debris from the mouth of the Okanagan River and along the connecting channel to Dog Lake (Skaha Lake). The cleanup was so successful that lake levels dropped dramatically and the wharves around the shoreline became higher and drier and then totally inaccessible. When a control dam was built at the mouth of the river in 1914, it was assumed the problem was solved. It was... for awhile.

In spite of the recurring floods, the community saw the potential for a sizeable park adjacent to downtown. A referendum was held in 1909, and citizens voted—146 to 43—in favour of paying David Lloyd-Jones $29,000 for the thirty-six acres. By 1913, the town was abuzz with a proposal to build a fine hotel in the new park. Attractive drawings were shown around and the Board of Trade made presentations to city council, stressing the value of this fine modern hotel and urging their support for the initiative. A plebiscite asking citizens if they supported the hotel proposal was held later that year. Most were furious at the thought and didn't support the proposal. The question of hotels, development and parkland would arise again, and again, in Kelowna. An orphaned five-acre parcel near the park entrance belonged to Bernard's niece, Dorothy Lequime, and it was another ten years before Kelowna and Dorothy, who still lived in San Francisco, agreed on a price for the remaining land.

ORCHARDS FLOURISH

These were great years for the real estate business. Where no orchards existed, agents nurtured a dream. The cachet of the Aberdeens continued to entice Brits and Scots to the valley while others came because of the lifestyle. Bernard Avenue was extended beyond the Knox Church to the top of the ridge and new residential areas grew up along Richter Street. The townsite grew southward along Pendozi Street and past the new hospital. Yet it was several more years before the low-lying land to the south of town, adjacent to Okanagan Lake, could be settled.

When the map of the new Kelowna townsite was deposited at the Land Registry Office in 1892, the street named after Father Pandosy appeared on the map as Pendozi. Though most of Kelowna was aware of the error, no one corrected it and the name was left misspelled for many years. In 1939, the new provincial government ferry was named the MV *Pendozi* though everyone knew it wasn't correct. One hundred years after the good priest arrived in the Okanagan Valley, the historical glitch was corrected and his street was finally renamed Pandosy Street.

Orchard development continued beyond the townsite: the Bankhead orchard's pear trees covered the area east of the city boundary, including a line of fast-growing Lombardy poplars that had been planted as a windbreak. Orchards appeared on the KLO benches while the South Kelowna Land and Orchard Company, farther to the south, declared the Bellevue Hotel—the original Thomson homesite—the centre of the Okanagan Mission townsite. Its four thousand flat acres were planted in tobacco, hay and orchards. East of the Rutland orchards, Belgo-Canadian Land Company, funded with Belgian capital, planted six thousand acres, imported workers from Italy, and built a fourteen-mile irrigation ditch from the north fork of Mission Creek. The Central Okanagan Land Company paid $100,000 for 1,665 acres of rangeland, on the northeast boundary of the Rutland orchards. This was the northern gateway to Starvation Flats, or Dry Valley, and it didn't take long for the company to option another six thousand acres and begin an impressive cross-Canada campaign to sell the properties.

Marketing the agricultural possibilities of Dry Valley seemed a bit of an oxymoron so the company ran a contest to rename the area: the winner would receive one hundred dollars. Various suggestions were offered, including "Hardpan Hollow" and "Alkali Akres," but "Glenmore," with its Scottish meaning of "beautiful valley," was more to the company's liking. Two submissions suggested the same name and the winners shared the prize money. Private railway cars brought prospective buyers from Eastern Canada. Most were city dwellers with little or no experience on the land, with orchards or even with farming. Many had selected their lots from maps and signed purchase agreements before leaving home, and several weren't happy with what they found upon their arrival. Lot sizes ranged from ten to sixteen acres and pricing was based on the distance from Kelowna: four hundred dollars an acre half a mile from town; three hundred if three miles; and two hundred and fifty for three and a half miles and more. The company's assurances that "Glenmore will be settled by a very superior class of people" had a decided allure. Some purchasers never lived on the land and hired the company to clear it and plant and harvest their crop. Others found managers to do the work for them. The company had engaged Dominion Trust Company of Vancouver to finance their development and irrigation system by issuing $500,000 in bonds. By 1914, $100,000 of the debt had been retired but when Dominion Trust collapsed later that year, the Central Okanagan Land Company was forced into liquidation.

Not all promoters were honourable and for a time, the valley seemed overrun with real estate agents. A 1912 Royal Commission lamented that many individuals had suffered much injury and the province's reputation had worsened at the hands of those who misrepresented the conditions and earning potential of the orchards. Even reputable companies were inclined to embellish the benefits and prestige conferred on owners of Okanagan land.

WATER — ALWAYS AN ISSUE

Water became crucially important as the Okanagan Valley moved beyond cattle ranching to more intensive agriculture. Early settlers established themselves close to creeks and built simple dams to divert the flow of water into furrows cut between rows of trees. Other times, heavy spring runoff flooded large acreages and the resulting soak would suffice for the season. Disputes were inevitable: water would seep through dirt trenches and flood neighbouring fields; upstream users diverted creeks and downstream users didn't get the water they felt they were entitled to. The district engineer and the water bailiff mediated but if they couldn't reach an agreement, lawyers were hired and a judge was left to decide. Other times, frontier justice ruled as with the lady in Okanagan Mission who sat on the control gate of the irrigation channel with shotgun in hand and resolved things her own way.

The Kelowna Story: An Okanagan History

Okanagan orchards would never have survived without irrigation. Various types of systems were built, ranging from ditches (top left photo), to elevated flumes (lower far left photo), to siphons that ran over hillsides (above photo) and pipes suspended across creeks (left photo). Water was carried from upland lakes and creeks to the valley floor.

| KELOWNA PUBLIC ARCHIVES 3028, 1574, 1575, 1658

Apple packing for the Kelowna Growers Exchange (KGE) at the Occidental Packinghouse circa 1910. | KELOWNA PUBLIC ARCHIVES 5656

Water from Mill Creek ran in open ditches up and down residential streets for many years. Several ponds were scattered through Bankhead and served as reservoirs and swimming holes in the summer and skating rinks and sources of ice in the winter. (Most of these ponds have since been filled in.) Development companies quickly understood their success was dependent on the availability of water. Irrigation was such a substantial part of initial development costs that the early systems were small, often makeshift and sometimes barely adequate. The intent was to use the income received from selling the lots to improve and then expand the irrigation systems. Engineering expertise was sometimes available and sometimes in sync with local conditions, though often not. When flumes and pipes were used for short periods of time they rusted and split while the alternating freezing and thawing of the Okanagan winter destroyed even the most simple of systems. Cattle wandered through or over furrows and ditches, weeds grew in and around, gophers dug their own diversions and inexperienced construction crews were just glad to have a job and weren't driven to excellence.

Most irrigation companies were subsidiaries of the privately owned development companies. As the economy slowed in 1913 and the Great War followed, settlers, and the growth they brought with them, vanished. Few companies could deliver on their promises of irrigation and several were forced to liquidate. The prospect of Okanagan orchards and no irrigation was so alarming that the provincial government stepped in with loans so systems could at least be maintained. Planning was short term and there was little collective effort to deal with the ongoing and growing demands for water. The government loans had to be forgiven by the 1920s, when irrigations districts were created with a mandate to ensure that all orchards would have access to water for irrigation.

OF PACKINGHOUSES AND CANNERIES

As the number of orchards grew, the foundation was laid for what has become the recurring marketing dilemma of the industry. Some growers built their own packinghouses, found their own markets and remained independent. Others joined co-operative associations and pooled their packing and marketing functions. Small-scale co-op marketing had been going on for some years but serious competition from growers outside the valley led to the creation of the Kelowna Growers Exchange in 1913. By the time the war ended, markets had changed again and the majority of valley growers joined the exchange. Increasing amounts of small fruits and vegetables, grown between the rows of apple and pear trees, were also presenting marketing problems. Some were shipped to the Kootenays and subsequently to the Kettle Valley construction camps, but there was much more produce available.

Fraser Brothers built the Kelowna Canning Company in 1910, across from City Park. It was the first business in what would become a thriving Okanagan industry. Pumpkins, beans and tomatoes were canned before the company branched into soft fruits. When much of the building was destroyed by fire a few years later, the plant moved north of Bernard Avenue and changed its name to Western Canners Ltd. A wood-frame building was built over the swamp and bulrushes, and Chinese workers peeled the tomatoes by hand and were paid on a piecework basis. Cans were shipped to Kelowna from Vancouver in the same two-, three-, and ten-gallon sizes that had been used by the coastal fish canneries. Once the cans arrived in the cannery, they were filled, wrapped with "Okanagan Brand" and "Standard of the Empire" labels and shipped out of the valley. Soon the wooden building was replaced by a more substantial brick structure and a room was added to make sodas. The company began selling on the Prairies, but as the economy turned down and the bank refused further financing, they closed their doors.

By then, the Occidental Canning Company had already set up business in the old brick British North America Tobacco Company building with machinery from another bankrupt canner. Since seasonal workers were hard to find in town, men were hired in Vancouver, put up at the Occidental bunkhouse and fed in the company's communal kitchen. The bunkhouse was sold when local workers became available: European immigrants who settled in the Okanagan after the war, and the women who filled in during the war and stayed on the job. Most workers were "on call" yet few had telephones, so they arrived at the cannery door each day, hoping to get hired for one of the shifts.

The British North America Tobacco Company (BNATCo) and the cigars they manufactured were a vital part of Kelowna's early economy. Financial mismanagement caused the demise of the company though tobacco continued to be grown for several years. The building was subsequently converted for the Occidental Canning Company to use as a cannery. | KELOWNA PUBLIC ARCHIVES 3422

The Laurel Packinghouse was across the road from the loading bays of the Occidental Canning Company, where wagonloads of tomatoes were delivered for processing. | KELOWNA PUBLIC ARCHIVES 850

Tomatoes were a huge part of the cannery's business. Horse-drawn wagons loaded with tomatoes lined up along Ellis Street and around the corner onto Bernard Avenue. The smell of processing tomatoes and spicy ketchup wafted over the whole community. Men loaded cans onto dollies and moved them from one work area to another while the women sorted, cut, peeled or pared tomatoes and packed them into cans. The best tomatoes were canned whole while those that were soft or bruised were diverted to the juice line. Those just a step or two away from being thrown out were made into ketchup, and it was a demanding job. Large vats wrapped with copper coils were lined up along the outside deck at the rear of the cannery. As quantities of sugar and spices were added, the risk of burning was so great that once started, the stirring couldn't stop until the batch was finished. No breaks were allowed and if mealtime came midway through the stir, men ate with one hand and stirred with the other.

IT TAKES ALL SORTS

A curious diversity of people arrived in the new town. Some were worldly and chose their destination carefully, while others simply ended up in town. Some came with money, while many others were almost destitute. An unfettered lifestyle attracted those who wanted to be free of family and societal expectations, while others arrived earnest and determined to succeed. Some, even then, had decided to spend their final years in Kelowna.

Rembler Paul, a man of "roaming disposition and an adventurer in every sense of the word," retired to Kelowna in 1905. He brought his wife, Elizabeth, and his money, and built a large, stately home on Bernard Avenue. A full-time gardener was needed to look after the surrounding eight acres. Paul was seventy-four years old, unassuming in spite of his considerable wealth, and could frequently be found among the regulars at Lequime's store. He was always recognizable by his large, and immaculately groomed, bushy white beard.

The couple's son had died as a young man and though various of the four young grandsons visited occasionally, the Pauls were mostly on their own. Mrs. Paul became ill soon after their arrival and suffered the ravages of cancer for several years. Hoping to provide a quiet summer retreat for his wife, Rembler bought several acres of land along the lakeshore, about five miles north of town. A finely crafted log house was built on the property though Elizabeth only visited it once before she became too ill to venture that far from her bed in town.

Paul wanted to pay tribute to his family in a unique way, and decided to have a substantial tomb built into the hillside, near the log house. The needed materials were transported by wagon and stone boat through what soon became the Glenmore Valley, and when the horses could go no farther, the large steel door, cement, boards, wire reinforcements, nails and equipment were lowered down the hillside by rope through a shale gully, onto a flat landing above the lake.

A vertical cut was made into a large mound of earth and a fifteen-foot excavation was dug back into the hillside. The opening, which was nine feet wide and seven feet high, was lined with concrete and two concrete shelves ran the length of a central passageway: there was room for eight coffins. The date, "AD 1910," appeared above the vault's large steel door, near the top of the cement façade, and the door was locked.

Elizabeth was eighty-three years old when she died in 1914. Rembler was devastated and was joined by the town's leading citizens, "amid every manifestation of sorrow," as they followed the coffin from the Anglican Church to the foot of Bernard Avenue. Once assembled, they boarded a flotilla of boats for the journey along the lakeshore to the tomb. The day was sunny, the lake calm, and the procession followed the grief-stricken old man up the steep hill from the lake. It was a memorable and profoundly sad occasion.

Rembler died in Edmonton two years later, having travelled to the northern city to winter with a friend. His body was returned to Kelowna by train and boat, and the town's leading citizens again boarded small boats to follow the barge carrying Rembler's casket to his tomb. The mourners glanced through the small glass-covered opening in Mrs. Paul's copper casket as they lowered her husband onto his shelf, and reported that she looked perfectly preserved. Paul had left instructions and provisions for the tomb to be cared for, but this never happened. After a few years, vandals had destroyed the lock and access to the tomb became impossible.

The property changed hands a few times but was never occupied year-round, and vandals continued to destroy what was left of the house and access the tomb. A subsequent owner eventually demolished the house and had earth and rocks mounded over the face of the tomb. The City of Kelowna bought the property and created the Paul's Tomb Park, which is accessible by boat, by trail from Poplar Point or from the lower Knox Mountain lookout. The paths all converge in a small open meadow that feels strangely peaceful. If one searches the low semicircle of hills at the back of the meadow, one may find the "AD 1910" on the tomb's façade. Other than lilacs and the odd fruit tree, there is little evidence that Rembler and Elizabeth Paul ever existed, though they still remain quietly entombed in the park.

Early Kelowna attracted more than just the well-to-do and the earnest; it also had its share of bloody murders and violent deaths. On March 12, 1912, the escapades of Boyd James alarmed the whole valley. Boyd was a shifty character, an American army deserter who didn't have much regard for Canadian laws. He came by his ruthlessness justifiably as his father was the brother and partner of the notorious American outlaw Jesse James. Boyd had been working for the Kelowna Land and Orchard Company for awhile and was known to a few locals. Deciding he'd had enough of orcharding, he headed to Charter & Taylor, the general store and post office in Okanagan Mission, one afternoon with his .45 Colt revolver drawn. He held up the three occupants, including a young boy, Randall, who quickly ran out the door, eluding the bullets Boyd fired after him, and headed for the bar of the Bellevue Hotel. A search party quickly headed out to apprehend the culprit but Boyd James had done his homework. His partner in crime, Frank Wilson, was waiting on the lakeshore with a boat, ready to depart.

The two men headed down the lake and appeared in Penticton a couple of days later. Word of the robbery had already travelled down the valley, and the two men were recognized in a bar, and arrested. The robbers had to be returned to the scene of the crime and were soon secured in irons. With Police Constable Aston as the escort, the trio booked into a stateroom on the SS *Okanagan* for the overnight trip to Kelowna. James and Aston got into a scuffle. The Penticton police had missed the revolver hidden in James's shirt when they

Rembler Paul built a tomb into a hillside on his summer property, where both he and his wife, Elizabeth, were buried. The log home and tomb were repeatedly vandalized: the house was eventually demolished while earth and rocks were mounded over the entrance to the tomb. This is now the location of the Paul's Tomb Waterfront Park. The Pauls remain entombed at the site. | KELOWNA PUBLIC ARCHIVES 4179

arrested him, and Aston was shot. James grabbed the key, unlocked their handcuffs, robbed their victim, took his gun and then casually headed to the dining room and ordered breakfast.

The *Okanagan*'s first stop the next morning was at Peachland. James and Wilson jumped onto the wharf before the gangplank was lowered and headed for the hills. The purser thought it curious, as no passengers were scheduled to get off at the settlement. An old-timer who had seen the pair earlier in Kelowna recognized them and was curious about their rapid departure. The purser thought they were stowaways and yelled at them to return. They kept on going. The old-timer headed to the ship's saloon for the trip down the lake and walked in to hear the guests whispering about gunshots and muffled sounds. Seeing the women passengers becoming more and more nervous, he notified the purser. Upon investigating, Aston was discovered lying on the floor in a pool of blood with a bullet hole in his forehead.

Rembler Paul's log home, five miles north of Kelowna, was badly damaged by vandals and eventually demolished. | COURTESY
OF DIANA KNOWLES

Kelowna Flourishes, 1905–1930

The finest carload of Jonathans ever exhibited at the National Apple Show in Vancouver. The judges in the foreground awarded first prize in the grand sweepstakes to the Kelowna exhibit in 1910. | KELOWNA PUBLIC ARCHIVES 3081

The *Okanagan* soon pulled into the Gellatly wharf (today, in Gellatly Bay Park in West Kelowna), where the old-timer got off and telephoned back to Peachland to tell them of the murder and warn them about the fugitives at large. It was too late—the men had vanished. The alarm was spread with orders to catch the pair, dead or alive. Posses were organized, every trail and roadway was manned, and every beach was searched. There was no sign of the fugitives. The next evening, two men who had been camping at Powers Creek, near Westbank, came to town for their mail and supplies. Everyone was talking about the shooting and the story emerged about how the partners had encountered two weary men as they headed back to their campsite earlier in the day. The men had obviously been walking for some time and accepted the offer to share a meal, and then offered to pay for it. The offer was refused and the two men departed... toward Westbank.

Everyone was certain the two strangers were the fugitives. The men joined the posses, mothers kept anxious watch hoping no strangers came to their doors and wives cast fearful glances into the dark as their armed husbands scoured the countryside. The night turned to day and no one had been arrested. Finally, word came back down the lake that two armed ranchers had captured James and Wilson just as they sat on a log to rest. The capture had been made near Wilson's Landing, about five miles north of the ferry wharf. The next time the prisoners found themselves on the *Okanagan*, they were securely bound and tied on the foredeck, and again headed to Kelowna.

Tales of the Okanagan's greatest manhunt were told over and over again. Aston died, so the murder, the escape and the recapture occupied locals for weeks. On the day before his trial, James managed to saw most of the way through his shackles with a hacksaw blade he had earlier hidden in his shoe. A sharp-eyed prison guard noticed and spoiled the escape. The trial found James guilty of murder and sentenced him to death by hanging. The prisoner made one last desperate attempt to escape on the day prior to his hanging. Hoarding the black pepper that had come with

Early bush mills were set up near the forest and moved when the largest trees in the area had been cut. Boards would be sawn at the bush mill and hauled into town to be finished into dimension lumber or fruit boxes. | SHARRON SIMPSON COLLECTION

his meals, the murderer blew it into the face of the guard as he opened the cell door. Though temporarily blinded, the guard had the wits to push James back into his cell and relock the door.

Justice was swift. James was hanged at the Kamloops jail on August 9, 1912, just five months after he had robbed the Okanagan Mission store. Frank Wilson was found to be an unwilling accomplice and was so fearful of James that he begged to be kept in custody until after the hanging.

In spite of the intervening dramas, Kelowna's business community continued to expand. Soft red bricks were made out of Knox Mountain clay and used in the new buildings along Bernard Avenue. Frank DeHart took fruit marketing to another level by convincing growers he could create displays that would not only showcase their apples but also increase awareness of the valley's fruit-growing potential. This became a popular way to advertise the Okanagan's orchards, especially when the displays won prizes in New Westminster, Toronto, London and Spokane, Washington.

The Kelowna Saw Mill circa 1912. The wagon and white horse would now be standing in front of Kelowna City Hall. | SHARRON SIMPSON COLLECTION

The Kelowna Story: An Okanagan History

113   Kelowna Flourishes, 1905–1930

It also took awhile for growers to decide how best to package their apples. Eastern orchards used barrels that held up to 150 pounds but they were heavy and difficult to handle. Washington state's apple industry, the Okanagan's nearest competitor, was using wooden boxes that weighed 40 pounds regardless of the size of the apples. Okanagan orchardists experimented with a larger box but ultimately decided the standard forty-pound American box worked best for them too. The boxes could easily be made locally. The tall, large-diameter ponderosa (yellow pine) trees covering the lower elevations of the valley had been named by David Douglas for their ponderous size. At seventy-five to ninety feet in height, the straight trunks of these trees were ideal for making fruit boxes as the branches started far up the trunk and the boards were generally knot-free. A vibrant new wooden fruit and vegetable box industry began and over the next thirty or so years, over 700 million wooden boxes were built and shipped out of the valley. So many boxes left the Okanagan that people throughout the province and on the Prairies started calling them "Okanagan furniture." They were reused as bookshelves, cats' beds, rabbit hutches, nests for hens, feed boxes for cattle, milking stools, children's cribs, dressing-table vanities, desks and, when nailed to the shady side of a cabin, refrigerators.

Early bush mills were set up near the forest and loggers cut the trees for horses to haul, by wagon or sleigh, to the nearby mill which was likely no more than a roof over a saw. If the trees were higher up the hillsides, horses would haul the logs to the cliffs overlooking the lake and drop them over, where they would be collected and towed to a lakeside sawmill. Logs would also be loaded into concave-shaped troughs at the highest elevations and sent careening down the hillsides into the lake. Liberal doses of bear grease were slathered over the troughs if there was a risk of the logs getting stuck, and by the time they reached the cliff above the lake they would be roaring along at a smoking sixty miles an hour. A lookout with bugle in hand would be posted wherever the chute crossed a road to warn of the impending danger.

Most communities in the region used wood-frame construction and the demand for lumber grew as more settlers arrived. As the apple trees grew larger, wooden orchard ladders up to sixteen feet tall were needed; expanding irrigation systems needed flume lumber; and more boxes were needed as increasing amounts of fruit was shipped out of the area. Various small sawmills made box shook—the individual parts of a box—and wrapped bundles of twenty-five different pieces with wire. Boxes were usually assembled by the packinghouses though some growers set up areas in their orchards and assembled their own boxes. Before long, a number of highly skilled box makers began following the ripening fruit up the valley and making boxes as they went. Each one had a workbench, specially honed axe handles and a uniquely organized work space. Box makers were paid on a piecework basis and the very best could assemble a thousand boxes a day. The ten dollars they made was well in excess of what almost everyone else was making at the time.

Stanley Simpson arrived in the Okanagan a few years before there was much of a demand for boxes and worked as a carpenter in Penticton. In the middle of the summer of 1913, Stanley and Mr. Etter, with whom he had been working, heard about a carpentry business for sale in Kelowna. The timing was opportune as their Methodist Church was planning a picnic in Kelowna and had booked the SS *Okanagan* for the trip. The two men took time out from the festivities and headed down Bernard Avenue, around the corner on Water Street and down the lane behind the fire hall. After looking at the shop and its equipment, they put twenty-five dollars down, arranged a loan for the remaining three hundred and bought the business. The new partners then rejoined the picnickers, returned to Penticton, packed up and moved to Kelowna.

The first few months of their new venture were promising but it wasn't long before the economy slowed and World War I broke out. The partners soon realized the business couldn't support them both and with a toss of a coin, the partnership ended and Stan took over. He scraped by doing whatever jobs needed doing: he built screen doors that were guaranteed not to sag, made odd bits of furniture, sharpened saws, repaired the jail and became known as a hard-working and reliable businessman. When the war was over and the economy picked up, S.M. Simpson Ltd. became a sash and door factory and moved along the lane to Abbott Street and into the fire-damaged Kelowna Canning Company building.

A few years later, Stanley, by now known as S.M., began buying rough lumber from different sawmills and from the independent loggers and started making apple boxes. He soon realized the risk of having to buy the lumber he needed from others and decided to get into the sawmill business himself. His first bush mill was set up with a partner and ran for just over a year before the area was logged out. The saw and shed were packed up and moved into another valley and then another, each time growing a little larger and adding a little more equipment. S.M. Simpson Ltd. had soon expanded into the sawmill business.

Box making usually began in March so a good number of boxes were on hand when the fruit was ready to be picked. Stan's shop remained on Abbott Street but space was at a premium: long rough boards were brought in from the bush mills, passed through the windows facing City Park, re-sawn or planed to the needed size and sent on to the box-making area. Saw blades were thick so mounds of shavings, slabs and sawdust accumulated everywhere, including in the lane behind the building. The city's curling rink had been built behind Stan's operation and when the ice melted, he rented the building and stacked it to the rafters with wire-wrapped bundles of shook. It didn't take long for the company to expand beyond apple boxes, and soon they were making specially sized prune boxes, plum crates, cabbage crates, cherry lugs and asparagus boxes that were lined with moss to keep the spears crisp. Over the next few years, Stan bought grape baskets and tin tops made of veneer from box makers on the Lower Mainland and resold them to the local growers for grapes, tomatoes and soft fruit.

The expanding mounds of sawdust and shavings were becoming an enormous challenge to work around as well as a growing fire hazard. The meandering Mill Creek was only a short block south of Stan's factory and the surrounding land was waterlogged for much of the year and worse during spring floods. It couldn't be built on and was of little value and up for sale. Stan bought several acres and carted load after load of the waste wood and sawdust to the area and spread it over the land, sometimes up to many feet deep. The area is now part of Kelowna's Heritage Corridor and if homeowners dig down a few feet today, they will likely find the still-preserved remnants of the sawmill and box factory.

David Lloyd-Jones's Kelowna Saw Mill was only a few blocks north of Stan's sash and door factory and box plant. It had been in the same location since before there was a Kelowna and had remained successful by collecting logs from around the lake and storing them in booms just north of Bernard Avenue. Stan decided it made more sense to bring logs to the mill rather than taking the mill to the trees, as he had been doing. Before the war, plans had been in place to build a cannery on land adjacent to the summer camps at Manhattan Beach. The plan had been shelved, the land was for sale, and though it often flooded and was wet for much of the year, Stan knew he could make it work. Just as the Depression was about to unfold, he bought the property, called it his Manhattan Beach operation, hooked a telephone on a pole in the yard and finalized plans to build a sawmill, a box factory and a veneer plant.

TO KELOWNA—BY BOAT

Kelowna, being at the midpoint of the Okanagan Valley, always seemed to have transportation issues. Vernon and Penticton were both railway destinations and had priority in accessing boats to carry both freight and people to their towns. Kelowna, on the other hand, struggled to make itself relevant in valley transportation plans. Canadian Pacific launched the SS *York* in 1905 to carry the freight that had been crowding passengers off the decks of the *Aberdeen*. It wasn't long before the company's wharf at the foot of Bernard Avenue became too small and though it had bought adjacent land, expansion opportunities were limited. The company began looking at the bays at the foot of Knox Mountain. Mindful of what happened to Prairie towns bypassed by the railway, the *Kelowna Courier* took the CPR to task, accusing it of pulling a grand bluff on the city in an attempt to find cheaper land. The newspaper called the railway committee "overbearing and arrogant" and accused the company of "soulless greed" and of being "an avaricious corporation."

Whether the outburst convinced the railway to reconsider or not is unknown but it soon decided to buy the vacant land just north of the Kelowna Saw Mill. Construction got underway for a 315-foot-long landing slip, and freight sheds and new tracks were built across Water Street. The area was away from the business district but it wasn't long before the packinghouses, canneries and fuel-supply companies took up the CPR's offer to build spur lines for anyone who would ship on its railway. The area wasn't large and it was quite an accomplishment for seven and a half miles of track to be wound around the buildings. Teams of horses were used to move railcars around the area as the company's usual switching engines couldn't work in such confined spaces. Two crews worked round the clock during the peak of the fruit season to keep the yard working and the barges efficiently loaded and unloaded before they departed for Okanagan Landing or Penticton.

The SS *Okanagan*, the lake's second sternwheeler, was launched from Okanagan Landing in 1907. Vernon had again declared a half holiday to mark the momentous occasion and a large crowd gathered on the shore. Many passengers had already gone on board to experience the excitement of the launch and the inaugural trip. Everyone watched and those on board held their collective breath as the boat started down the slipway… and then stalled. It had become hung up on the stringers. The launch crew tried every imaginable manoeuvre to dislodge the vessel but nothing worked. The *Okanagan* remained suspended and the stranded passengers

STOPS FOR THE
S.S. Aberdeen
S.S. Okanagan
S.S. Sicamous
Circa 1892~1936

The *Aberdeen*, *Okanagan* and *Sicamous* had several regular stops as they travelled from one end of Okanagan Lake to the other, and then back again. Settlers could also light two fires on the beach or hang a flag to signal they needed service. The boats would nose onto the beach if no wharf was available.
| NEIL THACKER

eventually had to be transferred to the nearby *Aberdeen*. No one seemed too worried and people soon departed for the Strand Hotel in Vernon to celebrate the launch that didn't happen. The crew had much better luck the next day when the *Okanagan* quietly slipped into the lake, without an audience and without fanfare.

The CPR's largest, most luxurious and last sternwheeler, the SS *Sicamous*, was launched in May of 1914 with even grander expectations than her sister ships. One of the largest paddleboats ever launched in BC, she was soon referred to as "The Queen of Okanagan Lake." The ship was beautifully finished: five saloons were available to passengers, along with the main deck observation lounge, which boasted a grand piano; the ladies had their own lounge, while the gentlemen had a smoking room. The dining room was sixty-five feet long and two decks high; service was to the highest standard with crisp white linen, crystal and silver, and each table was graced with its own electric candelabra. Electric fans were kept on the sideboards to keep passengers cool during the summer while hot meals were prepared on the lower decks by three Chinese cooks and sent to the dining room by dumbwaiter.

The thirty-seven staterooms were accessed from the second-floor gallery, which wrapped around the dining room. Though the trip from Okanagan Landing to Penticton only took a few hours, the morning departure was early and passengers often boarded the night before, paid their $4.75, and enjoyed the superb service along with a good night's rest. Those wanting to pay a bit less did without the ensuite bathroom and used the public facilities… which were, as was usually the case, emptied into the lake.

Sunshine streamed through stained glass skylights and the lounges and staterooms were finished in BC cedar, Australian mahogany and Burmese teak. Such elegance had never before been seen in the Okanagan Valley.

In spite of its stylish beauty and the luxurious travel it offered, the *Sicamous* also signalled the end of an era. World War I was declared a few months after the launch, lake traffic diminished and the *Sicamous* never lived up to its billing as transport for happy travellers and optimistic newcomers. Instead the boat's whistle haunted the valley during the war. The boat carried news of the death of a son or husband and several short sharp blasts on the whistle as it approached a wharf signalled the return of a wounded soldier. Everyone within hearing distance would silently gather at the shore.

By the time the war was over, people could travel between Vernon, Kelowna and Penticton by car: Okanagan Lake was no longer needed to get from one end of the valley to the other. The CPR was losing money and withdrew the *Sicamous* from service in 1931, although the valley's Boards of Trade complained so vigorously that the boat returned for another four years. In a further effort to cut costs, the CPR removed the ship's top deck and the "Queen of Okanagan Lake" was reduced to being a fruit barge. Two years later, the *Sicamous* was docked at Okanagan Landing, and left to be buffeted by winter storms and baked by the summer's heat for the next twenty years.

The valley's two railways, the CPR and the KVR, provided service to both Vernon and Penticton and used tugs and barges to tie the two systems together. Laden barges were attached to the sternwheelers for a few years but it was a far from satisfactory arrangement and conventional tugs and barges were soon brought in as replacements. Boxcars were loaded directly onto barges that had been fitted with tracks. Most of Kelowna's packinghouses and canneries were using the tugs and barges to ship their goods out of the valley by the early 1920s. The CPR increased its fleet to include the MV *Naramata* (1914), the SS *Kaleden* (1910), the SS *Castlegar* (1911) and eventually the SS *Kelowna* (1920).

The SS *Sicamous* under construction at the Okanagan Landing shipyard, circa 1914. The ship was launched sideways down the stringers into the lake. | KELOWNA PUBLIC ARCHIVES 6196

Kelowna quickly developed a love affair with automobiles: they were both a curiosity and a menace. Roads were the still-used wagon trails and the noisy erratic vehicles terrified the horses and often sent them bolting into the bush. Bernard Avenue had been made wide enough for a horse-drawn wagon to turn around but when automobiles used the same street, its wide open spaces "encouraged" speeds in excess of the legal ten miles per hour. Drivers parked their cars wherever they stopped and then drove in any direction they wanted instead of keeping to the left, as they did in Britain. A letter to the city council pleaded that cars be banned from the streets for at least one day a week so "country folk" could come to town and not risk having their horses bolt.

The mail from Vernon came on the first car to arrive in Kelowna in July 1905. However, dirt trails made worse by rain left service so unreliable that horses were soon back on the job. The lack of roads did nothing to quell buyers' enthusiasm and vehicles were often pre-sold long before they arrived on the wharf. Road travel northward was relatively easy but the primitive trail along the east side of Okanagan Lake was out of the question. On the west side, the narrow winding wagon road to Penticton challenged all car drivers. Most of the small boats and scows that carried cars and cattle across the lake travelled between Siwash Point on the west side and the wharf at the foot of Bernard Avenue on the east. The west side ferry wharf was called "Westbank," which caused some confusion as this was also the name of the town six miles to the south. The route between the two wharves was known as "the Narrows" as it was—and is—the narrowest part of Okanagan Lake. This was also the point where the lake usually froze and ice accumulated in the coldest of winters. When the first government ferry service between Westbank and Kelowna was offered in the mid-1920s, the public was assured that the boat would be "armed with devices designed to repel attacks from the Ogopogo."

Len Hayman, one of Kelowna's legendary and more colourful characters, captained a succession of ferries across Okanagan Lake. The *Aricia* was one of the more substantial at twelve and a half tons and was equipped with a passenger cabin, a pilot house and, uniquely, a lifeboat. When demand increased and included cars, Hayman added a scow that could carry up to eight vehicles. Though he was well experienced, he still ran into trouble on the unpredictable lake. On one memorable trip, the captain cast off from Kelowna into a stiff wind with six cars and nineteen passengers. All was well until he was just about to pull into the Westbank wharf and was broadsided by a swift gale from the north. Even with the engine at full throttle, there was little Hayman could do: he cast off the scow and its cargo of automobiles and then fought to keep the boat away from the rocks. The scow bounced off the boulders and disappeared down the lake.

The passenger boat, however, hit the rocks and stuck fast. Waves washed over the stern, the lifeboat filled with water, and then the gas line broke and the passengers were being gassed. They panicked. Hayman threatened to throw them all overboard if they didn't shut up and behave properly, and he finally managed to lower the lifeboat, bail it out and get the passengers to shore. One of the few who had managed to maintain his composure was dispatched to the dock to telephone one of the captain's friends in Kelowna with orders to bring over another boat. When the friend arrived, the pair headed down the lake to collect the scow. Even with the drama, all passengers and cars were delivered to the Westbank dock only an hour and a half later than their scheduled arrival time. But when the travellers collected themselves and their belongings to continue

The MV *Aricia* pushing a scow carrying an automobile. Behind is the SS *Okanagan*. | KELOWNA PUBLIC ARCHIVES 6267

their journey south, they soon discovered all was not well. The road from the wharf was blocked by trees that had succumbed to the same northerly gusts that had sent Captain Hayman and his ferry onto the rocks. Some likely thought it would have been better to have stayed at home.

Fifteen years later, the *Aricia* was replaced by a vehicle ferry, the MV *Kelowna–Westbank*, a wooden-hulled vessel with a fifteen-car capacity. It wasn't long before the boat became known as the MV *Hold-up* because the service was so bad. When the lake froze over or ice jammed the Narrows, no sailings took place, mail wasn't delivered and stores weren't supplied. People walked if they wanted to cross the lake, or found a horse and sleigh or perhaps a motorcycle and sidecar to carry them to the other side. The incensed public had little influence on the government in Victoria and inadequate service was the norm for the next twelve years.

The MV *Kelowna–Westbank* was the first real car ferry to cross Okanagan Lake. Not held in high regard by the locals, the ferry was soon dubbed the MV *Hold-up* because of the terrible service. | KELOWNA PUBLIC ARCHIVES 6282

FINALLY... KELOWNA'S RAILWAY

British Columbia's economy boomed between 1911 and 1913 and rail companies promised to lay new track all over the province. Most needed the provincial government to guarantee their loans, but that wasn't a problem, and it looked like the long-anticipated rail line to Kelowna would soon be a reality. The Canadian Northern Railway bought land for a rail yard in Kelowna's north end in 1912, and during the next two years completed surveys, purchased rights-of-way and started work on the grading and bridges. The route to Kelowna would run south from Kamloops, through Grand Prairie (Westwold), Armstrong and Vernon, and on to Kelowna. The provincial debt soon ballooned out of control, however, in part because of its railway loan guarantees, and most rail construction ceased.

The CNR station became a landmark when it was opened in January 1927. In addition to the express, baggage and ticket offices, ladies were provided with their own waiting room and gentlemen with their own smoking room. The station building is on the National Historic Register and has been converted for commercial use. | KELOWNA PUBLIC ARCHIVES 3580

Right after the war, railways' finances were in such disarray that the federal government forced amalgamation of five of the most financially troubled railways, the Canadian Northern among them. The new company became the Canadian National Railway (CNR). Work on the Kelowna line picked up where it had left off five years earlier; things moved a little faster than anticipated when the CPR agreed to share part of its track along the route. The railway's arrival was a historic and long-awaited event and plans were made to ship the 1925 fruit crop directly from Kelowna. The city was abuzz with speculation about the location of the new passenger depot. Since the two rail companies were now working together, everyone hoped the CNR would build its terminal near the CPR passenger wharf so boat travellers could easily transfer to the train. There was a limit to the co-operation, however, and CN carried on with its original plan to build a terminal closer to their rail yards. The city fathers were dismayed as they were certain it was too far from the business district to be well used.

The construction crew was still laying track about a mile and a half from the terminal on the morning of Thursday, September 10, 1925. A civic holiday had been declared for that afternoon, to welcome the first train, and all of Kelowna was encouraged to celebrate the momentous occasion. However, as the *Kelowna Courier* later reported, there was a "proverbial slip between the cup and the lip"—the track sagged just as the engine crossed the city boundary and the train tipped over at a precarious angle. The spongy railbed was apparently caused by nearby Brandt's Creek and a previously undiscovered Native burial site. The celebration was cancelled, all work on the track ceased and a "gang of husky labourers strove with such appliances as were at their command to right the engine and get it once more on the rails."

Undeterred, 1,500 citizens showed up again the next day to celebrate the train's actual arrival and schoolchildren were happy to have another holiday. Mayor Sutherland joined railway dignitaries to hammer the ceremonial golden (actually gilded) spike into place as the jubilant crowd showered the construction crew with apples and "luscious musk melons." When the train's whistle sounded promptly at three o'clock as the engine pulled into the station, it was answered by the whistles of all the factories around town. Kelowna had good cause to celebrate: the Shuswap & Okanagan Railway had arrived in Vernon thirty-four years earlier and the Kettle Valley Railway had chugged into Penticton ten years earlier. Finally, it was Kelowna's turn.

CN passenger service began a few months later with an oil-electric car, and passengers likened it to a long-distance streetcar ride. The trip to Kamloops took four hours and forty minutes and included a stopover in Vernon for lunch. When the demand exceeded the capacity of the initial car, it was replaced by a steam train with first- and second-class passenger, baggage and express service. The CNR then built a wharf half a mile north of the CPR wharf and added tug and barge service, using the *Pentowna*, the *Radius* and three other tugs identified only by number.

JOLLY GOOD!

The Okanagan in the summer looked like one great sports field. Competition was fierce as each community fielded lacrosse, baseball (rounders), football (soccer), rugby, tennis and cricket teams. Sometimes the same people were on every team. Many arrived in the Okanagan after some years in the British military and brought horse racing, polo and gymkhanas with them. The first golf tournament on the BC mainland was held in Kelowna in 1899 on a small course just north of Bernard Avenue and east of the Kelowna Saw Mill. This was built around marshes, downed trees and the few remaining pines, but the *Vernon News* nonetheless observed that "we anticipate that Kelowna will some day be as well known for golf as for tobacco, cricket, or any other games or vegetables."

The Bankhead Orchard Company had set aside sixty acres of undulating meadow by 1914 for a nine-hole course, and imported a greenskeeper from St. Andrews, Scotland. Little happened during the war but by 1920 the interested agitated for a better facility. The Kelowna Golf Club was soon formed and, after searching around the community for a suitable site, it purchased land across Glenmore Road from the town's original course for the "huge" sum of $5,500. The shack that had previously housed the Chinese men working in the orchard was fixed up for a clubhouse though a toolshed was built closer to the first fairway with a "Ladies' Toilet" attached. The men were apparently left to their own devices. The club's board felt such confidence in their course that they placed an advertisement in the CPR pamphlet *Golf in Canada, 1921–1922*. They noted that their "humble club house [was] somewhat lacking in refinement."

THE KELOWNA REGATTA

It was about 1924 when the non-Native community took over N´ha-a-itk and transformed the fearsome lake monster into Ogopogo. The name came from a popular British music hall ditty: *His mother was an earwig, His father was a whale, A little bit of head, and hardly any tail, And Ogopogo was his name.* The renaming also transformed the legendary fierce monster into something more benign… and vegetarian.

In usual fashion, each valley community has claimed Ogopogo as its own. The dispute led to hard feelings when Kelowna's statue of Ogopogo disappeared from its pond at the foot of Bernard Avenue. The creature, minus its tongue, was discovered in an army hut in Vernon a few weeks later. No one admitted to any wrongdoing, though the Ogopogo was soon embedded in cement to make sure it stayed "home" in the future. Sightings of the monster were often dismissed as Regatta publicity stunts, as most sightings were during July and August… but then again, isn't that the most logical time for the creature to be about? Winters were surely spent hibernating, and when the lake was frozen, it couldn't have surfaced. Many "responsible non-drinking citizens" were convinced that Okanagan Lake was home to some kind of curious aquatic creature, and that remains true today.

British settlers also brought their English regatta traditions with them, and by 1906 the first Kelowna Regatta was underway. Soon it became the city's signature summer event. Spectators gathered on the CPR wharf to cheer on the sailors, canoeists and rowers in the bay though it wasn't long before the crowds grew and spread farther along the beach to the original Lequime wharf and warehouse. The Kelowna Aquatic Association Ltd. was formed a few years later and sold twenty-five-dollar shares to pay for

This early 1930s depiction of the Ogopogo on an apple box label portrays a fearsome snake-like creature who devoured apples—and perhaps anything else that came its way. | KELOWNA PUBLIC ARCHIVES 6109

a pavilion and diving stand a little farther along the beach. Separate bathing cubicles for women were built west of the pavilion, while men had to use the boat storage space under the pavilion.

The Kelowna Regatta had already become a two-day festival by 1912 and was attracting over two thousand spectators. A tea room was added along with an eight-hundred-seat grandstand, with "KELOWNA" painted on its roof. Competitors "tilted" each other out of canoes and challenged each other in the swim across the lake, and children scrambled to catch a greased pig that had been dropped into the water. The pig always managed to evade the swimmers by squealing off into the park with the children in hot pursuit. Gas launches and sailboats continued to compete, though the war canoe races generated the fiercest rivalries. Men's, ladies' and mixed teams gathered from throughout the valley and the races were often so close that spectators would be leaping out of their seats, yelling themselves hoarse, with enthusiasm. Evening shows were added to the sporting events with displays of gymnastics and the "high-kicking" Gladstone sisters, who were also appearing at Kelowna's Dreamland Theatre. In the usual Okanagan tradition, a ball wrapped up the event. Kelowna summers and the Regatta were inseparable for many years to come.

Kelowna Flourishes, 1905–1930

The Kelowna Regatta circa 1907 (right photo). The building and wharf were originally built by Bernard Lequime when he moved his sawmill to the Kelowna townsite. The beach faces north and is part of what became City Park. As the Kelowna Regatta grew, a tea room and a grandstand were added (below photo). It was the first sight as the paddlewheelers rounded the point and pulled into the Kelowna wharf.

| KELOWNA PUBLIC ARCHIVES 2103, 4079

City Park

The lakeshore in Kelowna's City Park is remarkably quiet today, in comparison to earlier times. The north-facing beach was the first location of Lequime's wharf and warehouse, and the location of the town's earliest Regattas. With the construction of the first Okanagan Lake Bridge, water patterns changed and the sand from this beach was pushed northward to Manhattan Beach. The point of land farther along the waterfront was the location of the Aquatic Centre, the Ogopogo Stadium, the Athans Diving Tower and an open water swimming pool. Today, an old building, some pilings and a small wharf are all that remain of Kelowna's once bustling and vibrant summer gathering place. The area is accessible via the walkway at the foot of Bernard Avenue. | STUART KERNAGHAN, XYPHOTOS.CA

AROUND THE TOWN

Okanagan Mission

Kelowna was still not much larger than the original Lequime acreage when the neighbouring areas began to take on their own unique identities. Okanagan Mission became a magnet for all things British and since it could only be reached along the muddy and often disappearing Swamp Road, it happily developed on its own. Even after an alternative route from Kelowna was built in 1912, the road was so close to the lake that cars were usually mired in sand during the summer and overwhelmed by snowdrifts in winter. It remained that way for years.

The South Kelowna Land and Orchard Company lavishly promoted the area and British settlers came to clear land or take over the properties of those who had come before. They built large homes and planted orchards; they also build drying sheds for their tobacco crops. The post office moved to the Bellevue Hotel, the Okanagan Mission Supply Company was nearby and St. Andrew's Anglican Church was consecrated in 1911. The townsite was essentially complete when the school moved from its earlier Swamp Road location to the lot across from the church. The wharf at the foot of the road to the Bellevue Hotel (the original Thomson home) had the *Aberdeen*, *York* and *Okanagan* dropping off freight and passengers. Access to the hotel was easy and its elegant dining room and well-stocked bar soon became the social centre of the community.

Okanagan Mission's heyday was during the construction of the Kettle Valley Railway. The MV *Kaleden* delivered large caches of dynamite, powder and other supplies to the wharf, which were then loaded onto wagons and hauled past the Bellevue and up the hills to the construction site. A tent camp for workers was built behind the hotel along with a makeshift hospital staffed by a doctor and two nurses. Residents were aghast at how the construction workers' behaviour transformed their usually sedate community. A statuesque blonde, soon known as "Lady Godiva," took to riding her great white steed along the lakeshore with little other that her flowing locks to cover her. Construction workers told the story of the fellow who was heading back to camp carrying a large amount of whisky, along with his half-empty flask. The climb was long and he was tired and soon lay down for a snooze—and was found later in the winter, frozen solid.

Then there were the three young fellows who lived in what was known locally as "Buckingham Palace"... really a precarious lean-to.

Having time on their hands after a Saturday afternoon at the bar, they spent the evening using their neighbour's chimney for target practice. Their aim wasn't the best and their neighbours had to avoid the area for hours. The Ritz Hotel was at the bottom of the Mission hill and the resident ladies were apparently available to entertain anyone passing their door. During the languid days of summer when the unrelenting heat made life almost unbearable, the ladies were known to cool off by slipping into the irrigation ditch running along in front of their hotel and St. Andrew's Church. The water inevitably dammed up and overflowed onto the road, and those attending church would have to navigate through the mud and puddles.

The Countess Bubna of Austria, owner of the Eldorado Ranch, built a half-timbered, gabled luxury private hotel on the lakeshore in Okanagan Mission in 1926. Named the Eldorado Arms, it was to accommodate her friends and the friends of friends who came to visit: if she liked them they didn't have to pay but if she didn't, or their connections were too remote, they paid for the honour of staying at her hotel. Bathrooms were communal, verandas were screened, tea was presented on the lawns and the staff quarters housed the retinue of servants who accompanied the guests. Visitors more or less disappeared during the Depression and the hotel opened to the public. A few people, usually spinsters or widows, arrived from Kelowna each summer to spend a few weeks or even most of the summer in the small upstairs rooms, enjoying the gradually fading elegance of the lakeshore hotel.

Though Mission residents sometimes talked about officially incorporating as a town, nothing ever came of it. A letter appeared in the *Kelowna Courier* in 1930 from a disgruntled resident who complained about the area's unjustified reputation as being the home of the idle rich. Most residents, it stated, including the letter's author, were simple farmers who were paid the same for their crops as anyone else in the valley, and the comments were mean-spirited and ill-founded.

Rutland

Settlers from the Prairies and overseas continued to arrive in the Rutland area, and they bought land and planted orchards in the surrounding communities: Black Mountain, Hollywood (after Hollywood, California), Joe Rich (after a pioneer settler) and Belgo (after the Belgian Orchard Syndicate), which were more geographic areas than communities, though some had their own schools. Before long the Rutland townsite attracted a collection of small stores, a school, a post office and churches. The Farmers' Exchange packed apples for a number of orchardists until McLean and Fitzpatrick set up their own packing operation and marketed their apples under the Zenith Brand label. When the CNR built its tracks through Rutland, Mc & Fitz, as they became known, moved their plant to the rail line. These were challenging times for the newcomers: some years were plagued by drought, or apple scab and low apple prices. Many took jobs off the farm because they needed the income while others grew onions, tobacco, asparagus, raspberries or flowers and seeds. The Cross Cannery was built adjacent to the rail line and became the first in the area to can locally grown asparagus.

Kelowna's Chinatown shrank as the early share-croppers grew older and the federally imposed Head Tax cut off the flow of new immigrants. Yet Kelowna's Asian population grew when Japanese residents in Vancouver were confronted by anti-Asian riots in 1907, and many decided to leave the city. When the labour bosses from Vernon's Coldstream Ranch went to Vancouver to recruit workers, many Japanese families came to the Interior and some moved south to Rutland. They too had originally come to Canada expecting to strike it rich and return to their homeland. Instead, their reality became back-breaking labour and share-cropping on the area's vegetable farms. Some returned to Japan to marry or arranged for brides to sail to Canada; their children attended local schools along with Japanese school, where they learned their country's history and traditions. These families were usually frugal; they lived with few comforts, endured being strangers in a sometimes unwelcoming community and relied primarily on each other.

The first Indo-Canadians, mostly Sikhs from the Punjab, were hired by CPR labour recruiters in India and came to Canada to build the railway. Many of those who stayed in BC gravitated to Vancouver and found work in the sawmills; others drifted into the Fraser Valley and the Okanagan to work on farms and orchards. Some returned home but many who stayed experienced the growing anti-Asian violence in Vancouver. The animosity had begun to spill over to the Indo-Canadian community by 1914, and some chose to leave the coast and settle elsewhere, including in Rutland and Ellison, near Kelowna. Starting out as share-croppers, many new arrivals bought a few acres of bush, cleared and planted, bought more, repeated the process and grew acres of vegetables. They arrived expecting to work hard and did, and then infused their children with the same work ethic. They bought more land, sent their children to local schools, expanded their business interests and gradually became involved in their new community. By the beginning of the 1930s, Rutland had an ethnic diversity that was noticeably lacking in the other neighbourhoods.

Glenmore

The Central Okanagan Land Company continued to market its Glenmore properties in Toronto and Montreal. In spite of a fair number of settlers arriving from Britain, the area didn't have quite the same cachet or notoriety as Okanagan Mission. The Glenmore newcomers seemed much more earnest, and intent on getting their orchards planted and properly irrigated. Flumes were generally routed near the homes with a pipe and tap either in the yard or indoors. When the irrigating season came to an end, nearby cisterns were filled to ensure families had water over the winter. Drinking water was another matter, and for many years Glenmore residents carried five-gallon milk cans or barrels in the back of their pickups whenever they came into Kelowna. A drinking-water tap was installed across from the Kelowna Golf Club so drinking water could be collected on their return trip.

With only 270 residents, Glenmore was unique among its neighbours when it incorporated in 1922. Its reeve and councillors governed its 3,760 acres and paid attention to the orchards along with controlling the coddling moths and the mosquitoes. Glenmore had many ponds, and since much of Kelowna was built on swamp land, both communities were consumed with trying to find ways to control the pesky critters. One of the more curious efforts to locate the mosquito breeding grounds led to the dusting of a few ponds with coloured powder and then asking people in both communities to gather every mosquito they killed and put each in a separate envelope. They were to note the date, time and place of the kill. The envelopes were then mailed to the provincial entomologist who created a picture of where these mosquitoes began their life, their flight range, how long it took to get to their destination and their date of death. Hundreds and hundreds of envelopes were received, though no solution was ever revealed. Later, when DDT was introduced after World War II, great areas of low-lying land were drenched with the pesticide.

Though Glenmore had many ponds, few were swimmer-friendly. The municipal council thought they had solved the problem in 1927 when they bought lakeshore property at the foot of Knox Mountain, near Kelowna's northern boundary. Farmers brought their horses and equipment, levelled and filled the land, and created a bathing beach. They soon added two dressing rooms and a kitchen, a wood stove and a nearby woodpile so families could boil water for corn and make a nice cup of tea. It was a great alternative to the irrigation flumes and a welcome respite from the summer's heat. When the Depression arrived a few years later, however, transients who had ridden the rails to town learned of the building, the stove and the woodpile and took them over. The Glenmore families abandoned the beach and the community's first and only experiment of having its own slice of lakeshore ended.

CHAPTER FOUR:

And We Thought We Would Be Spared, 1930–1940

The Depression was slow to arrive in Kelowna. So slow in fact that many were saying it really wasn't a Depression at all, just negative thinking, and if we all pulled together and thought more positively, everything would be fine. The previous twenty-five years had been eventful for the new community and about 4,500 people now lived in the town and surrounding areas. There were few signs that life would not continue as it had been, and news stories in the *Kelowna Courier* were about valley-wide badminton tournaments and whether the Kelowna Growers Exchange was a better way to sell apples than the wherever, whenever tactics of the independents. Yet all was not well. The Royal Anne Hotel's New Year's Eve celebration in 1930 was marred by the death of a young man who climbed outside through a small third-storey bathroom window thinking he could cross the narrow gap and climb back in through the adjoining bedroom window. The sheer brick wall gave him little to hang on to and he fell to the street. By the time Dr. Knox was called from the dance floor inside the hotel, it was too late. It was not an auspicious beginning to what would become a troubled decade.

Though the CNR had arrived a few years earlier, Kelowna was certainly not on the mainline. The train pulled into the station, stayed for an hour or so and departed on the same track: Kelowna was a destination, and an unlikely stop on the way to anywhere else. The community remained somewhat isolated and the first news that times might get tougher was a paragraph in the newspaper about plunging Prairie wheat

The Royal Anne Hotel evolved from the early Palace Hotel on the north side of Bernard Avenue. This building was destroyed by fire in 1971. A modern version of the hotel remains part of downtown Kelowna today. | KELOWNA PUBLIC ARCHIVES 5809

prices. Then the apple shippers started having trouble getting the prices they wanted for the remainder of the 1929 crop.

Otherwise, life in the area was more or less unchanged. The hospital held its annual egg drive and collected two to four hundred dozen eggs, which were preserved in waterglass to keep them fresh; the talkies were showing at the Empress Theatre and matinees cost fifteen cents; and electric refrigerators with the motor on top began replacing ice boxes. Tobacco was still trying to make a comeback, but while the Okanagan product was of good quality, marketing had been a disaster and more money had been lost in various tobacco ventures than with any other crop grown in the valley. The Royal Anne Hotel and the Eldorado Arms in Okanagan Mission remained busy with parties and celebrations through the troubled years ahead, even if there were fewer out-of-town visitors.

Then, oil was discovered—or at least the likelihood of oil—in the bowels of the earth in East Kelowna—or Okanagan Mission, or Bankhead—and the promises of promoters galvanized the community in the dreary winter of 1930. A local syndicate obtained leases and raised money, and a geologist, with the aid of a divining rod, agreed that a vast pool of high-grade oil would be found two to three thousand feet down. The junction of Mission and Canyon Creeks soon became the location of Okanagan Oil & Gas Company Well #1. Several hundred spectators arrived to watch the construction of the eighty-foot derrick, and later the building of comfortable quarters for the crew. Grote Stirling, MP, came to mark the "auspicious occasion" as Mrs. Rattenbury, the wife of the mayor, and Mrs. McKenzie, the wife of the promoter, broke a bottle of water over the rig (reflecting the lingering restraints of Prohibition). The International Pipe Line Company promised to connect Kelowna with Vancouver once commercial quantities of oil had been confirmed. Assurances were given that the Kelowna deposits would likely exceed those of the Turner Valley, in Alberta. The machinery ran twenty-four hours a day, schoolchildren visited the site with their teachers and the appeal for financial support continued amid promises of greater prosperity than anyone could ever imagine.

Then… equipment began to break down, the project was delayed awaiting replacement parts and investors were admonished that they must expect these kinds of setbacks. Ten months after drilling began, the crew reached 2,102 feet and gas was now suspected. It looked amazingly like the wells in Viking, Alberta, that supplied the city of Edmonton with natural gas! Then the drill broke and it took five weeks of "fishing" to dislodge and remove it. Delays and shutdowns seriously interfered with the promoters' fundraising efforts early in 1932. Over two hundred people gathered a few months later to hear the company's "frank" presentation about the undertaking. In spite of an Ottawa geologist's negative report, several of those in attendance promised to give favourable consideration to the company's appeal for just a few more dollars. Everyone was fascinated and hundreds travelled to the well site each Sunday to see progress unfold before their eyes.

A great flow of water was discovered at 1,900 feet, along with a black carbonaceous layer of shale… and then more water. Further delays followed but with funds arriving from investors in Nelson and Trail, drilling started again. Success was so close and the promoters were so doggedly determined—their faith in the project never faltered. However, as 1933 drew to a close, and after many stops and starts and explanations and assurances, the taxes hadn't been paid and there was no money in the treasury, so the shareholders called a meeting and suspended operations. Drilling had reached 2,740 feet, yet the promoters pleaded with investors

Oil fever gripped Kelowna during the early 1930s. Promoters made promises and sold shares, and schoolchildren visited to view their future. As two wells were drilled, one at the meeting of Mission and Canyon Creeks and another in Okanagan Mission, crowds gathered to watch history unfold. Sadly, nothing came of the venture. | KELOWNA PUBLIC ARCHIVES 929

not to be discouraged as a rich oil field was sure to be found at just 3,500 feet…

The promise of oil was about the only bright spot in the community as the reality of hard times elsewhere in the country started to become apparent. The selling price of the previous year's apples continued to fall as the new crop began ripening on the trees. Transients arrived in Kelowna for the 1930 picking and packing season and then stayed on. Kelowna formed a Central Relief Committee to augment the efforts of other levels of government in dealing with the unemployed and indigent, with each paying one third of the costs and the city administering the funds. With about 4,500 people living in Kelowna and the surrounding area, and 111 unemployed at Christmas that year—61 of whom were married, with 44 of those having one or more children—it was a considerable burden. Little did they realize that the number would double and then triple over the coming years. Single men were sometimes housed in the old exhibition building in the north end but they were evicted as soon as the weather turned warm. Other years, the building was rented to store unsold onions and the men were left without a roof over their heads.

Most of those arriving in Kelowna had jumped off the transcontinental trains at Kamloops and hitched a ride on the CNR southward. It wasn't long before a "hobo jungle" appeared north of the tracks. It was called "Honolulu City" by its inhabitants, and whether the name was because it was that good or because it was as close as the inhabitants were likely to get to the real thing has been lost to time. Unlike many other "jungles," Kelowna's was an orderly place with rules and regulations, and was organized enough to send delegations to city council to lobby for better conditions. Council was dismissive, as the men were not Kelowna residents and they had no right to petition on any matter, and sent them to the provincial government office. When council asked why they shouldn't call out the Rocky Mountain Rangers to run the squatters out of town, they were told that such action would result in the men scattering and likely sleeping in people's cellars, camping in their barns and perhaps even stealing whatever they could lay their hands on. It would be wiser if council let the orderly Honolulu remain as it was.

Residents who still remember those times recall few problems. Men would knock on doors offering to work for a meal and then leave a coded message scribbled on the gatepost so those who came along later would know if the householder was generous... or not. If specific skills were needed, locals would head to Honolulu looking for a paper hanger or a painter and usually returned home with the helper they needed. In the early years, Kelowna developed a number of water and sewer projects to employ the transients, but those opportunities soon vanished and the single men either left town or went to the federally run relief camps. There was no point in allowing women to register for relief as no suitable employment was available for them.

The federal government became increasingly alarmed at the political agitation, anger and unrest infiltrating the ranks of the unemployed. By 1932, several relief camps had been set up across the country. Two of these "concentration camps," as the locals called them, were nearby: Wilson's Landing on the west side of Okanagan Lake just minutes from Kelowna, and Oyama, along the road to Vernon. Men were sent out each morning with picks, shovels and wheelbarrows to build roads and survey camps. They soon became known as the Royal Twenty Centers, as that is what they were paid each day for their efforts. Rather than containing the disenchanted, the camps proved to be a fertile breeding ground for Communist agitators and recruitment centres for the protest marches that marked the Depression years.

MADMAN ON THE LOOSE

Life in Kelowna was usually uneventful and the town's history held little drama. That changed early in 1932 when the *Courier*'s headline read: "Death stalked in the wake of a madman on Tuesday afternoon, when this Okanagan city was the scene of two cold-blooded murders." On January 19, between the hours of five and six p.m., Chief Constable David Murdoch murdered Jean (Genevieve) Nolan and his former deputy, Archie McDonald. Miss Nolan had been shot in the rotunda of the

Mayfair Hotel (earlier named the Lake View Hotel) where she had sought refuge from the gunman. The ex-deputy had been shot in his own home, just minutes away, on Lake Avenue. Word of the murders spread quickly and people were panic-stricken: doors were locked, porch lights were turned on, and people fled downtown. Terrified residents were even more alarmed to hear the murderer had visited the offices of the lawyer, T.G. Norris, and the police commissioner, Dr. Boyce, within that same hour.

By seven that night City Constable Sands had been advised that the murderer was likely Murdoch and went to the chief's house to take his wife and son to a safe place. Before doing so, and while other officers watched the house, Sands went to a nearby telephone office and called the chief's phone number. When the son answered, he assumed that only the child and his mother were at home and returned. When Mrs. Murdoch opened the door, the constable immediately spotted Chief Murdoch's blue coat and fedora lying on a chair. Quickly drawing his pistol, Sands walked into the kitchen and found the fugitive calmly sipping a cup of coffee. Declining the offer to join him, Sands arrested his chief and took him down the street to the lock-up.

An inquest was held the following day and as the details unfolded, the newspaper pondered the motives for such drastic behaviour. It also cautioned readers that the police chief had not yet been found guilty and, in the best traditions of British justice, he was not guilty until the court made that finding... and then speculated as to why Murdoch had murdered his two victims. Jean Nolan, the pretty auburn-haired girl who was twenty-four or -five, had been in town only a few days but was a known police informer who might have worked with Murdoch before he came to Kelowna. Dr. Boyce later testified he was sure she was at least thirty. Archie McDonald and the chief had also been involved in an altercation during the previous year's Regatta, and Murdoch was reportedly convinced his subordinate intended to kill him. The deputy had been charged with assault, and when the charges were dismissed Murdoch felt the court had "crucified" him. McDonald lost his job in spite of his innocence.

Several witnesses testified at the preliminary hearing a few days later and a different story began to unfold. Questions were raised about Murdoch's mental state and when local doctors were asked about his condition, they said he "was in an unbalanced state of mind at the time." Letters written by Murdoch to Nolan were introduced: some were in

The Kelowna Story: An Okanagan History

verse; some rambled on for pages; some were signed, others were not. The game warden, Mr. Maxson, who doubled as a special constable, said they had all been written on the police station typewriter. Nolan had subsequently given the letters to McDonald who passed them on to the clerk at Mr. Norris's law office; Norris had represented McDonald on the dismissed assault charge.

Jean Nolan had been shot at seven times: Murdoch fired on her twice outside the hotel and five times in front of the dining room doors in the hotel's rotunda. One bullet pierced her heart and witnesses claimed she was still moaning when Murdoch ran from the hotel. None of the bullets stayed in her body and those shown in court had been extracted from the door frame of the lobby's telephone booth and from the dining room floor. Murdoch had run from the hotel, through the main entrance to City Park, past the playground, past the baseball diamond, across the bridge and onto Lake Avenue, where he made his way to McDonald's house. The ex-deputy was found on the kitchen floor with his hands under him, his legs crossed and a broken dish of vegetables on the floor beside his head. There was no pulse. Though some witnesses had trouble identifying Murdoch in the January gloom, a distinctive notch on the heel of his boot had left a clear track in the snow and his route had been easily identified. Mrs. Murdoch, who "controlled her emotions well," sat in the courtroom all day. Murdoch was committed for trial and held for five months at Oakalla Prison, near New Westminster, until the spring assizes in Vernon.

After hearing more or less the same evidence admitted at the preliminary hearing, the jury deliberated for three hours before returning to the courtroom to admit they were unable to reach a verdict. Five months later, a second jury was called to hear the evidence at the fall assizes. It was more or less the same evidence as had been heard at the first trial. The jury deliberated for another three hours before returning to the courtroom to declare they too could not agree on a verdict. The defendant never testified and his counsel never challenged the facts: he had murdered the two victims. Neither jury could reach agreement on the defendant's mental state: had he been sane… or not?

A third trial got underway a week later and this time both sides called in medical experts from New Westminster and Vancouver and delved deeper into the chief's past: he had been an illegitimate child and felt everyone was against him because of it. He obsessed and blamed his past failures and job losses on the circumstances of his birth. He had initially felt Kelowna was remote enough that his past would remain hidden, but his behaviour had recently become strange. Those who noticed thought he was overworked and that a holiday, or less work, or going to church, would cure him. When a colleague from Penticton told him that Nolan was a dope peddler and a prostitute, Murdoch called her a "wrecker of men's souls" but remained convinced she was still the only woman for him. When he discovered that Nolan had delivered his precious letters to McDonald, Murdoch either lost contact with reality or planned the murder of his victims.

The experts diagnosed Murdoch with "paranoia simplex… which causes the patient to suffer the delusion of persecution. The progress of the disease was typically slow and is usually more pronounced in middle life." They said the patient simply did not know what he was doing when he fired the gun and was not capable of the intent to murder. By then, everyone was getting tired of the case. When the third jury had been deliberating for five hours, the judge called them back to the courtroom and told them he would not accept another disagreement. An hour later, the jury returned with a guilty verdict, though they added a strong recommendation for mercy because of the defendant's proven mental instability.

The judge refused to accept their verdict so they had to make a choice: either a clear verdict of guilty or a clear verdict of not guilty because of insanity. The jury finally agreed to the latter. Murdoch was committed to a mental hospital for the criminally insane for the remainder of his natural life. The conviction was for the murder of Jean Nolan, and he was never charged for the murder of his former deputy.

GLIMMERINGS OF HOPE

As the Depression deepened, more of Kelowna City Council's time was taken up dealing with the fallout: the federal government's count of the unemployed didn't match the city's and the funds the city was sure they were owed didn't arrive. With less tax revenue, city staff were forced to take pay cuts and then the hospital wanted to know who was going to pay for the men coming in from the "concentration camps." Relief for work was a nationwide mantra even if "work" meant selling apples on a street corner: that, at least, was better than standing in line for the dole. City council worried and sent notices to all householders warning them to save their wages and store and preserve fruits and vegetables.

Although unemployment and a sense of hopelessness pervaded much of the country during the 1930s, Kelowna moved on, sooner than most cities. By the end of the decade, voters approved tax hikes to pay for new schools as well as a concrete and fireproof hospital.

W.A.C. Bennett—Cecil, or "Cec" as he was known to his friends—arrived in Kelowna with May, his wife, and children Russell (R.J.) and Anita at the beginning of the 1930s. He had been involved in the hardware business in Alberta before deciding to look for opportunities in BC. Perhaps foretelling later developments, the Bennett family had to travel through the US to get to BC, as no highway yet connected the two provinces. The thirty-year-old Bennett first headed to Victoria but decided there might be better opportunities elsewhere, and soon discovered that David Leckie, Kelowna's hardware merchant since 1904, was looking for a buyer for his business. Bennett bought the hardware store and the two-storey brick building on Bernard Avenue, and then spent the rest of the Depression watching the inept and inadequate handling of Canada in crisis by his own Conservative Party and then the Liberals.

Because a number of Bennetts had already settled in Kelowna, Cec decided he needed to establish his own identity—and hopefully get his own mail—and soon became known as W.A.C. Bennett. Two years after arriving in town, a second son, Bill, was born. Cec joined a number of local business and social groups and then became involved with the local Conservative Party. He sought to become the party's candidate in the next federal campaign but soon realized the incumbent was well-entrenched and that it made better sense for him to turn his attention to provincial politics. The Co-operative Commonwealth Federation (CCF) had arrived in BC early in the Depression and before long had both radicalized and polarized the province's politics. As if biding his time, Bennett opened hardware stores in Penticton and Vernon and, although he was a teetotaller, joined his friend Cap Capozzi in a new business venture that soon became Calona Wines.

Bennett sought the Conservative nomination to run in the 1937 provincial election. He lost the nomination and his party lost the election, and his aggressive, independent style didn't endear him to his party's brass in Vancouver. He sought the nomination again four years later, and by that time had won over both the brass and the community, and soon headed to the legislature in Victoria. His arrival coincided with the release of the report of the Royal Commission report on Dominion–Provincial Relations, which identified BC's historic role as that of the spoiled child of Confederation. It offered the opinion that the province would never amount to much: it was isolated by the mountains, would probably always be in political chaos and would never have the wealth of the other provinces. No party held the majority in Victoria, and the Liberals and Conservatives formed an uneasy coalition to hold onto power. Much to the surprise of many, the CCF won the popular vote and became the official opposition. The coalition was plagued by infighting, the policies of the two parties were indistinguishable, little was accomplished and Bennett became frustrated. However, Kelowna now had a presence on the provincial stage.

In other areas, Kelowna was becoming less isolated when new technology connected it with the rest of the world. The first commercial radio station, CKOV, "the Voice of the Okanagan," emerged from an amateur predecessor thanks to James "Big Jim" Browne and his wife, who had arrived in Kelowna in 1914. Jim got his start with the amateur station but was intrigued with its potential. Finally granted a commercial broadcast licence in 1931, Jim soon began airing live broadcasts from a tiny house on Pendozi Street. Two ninety-foot cedar poles had been erected in the corner of the nearby Kelowna Saw Mill yard as transmitters. A carpet hung from the ceiling of the station to deaden outside noises, listeners loaned both recordings and money and the station's salesmen flourished. CKOV quickly became the voice of the community: lobbying for civic improvements, suggesting ways to control those pesky mosquitoes, reporting apple prices and broadcasting live lacrosse games from City Park and basketball games from the Scout Hall.

The station outgrew the house and needed a more secure transmission, so it moved to a new site on Lakeshore Road in 1938. Soon after, the CKOV signal was being picked up beyond Kelowna. The Canadian Broadcasting Corporation (CBC) was threading its way across the country at the time, and when Britain declared war on Germany in September 1939, the CBC withheld the news. Prime Minister Mackenzie King needed time to decide if Canada should join Britain or not and wanted to make the decision before telling the country. Big Jim had been monitoring US broadcasts and felt no compunction about keeping his listeners up to date on unfolding world events. Ottawa somehow heard of CKOV's unauthorized broadcasts and was not amused. The following day the station received a telegram telling them to cease and desist or risk losing their broadcast licence.

The *Kelowna Courier* had been a part of the community since 1904. Originally it was the *Kelowna Clarion*, then the *Kelowna Courier and Okanagan Orchardist*, and finally, with a new editor and publisher in 1939, it was renamed the *Kelowna Courier*. Early issues usually reflected the owner's view of the world—his politics, stand on local issues and general opinions—and were rarely unbiased or neutral. When the Depression took its toll on both circulation and advertising revenues, the *Courier* was sold to a company jointly controlled by the *Penticton Herald* and the *Vernon News*. Kelowna lost its independent voice. But when R.P. McLean arrived in town in 1938 and purchased the paper, he promised more balanced reporting and committed to print all the news, even if some people didn't want to see their names in print— they should have thought about that before they committed whatever it was that caught the editor's interest in the first place.

Aside from the Murdoch drama, life for many in Kelowna remained relatively unchanged during the Depression. A few businesses continued to advertise in the *Kelowna Courier and Okanagan Orchardist*, the Royal Anne Hotel and Eldorado Arms

The Willow Inn and Lodge

By the late 1920s, Mrs. Madeline DeMara decided Kelowna was ready for a new hotel. She oversaw the building of the Willow Inn and then ran the busy and popular hotel, which added a touch of elegance to the community. A large veranda was soon added along the front, cottages were built in the rear and a coffee shop was opened. With the ferry wharf across the street, Mrs. DeMara saw another opportunity and bought the adjacent land from the Kelowna Saw Mill. The Willow Lodge was built on the beachfront. The fine log building was a popular gathering place for families and visitors for many years. A.H. DeMara Insurance, a BA gas station and the Snack Bar were soon built alongside. | KELOWNA PUBLIC ARCHIVES 1164

were busy, and a campground had been set up in City Park, though most acknowledged that cabins would attract a better class of visitor. The elegant Willow Inn Hotel had been built in 1928 and linked to the nearby Willow Inn Cottages by a garden surrounding a fountain and goldfish pond. Located between Bernard Avenue and the Kelowna Saw Mill across from the ferry wharf, it became so popular that Willow Lodge, built from cedar logs trucked in from Lumby, was added in 1935. Both locals and visitors lounged in the gardens, played and partied on the beach, and moored their boats in the bay beside the public wharf.

TOO MANY APPLES

Few if any new orchards were planted in the Okanagan during the 1930s, though the weather that created the Prairie dust bowls made for near-perfect growing conditions in the valley. Orchards planted during the previous decades were maturing and producing more and more apples just as Prairie residents could no longer afford them. Also, so much emphasis had been put on production that the quality of the fruit began to suffer. There were too many culls—the undersized, insect-damaged or poorly coloured apples—and the packinghouses didn't know what to do with them. Orchardists had to pay to prune, thin and spray, pay their packinghouse to grade and pack, and then pay shippers to sell and deliver their apples to the wholesale market or fruit jobbers. It wasn't long before orchardists realized the apples that weren't good enough for the fresh market would cost them money. They had few options other than leaving them on the trees, ploughing under or hauling them to empty lots and leaving them to rot.

There was little to be optimistic about in the apple business and it wasn't the best time to try something new. Desperate times, however, demanded action. Louis Deighton from Oliver, at the south end of the Okanagan Valley, heard that Sunkist of California had just introduced the first fruit juice to the market. There was little to lose, and he figured he should be able to produce something similar with apples. With help from Ottawa and borrowed equipment, he experimented and improvised, and produced 1,500 cans of clarified apple juice in his first year of production. However, it wasn't an easy sell and his backers thought it was too much effort for such a small return, and abandoned him. Undeterred, Deighton produced forty thousand cans of juice the following year and then travelled the Okanagan and the Kootenays promoting and selling his new product. On a hunch, he sent juice samples to Vancouver General Hospital; when they ordered two thousand gallons, he knew he was on the right track. It wasn't long before the packinghouses began paying growers for their culls.

Initial juice production was low, though the Vernon Fruit Union got on board and began making juice at its Woodsdale plant in Winfield. The investment soon paid off when the Department of National Defence bought the valley's total output of juice during the war. Kelowna took awhile longer to get into the juice business. Modern Foods Ltd. began dehydrating apples in 1937 and went on to turn the peelings and cores into vinegar. The first year's operation wasn't a financial success and the plant closed. The following year, another group formed the Kelowna

Vinegar Syndicate and processed five hundred tons of cull apples into vinegar. It didn't sell and they too closed their doors. Gallons of vinegar were left behind along with a bill from the Kelowna Growers Exchange for the apples. Since the packinghouse didn't want to refinance the syndicate and no one else wanted to buy the vinegar, the KGE was left with a loss. Their manager, Bill Vance, didn't agree with the KGE board and was convinced apple by-products would be the growers' salvation. He put up his own five hundred dollars, bought the defunct plant and the vinegar, adapted his mother's pickle recipe to commercial quantities, and turned Mrs. Vance's Commercial Relish into a bestseller.

In spite of the successful relish, few apples were being diverted for dehydration, juice or vinegar. Orchardists were becoming increasingly desperate as the bills were piling up and no one was buying their apples. The majority agreed to pull together and to market and ship together. They also agreed that they would not bulk load the apples directly into the boxcars, though they knew this was a cheaper way to get their apples to market. A few independents remained, still determined to sell to anyone, wherever and however they could find a buyer. The two sides negotiated for days and finally agreed to have a single marketing and shipping plan. The independents later declared they had been intimidated and threatened, and felt they had little choice but to agree.

The growers were desperate. They decided they wouldn't deliver their apples to the packinghouses unless the shippers guaranteed them one cent a pound, or forty cents a box. If the shipper would not or could not make such a guarantee, growers would dump their apples before being charged for grading, packing and shipping. Vigilantes manned the three bridges into town from the surrounding apple-growing areas. They would not tolerate any monkey business. If truckers didn't have a written statement from shippers agreeing to the growers' terms, they were turned back. These were unprecedented measures but these were also unprecedented times: if the growers stepped beyond the boundaries of the law, well, so be it. It was war, and the growers' rallying cry of "A cent a pound or on the ground!" reverberated throughout the community.

Though Margaret Oliver looks quite happy perched on this mound of apples, the growers were not. There was no market for the small, poorly coloured, or insect-damaged apples and orchardists had to pay to have them trucked to empty lots around town and left to rot. | KELOWNA PUBLIC ARCHIVES 1386

Then word reached the organizers that railcars were being bulk loaded with orchard-run McIntosh Reds at the Rutland Cannery and Joe Casorso's Belgo Co-op packinghouse. The call went out and growers downed their tools, leapt in their trucks and raced to the cannery. Loading stopped immediately, and a council of war was convened. Mr. Cross, the cannery manager, denied any knowledge of the regulations and said he was only carrying out Mr. Casorso's instructions. Enraged growers wanted to unload the car but finally agreed to seal it before jumping back in their trucks and heading to the Belgo packinghouse. Another car of mixed-grade McIntosh Reds was being bulk loaded, again on Mr. Casorso's instructions. The manager was given the choice of having the growers unload the car or having it sealed. He chose the latter. Mr. Casorso, they were told, was in Vancouver and could not be reached.

Meetings were held up and down the valley to sign up other orchardists. It took a couple of weeks before things began to unravel. Joe Casorso, son of Giovanni Casorzo, who had extensive holdings in the Rutland area, had convinced the Rowcliffes at Hollywood Orchards and their growers (mostly "foreigners") that their salvation lay in the bulk shipment of apples. They were adamant and claimed they'd "blow to hell" anyone who laid a hand on their fruit. The police were called to the packinghouses and although the crowd remained orderly, power was cut to the loading bays and windows were broken. Bonfires were lit beside the tracks as sympathetic citizens gathered and handed out coffee and refreshments. Casorso promised not to move any cars that night.

It didn't take long though for rumours to start up again: two… and then seven railcars of apples were reportedly being bulk loaded. The growers pleaded with local railway agents and then sent telegrams to the presidents of the CNR and the CPR. When they didn't get a response, they sought an injunction against the railways to prevent them from moving the cars. That involved a trip to Vernon and back, finding the appropriate judges and preparing the legal papers, and growers were worried the trains might leave before the injunction could be served. A call went out to mobilize. The group said they were not promoting any unlawful activity, only mobilizing their supporters in an act of self-defence. If it was unlawful for them to lay hands on the loaded cars once the railway had taken charge of them, that was fine, but they also noted that it was not an offence to stand on the railway track.

So they did. The head of the growers' group declared, "We are peaceful citizens defending our right to live. We will take a walk on the railway tracks and if I lie down and go to sleep on the ties, I will expect you to see that I am not run over by a freight train." The women and children were less restrained with cries of "Over our dead and mutilated bodies!" Train crews, not surprisingly, backed off and the growers and their supporters gathered around bonfires and sang well into the early morning.

The Kelowna growers won that battle but the war continued. Orchardists from the Kootenay, Creston and Grand Forks areas hadn't signed on to the cent a pound campaign and continued to sell their apples anywhere they could, for whatever price buyers were prepared to pay. As it turned out, Kelowna's growers shipped their apples later in the season and most sold for more than the cent a pound they had been demanding. Marketing by co-op, individually or by legislation remained a thorny issue in the industry for many years.

A VALLEY FIRST: DOMESTIC WINERY AND BY-PRODUCTS LTD.

The wine industry arrived in Kelowna in 1931. Though prohibition was no longer the law, the government restricted liquor sales and the *Vancouver Sun* declared that "the establishment of wine industries in British Columbia is a step towards the reduction of alcohol consumption. It is a step towards temperance and towards real moderation." Giuseppe Ghezzi, a representative of wine expert Professor Eudo Monti, Ph.D., of Turin, Italy, had just come to town, bringing samples of wine and cider made from Okanagan apples shipped to the Old Country. The beleaguered orchardists were hopeful that a new apple-based wine would use a good portion of the apples they would otherwise be throwing away.

A syndicate was formed with a well-connected board of directors, including teetotallers, hardware merchant W.A.C. Bennett and grocer Pasquale ("Cap") Capozzi. Their company was called Domestic Winery and By-products Ltd., and they ordered their machinery from Italy. Mr. Ghezzi's son Carlo arrived to become the winemaker and Professor Assenelli, a chemist and specialist in sparkling wine and champagne, also came to lend his expertise. A cement building in Kelowna's north end became their winery, a refrigeration plant was added and four thousand gallons of apple juice was soon ready to be made into apple wine. Later, apple juice was added to Concord grape juice to make the Italian-style wines as well as their premium champagne.

The following year, BC government liquor stores ordered a thousand gallons of wine and the company began selling the "Okay" label in attractive twenty-six-ounce and gallon jars: there was Okay Clear, a sparkling white wine, and Okay Port, a rich flavourful red. Doctors in town for a medical convention the following year visited the plant and without exception heartily endorsed its wine. The local newspaper was somewhat reserved in its assessment and noted, "it is not unlikely that this will become one of the Valley's most important industries." Kelowna's Italian community was enthusiastic and many worked in the plant, while others became shareholders.

Some orchardists were a bit dubious about the viability of the new industry, though the public flocked to demonstrations and eagerly sampled the new product. As the market grew, the company realized that its "Okay" branding wasn't very optimistic and in 1936 ran a province-wide competition to come up with something classier. The winner was from the Fraser Valley: the suggestion of "Calona Wines" was seen as much more suitable. Giuseppe Ghezzi soon moved onto the Yakima Valley and eventually California, though his son Carlos Brena Ghezzi continued on as winemaker. Calona Wines became a familiar brand in the government liquor stores: the twenty-five-ounce Calona Champagne cost $1.90; the forty-ounce Calona Red, seventy-five cents; and a gallon of twenty-eight-percent proof Calona Dry Red, Italian type, $2.85. It was just the beginning.

AN ESTABLISHED BUSINESS EXPANDS

At the onset of the Depression, Stan Simpson was already building his new sawmill at the Manhattan Beach location. A veneer plant was soon added, though box production remained at the Abbott Street plant. When growers began using sacks instead of boxes and then bulk loading their apples, Stan must have wondered if he had a future in the business. The success of the Cent a Pound campaign sustained him for awhile, but he knew he would have to adapt. When the new box factory opened at Manhattan Beach in 1933, the assembly line ran round the clock to build a simpler, lighter, topless crate that held fifty pounds of apples.

As Simpson had planned, the veneer plant gave the company more flexibility and it soon began manufacturing veneer berry boxes, tin tops and grape baskets. The companies that had previously been supplying these containers, for resale to the growers, soon began a price war. Undaunted, Stan continued producing—and the outsiders eventually gave up. The logs used in the veneer plant were dumped in vats of hot water to soften the wood before long thin sheets of veneer were peeled off, scored and made into berry boxes and tin tops. By the mid-1930s, between

1.25 and 1.5 million tin tops were being produced each season. Sheets of tin measuring twenty by sixteen inches and six inches thick were shipped from England and on to Kelowna by rail; a single layer would cover the floor of the car. The tin was cut into narrow strips that would be wrapped around two pieces of veneer while a leg-operated crimper secured the tin around the top of the basket. It was a hazardous job as the tin was sharp and gloves didn't help. Most of the women operators said their hands toughened up by the end of the year. Experienced workers could produce about 2,000 containers on an eight-hour shift. About 940,000 tiny veneer berry cups were also stapled together and packed into two-layer crates before being shipped to North Okanagan strawberry and raspberry growers. About 75,000 grape baskets were made and assembled annually for the table grape industry.

Apples were always shipped out of the Okanagan Valley in new wooden boxes. But the solid lids were replaced by veneer tops and bottoms, and since Stan Simpson had the only veneer plant in the Interior, the company made and sold the lids to other box manufacturers. Over 10 million were made in a season. With the new sawmill on the lakeshore, logging contractors dumped their logs at various booming grounds around the lake where they were picked up by a succession of company-owned tugs and hauled to the mill. The first tug, the *Klatawa*, was bought from ferry captain Len Hayman in 1932.

During the Depression, small groups of men would gather outside the mill office looking for work even when they knew none was available. Other times a few old employees would arrive, load the sawdust trucks and deliver the fuel to homeowners who had no other way to heat their houses. When he had no money to pay them, Stan told his workers to go to Capozzi's City Grocery and charge what they needed, and he would guarantee their bill. He rarely, if ever, had to cover a bad debt. By 1937, when the politicians were insisting the worst of the crisis was over, fire wiped out Stan's office and his blacksmith and machine shops. The midday July winds were fierce and most of the efforts of the firefighters were used to prevent the flames from leaping across the narrow road to the sawmill and box factory. The cause of the fire was never discovered and crews soon set about replacing the buildings.

Two years later, when the box factory was running round the clock to ensure enough boxes were ready for the upcoming fruit season, an early morning fire destroyed the sawmill and veneer plant. Only the heroic efforts of the firefighters saved the box factory. A bottle of kerosene

Women operated most of the specialized equipment used to manufacture apple box tops and bottoms. Over 10 million of these unitized pieces were made in a season. | SHARRON SIMPSON COLLECTION

and oiled rags were discovered two days later behind a pile of lumber. The fire was of "incendiary origin." Stan set up a portable mill in the yard, added an extra planer to the one that had been rescued from the burning sawmill and began cutting lumber for the box factory. He also cut the heavy timbers needed for the joists in the new sawmill and veneer plant. The packinghouses got their boxes on time, and Stan searched for the best and newest sawmill and veneer plant equipment from across the continent. The veneer plant was back in full operation by July 1939, though the building was still without its roof. The portable mill kept producing lumber until the beginning of September when the new sawmill could be started up. By that time, Canada had declared war on Germany.

KELOWNA WAITS IMPATIENTLY

Kelowna was exasperated with the MV *Hold-up* as it continued to live up to its reputation for terrible service. Car traffic had increased but the ferry could still only carry its original fifteen cars, and angry drivers and passengers were left waiting endlessly for later sailings. Winters had been so cold that the lake froze over several years in succession and the ferry was left icebound. Passengers waited and waited, businesses ran out of supplies and politicians were immune to pleas for help.

The community was so fed up they decided to solve the problem themselves. Father Pandosy's old trail had always enticed people into thinking that a road along the east side of Okanagan Lake was a possibility. The road south from Kelowna had been started a few years earlier and a survey camp had been built by men from the relief camp, but little real progress had been made. Things were more promising at the other end as a road between Penticton and Paradise Ranch, just beyond Naramata, was already built. From there, however, narrow footpaths and animal trails were the only way to reach Okanagan Mission.

Not everyone thought the road was a good idea, but when word of the project starting up again got out, the *Courier* reported that the news spread "like wildfire and has enthused hundreds of persons." The Kelowna Board of Trade mobilized volunteers: bulldozers were offered and work parties blasted rock, dug through the clay banks, toppled trees and worked with such enthusiasm "they put paid labourers to shame." Money poured in to buy dynamite and blasting caps. Thursdays and Sundays were workdays. Women turned up to provide tea and coffee for the workers and a few of the hardiest grabbed shovels and worked alongside the men. All were paid in "shovel shekels," which were redeemed for free goods or entered into a weekly draw for donated prizes. News of the project and the shekels spread to the coast and it wasn't long before stories began to appear in the *Toronto Mail and Empire* and the *Halifax Herald*.

The planned road from Cedar Creek though Wild Horse Canyon to Paradise Ranch would be sixteen miles long. Old logging roads could be incorporated in some areas, bridges had to be built across several creeks and the formidable grade from the lake to the entrance of the canyon had to be conquered. Most volunteers were unaccustomed to hard physical labour and sometimes fewer than anticipated arrived for their shifts. When work crews reached Deep Creek, they "hurled up a cabin… of neat appearance in a day with a husky door, three well fashioned windows and a hand carved

A frozen Okanagan Lake was always a challenge for the ferries. Tugs would try to keep a channel open between the Westbank ferry wharf, at the right of the picture, and Kelowna. People had the choice of walking across or finding a horse and sleigh. Sometimes a motorcycle with a sidecar was pressed into service but when one loaded with liquor sank to the bottom after encountering thin ice, people became a bit cautious. The motorcycle was recovered but the liquor wasn't. | KELOWNA PUBLIC ARCHIVES 2476

sign over the door declaring it Kelata Kabin." It was ready for anyone who wanted to spend a night or a week or two in the wilderness.

"On To Naramata Week" was declared in Kelowna in April 1937 and a well-attended banquet at the Royal Anne Hotel generated much enthusiasm for the road. The lake had frozen over that year so everyone was keenly aware of the need for an alternative route out of and into town. Volunteers came from all over the valley and as one crew blasted their way through the mountainside, another followed to round out the sharp turns and widen sections so two cars could pass. When volunteers arrived on site in the spring of 1938, they discovered the road had survived the winter and spring runoff and they were able to pick up where they had left off. However, their motivation was severely challenged a few months later when the provincial government announced it would replace the

MV *Hold-up* with a steel-hulled ferry. Still committed to an eastside road and not convinced a new ferry would solve all Kelowna's transportation problems, a small dedicated group continued to wrestle rocks, brush and trees through summer and into the fall. Then they encountered a large slough at the entrance to Wild Horse Canyon, just as work was wrapping up for the season. It could wait until next year. Progress was being made—a couple more years, they figured, and the road would become a reality.

The MV *Pendozi* was launched on May 18, 1939. The ferry had been manufactured in Vancouver, dismantled and shipped by rail to Kelowna, and reassembled. The Kelowna dock had already been improved in anticipation and the last corner of the steep hill leading to the Westbank dock had been cut back and widened to make a safer approach. This ferry was different from its predecessor as it could be propelled from either end, so it didn't have to be turned around before heading across the lake. It also had two lifeboats and enough life-saving equipment for 150 passengers.

Dignitaries came from all over the valley to celebrate the launch of the *Pendozi*. The Kelowna Board of Trade hosted a lunch at the Royal Anne Hotel for one hundred important people, schools closed early, businesses declared a half-day holiday and over three thousand residents and visitors gathered to watch Mrs. MacPherson, wife of the Minister of Public Works, swung a bottle of champagne against the ferry's steel hull. The *Pendozi*, decorated with flags and bunting, was quite a sight as she slid down the slipway and splashed into the lake. It took six weeks of fine tuning and various adjustments before the hourly sailings between 6:00 a.m. and 11:55 p.m. began. Plans to repair the MV *Hold-up* and keep it in reserve were scuttled when it was discovered the entire bottom of the old boat was rotten and falling apart. The new ferry was a great addition to the Okanagan highway system and everyone rejoiced at how much easier it now was to get from one end of the valley to the other.

The new ferry and the outbreak of war undermined the community's sense of urgency about the need for the Kelowna to Naramata road. Many volunteers became part of the war effort and interest in completing the project disappeared. The idea has never entirely vanished though: problems getting across the lake often raise the need for an eastside road. In the intervening years, two additional ferries were added to the Kelowna–Westbank service and two bridges have since been built across Okanagan Lake. Though rough vehicle access is available along the east side, only the adventurous actually drive it. The story of a few determined and tenacious pioneers is all that remains of the Kelowna to Naramata road... for the moment.

The Naramata Road volunteers were paid with "shovel shekels," which could be redeemed at local stores for donated merchandise. Though construction on the road ceased in 1939, the idea of a highway along the east side of Okanagan Lake has never entirely vanished. | COURTESY OF DOROTHY ZOELLNER

Many Kelowna citizens were so frustrated with the government's refusal to provide adequate service across Okanagan Lake they took matters in hand. A group of dedicated volunteers decided to build a road to Naramata, along the east side of Okanagan Lake, themselves. What they lacked in experience they made up for with enthusiasm. Construction went on for a few years before a new ferry and World War II intervened. | COURTESY OF DOROTHY ZOELLNER

When the Kelowna Aquatic Club's first diving tower wasn't quite high enough, those wanting greater adventure improvised. | KELOWNA PUBLIC ARCHIVES 657

ALWAYS TIME TO PLAY

Depression or not, "Canada's Greatest Water Show," the Kelowna International Regatta, continued. Competitors from nearby communities joined local athletes and filled in for the visitors and competitors from farther away, who stayed close to home. The Silver Jubilee Regatta of 1931 was notable as war canoe teams from the Growers Co-op and Independent Growers competed in friendly rivalry against each other: this was before they battled out their differences in the packinghouse yards. Youthful athletes competed in swimming, diving, plunging and racing the four-oared shells for the championship of Okanagan Lake.

To celebrate its twenty-fifth anniversary and "arouse extraordinary interest," the decision was made to hold the Regatta's first ever queen contest in 1931. The traditional Saturday-night Regatta Parade featured a beautiful yet empty throne, perched on a flatbed truck, with a huge question mark sign balanced on the seat. Then, as the *Courier* reported, "Kelowna's pulchritudinous aspirants to the crown and Queen of the Silver Jubilee Regatta" took part in the parade to the "stirring accompaniment of the bag pipes, the gala music of the City Band, and the melodious strains of the Kelownians Orchestra… and gave an optical treat to the large crowd of spectators."

The evening event began with wrestling and boxing matches, which were to be followed by the crowning of the queen, fireworks and the usual Regatta Ball. The contestant who sold the most tickets would be declared the winner: one ticket equalled fifty votes. Both the Independent

Growers and the Co-op Growers joined in and sponsored candidates in the hotly contested event. So hotly contested and complicated that it took so long to count the ballots—the winner received 88,000—that the coronation had to be deferred until the following day. By that time, the Regatta was over and the queen had no chance to reign. The decision was made to hold future queen contests on the first day of the Regatta, to avoid the "farce" the event was in its first year. All was not lost, however, as those attending the ball had an opportunity to win a round trip to Honolulu, Hawaii, a round trip to the 1932 Olympics in Lake Placid, New York, or an electric refrigerator. The winner chose Honolulu.

The Regatta's first "beauty parade" was held in 1931. The winner was chosen by ballot but the process was so complicated the winner wasn't announced until the following day. By then the Regatta was over. In the future, judges would choose the winner and the contest would not be left until the last day of Regatta. | KELOWNA PUBLIC ARCHIVES 2271

NEIGHBOURING COMMUNITIES

Okanagan Mission

Little changed in the communities surrounding Kelowna during the 1930s. A new road to Okanagan Mission was built farther back from the beach and the previous roadway was advertised as an ideal place for Kelowna residents to build summer cabins; lots could be purchased for $150. Electricity arrived in most homes for the first time when West Kootenay Power and Light Company strung in a line over the upper trail from Penticton. The Eldorado Arms began welcoming the public as Countess Bubna's friends were no longer visiting and its tennis courts were made available to locals. They often stayed for tea. Another oil derrick appeared in the Mission and while many hopeful—or delusional—citizens bought shares in the venture, they were no luckier than those who had invested earlier.

The roof of the Mission packinghouse belonging to the Kelowna Growers Exchange suddenly collapsed under the weight of wet snow in 1937. Before long, a meeting was called to see if there was interest in the community having its own hall. The vote was unanimous and a committee quickly canvassed Rutland and Peachland, which both had their own halls, to see what options were available. When a plan was adopted to build the hall, organizers decided to make it look like a barn

Life in Okanagan Mission centred around St. Andrew's Anglican Church and the elegant Eldorado Arms Hotel. | KELOWNA PUBLIC ARCHIVES 5598, 4958

and then paint it red to fit into its rural surroundings. Residents offered rough lumber and nails, the Badminton Club donated fifty dollars, the Women's Institute gave eighty-four dollars and the Okanagan Mission Sports Club gave the hall association just over two acres of land. A plant sale raised a further $30.65, a treasure hunt, $12, while others donated cement mixers and scrapers or offered their services as amateur carpenters. It was a great community effort and less than a year after the packinghouse roof collapsed, over three hundred people attended a dance to officially open the new facility. The building became the area's social centrepiece and was in constant use for weddings, dances and parties, and even as a schoolhouse and badminton hall. The building is still in use, and the outside was recently returned to its original red after spending too many years in a very solemn grey.

The land adjacent to old Swamp Road was first planted with lettuce and celery in 1932. The damp boggy soil supported the new crop for the next twenty years before it was phased out. Cricket and tennis remained popular in the Mission, though war repeatedly depleted the ranks of those participating. The first horseback riding club in the area started in 1931 with much enthusiasm for paper chases and gymkhanas, which drew riders and spectators from throughout the valley.

Forest fires were a frequent menace and in June 1930 a blaze that burned the hillsides above the community also threatened a number of farms. Twenty years earlier a fire had started at Cedar Creek and decimated the same hillsides. Residents often complained of the valley being full of smoke during the summers as uncontrolled fires were left to burn themselves out. The 2003 Okanagan Park fire burned over the same area again.

Rutland

Rutland residents often discussed incorporating themselves as a munici-pality, but when that didn't happen a variety of organizations took over some of the functions of local government. The Rutland Farmers Institute, organized in 1930, explored the possibility of incorporating but got diverted by the pressing need for a pound. Cows and horses were wandering across the roads and through the orchards and becoming both a hazard and a nuisance. Many meetings were held, few decisions were made and no pound was ever created. The organization ceased to exist in the mid-1930s.

Travelling between Kelowna and Okanagan Mission remained a challenge. Simeon's Okanagan Mission Auto Stage was of great assistance to those who didn't have their own car or didn't wish to drive through the potholes and mud themselves. | KELOWNA PUBLIC ARCHIVES 8585

The Rutland Parks Society was founded in 1929 by a group of public-spirited citizens who wanted to raise money and buy eight and a half acres for a swimming pool and playing fields. There was great support for the project, and when a child drowned in an irrigation flume the community pulled together and ensured a pool was built for all to use. A paddling pool and a pavilion were subsequently added, and a lifeguard taught swimming. All children under twelve were admitted free, and the facility soon became the community's most popular summer gathering place.

Grant MacConachie, bush pilot and general manager of Yukon Southern Air Transport, arrived in Kelowna in June 1939 to announce he was putting the city on the province's air map. An eight-passenger "luxurious air ship" was already providing three scheduled flights a week between Vancouver and Oliver, at the south end of the Okanagan Valley, and he intended to extend the service to Kelowna. Since Kelowna didn't have a landing strip, the company planned to use the Rutland airfield once it was extended into a neighbouring hayfield. MacConachie urged the community to remove the rocks from the runway as soon as possible so levelling could be done and the service started. While this would only be a "stub line" serviced by a four-passenger plane, Kelowna could expect better service once a site for a more substantial landing strip could be found. Two years later, Yukon Southern Air folded into the newly organized Canadian Pacific Airlines, with MacConachie as its CEO.

Glenmore

The small municipality of Glenmore stuck to its agricultural roots during the Depression. The irrigation systems built during the previous twenty-five years began deteriorating and when the Mill Creek Dam was condemned, construction crews and all their equipment had to travel more than ten miles up the mountain by packhorse to repair it. Then the miles of steel siphon were condemned the following year. The system had been built in 1910 and the inside of the pipe had been given a light coat of paint at the factory. It had begun to rust in its first year and keeping it in working order meant repairmen had to climb into the thirty-two-inch-wide pipe, scrape the inside with wire brushes to remove the rust and reapply two coats of paint. It was a terrible job—and unproductive, as the rust returned almost immediately.

Though Glenmore never had a town centre of its own, it did have a rich social life: the Vagabonds became the community orchestra and played at numerous concerts and dances over many years. The link to Kelowna further tightened when the decision was made to bus Glenmore children into town for school. It was the first school bus service in the area and since there was no such thing as a "school bus," benches were bolted along the sides of a flatbed truck with a canopy attached overhead. The vacated Glenmore School became the community's gathering place for many years.

A GRADUAL RECOVERY

As challenging as the Depression years were for many in Kelowna, other parts of the country had a much tougher time. Seventy-five carloads of fruit and vegetables left the Okanagan in the autumn of 1936 for the destitute still trying to survive in Saskatchewan and Manitoba. Money from Regina service clubs funded Kelowna's Prairie Relief Committee and paid for the digging, sacking and loading and for shipping the produce eastward. As the decade grew to a close, farmers and orchardists again realized they needed to find markets beyond the valley and began lobbying for the completion of the Hope–Princeton Highway, which would provide faster travel to Vancouver. Dr. Boyce sold 190 acres of Knox Mountain to the city for one dollar, to become a park. The park formed a natural boundary north of the city limits and the *Courier* prophesied that "before many years, the new park will be recognized as one of the city's most precious possessions… and it is entirely possible that before long, a road will be built to the summit and a small terraced lookout will be established." Twenty-five years later, the Stanley M. Simpson Knox Mountain Trust provided funds to build the road to the summit.

Euphoria swept across Canada in May 1939 as King George VI and his consort Queen Elizabeth began their cross-country tour in Quebec City. After years of bad news, hopelessness and anger the country was ready to celebrate. The royal tour was a perfect excuse, and nowhere more so than in the British bastion of Kelowna. The mayor issued a proclamation to welcome the royal couple, affirming that "They rule in the Hearts of the People… and the citizens of Kelowna, their loyal subjects, rejoice to be honoured with the priceless privilege thus to greet in person the man and woman who so royally and unobtrusively interpret the enduring though intangible ties of Empire… we pledge our unswerving devotion."

That Their Majesties would get no closer to Kelowna than Revelstoke, about 200 miles away, was irrelevant. Thirteen special railcars filled with Boy Scouts, Cubs, Girl Guides, Brownies, Sea Cadets and ordinary citizens left Kelowna and joined a similar contingent from Vernon. Hundreds of others were more than happy to drive through the pouring rain, over gravel roads at speeds rarely exceeding 30 miles an hour, to get to the celebration. Since the royal train arrived in Revelstoke in the afternoon and required servicing midway through the mountains, most people decided this stop would give them the best opportunity to see the royal couple.

Thousands gathered and happily waited in what the reporters called a "Scotch mist." The "mist" was unrelenting for awhile and people huddled under umbrellas, blankets, coats and even a roll of tarpaper that suddenly appeared. Seats were at a premium so cushions, blankets, newspapers and apple boxes were pressed into service. The Revelstoke Band, enhanced by a few members from the Kelowna City Band, played alternately with the Vernon Pipe Band. Just before the royal train pulled into the station, both bands played at the same time and the throng of reporters, who arrived just moments before, noted it was a "most noisesome reception." The din was terrific and the crowd collectively sighed with relief when the bands stopped playing. Then everyone broke into a rousing "God Save the King" as the blue and silver train, with the royal coat of arms emblazoned over its headlight, pulled into the station.

The Knox Mountain Pavilions

Stanley M. Simpson created a trust fund to pay for capital improvements to Knox Mountain Park. The first expenditure was for a road to the summit of the mountain, which was built in the 1960s. The Stanley Simpson Nature Pavilion, a children's playground and a picnic area were built soon after. The pavilion was subsequently vandalized beyond repair. Using the balance of the trust fund, along with some funds from the city, a new pavilion, a caretaker's residence and public washrooms were built in 2004. At the official opening, the building was renamed the Pioneer Pavilion to honour all Kelowna's early pioneers, one of whom was Stanley M. Simpson. The pavilion can be reached via Knox Mountain Road.

| SHARRON SIMPSON COLLECTION

The royal couple mingled freely with the crowd. The king wore the same suit he had worn in the photos published in the *Courier Special Edition* the week before. The queen, however, wore the most stunning costume of any she had worn since arriving in Canada. It was a deep sky blue and reportedly matched her eyes. The royal couple walked along the railway ties and chatted with children and veterans, and when the crowd broke through the police lines, no one seemed to mind. The couple stayed much beyond their allotted time and the train's whistle could be heard trying to coax them back aboard to continue on to the next stop. Their loyal subjects were emotionally exhausted when the royals left, but waited patiently for the almost three hours it took the police to get the traffic organized so they could all head home. It had been a joyous celebration.

Canada declared war against Germany in September of 1939. The biggest issue in town at the time was whether Okanagan apples could still be shipped to their traditional British markets. Was there still enough cargo space on the ships travelling the Atlantic? Would Ottawa help market the fruit? Would shipping from Pacific ports and the Panama Canal pay? During the early months no one seemed to think the skirmishes would escalate into war. The *Courier* reported that merchants were pleased with their "excellent Christmas trade" and noted that "Kelowna was a gay city over the long holidays."

CHAPTER FIVE:

Despair and Recovery, 1940–1955

War became a reality in Kelowna when France was invaded in the spring of 1940 and the Battle of Britain began a few months later. The provincial police warned of sabotage and men from the local militia, the BC Dragoons, were dispatched to guard CNR and CPR bridges along the mainline. Extra guards were stationed around the armoury, the packinghouses, the power plant and the ferry when it docked overnight. Each edition of the *Courier* featured the column "Canada at War—A Review of Developments on the Home Front," and highlighted the opening of a recruitment centre and the forming of a civil defence unit of the over-thirty-fives and those too vital to the local war effort to leave town. They would be taught to deal with poisonous gas, incendiary bombs and high explosives, and learn basic first aid.

Kelowna had to be prepared, though air raids were unlikely. A long steady blast from the hand-cranked fire siren would let everyone in town know if enemy planes were approaching. Police cars would drive up and down country roads with their sirens blaring to warn those in rural areas. The alarms could be sounded any time of day or night but a night raid would be confirmed if the street lights had also been turned out. All windows and doors had to be blacked out at dusk and covered with heavy paper or blankets. If driving was absolutely essential, headlights had to be covered except for a three-inch-long vertical strip, a quarter of an inch wide. A pail, a shovel and a garden hose had to be kept at the ready to deal with the inevitable fires from incendiary bombs. The two-pound, highly inflammable magnesium tube bombs were filled with a mixture of powdered aluminum and iron oxide that would ignite fiercely hot blazes all over town. The fire department couldn't be expected to attend every fire and citizens had to be prepared to look after their own property.

War was costly and while higher taxes paid a portion, the public was expected to pay the balance by purchasing Victory Bonds and war savings certificates. A series of extraordinary campaigns between June 1941 and October 1945 raised billions of dollars for the war effort from ordinary Canadians. Communities and salesmen had quotas and each town had a "special names" list of those identified as substantial purchasers. The *Courier* ensured everyone knew their patriot duty and then celebrated when Kelowna was the first valley community to reach, and then exceed, its quota. Everyone, including children, was urged to buy "ribbons of silver," the twenty-five-cent stamps that could be bought at the grocery stores and fixed to a savings certificate until they totalled five dollars.

Fundraising campaigns were constant: the Red Cross asked for money for soldiers overseas and their families at home; a donation of one dollar would provide Prisoner of War Parcels for Allied soldiers; the "Bury Hitler Under Aluminum" campaign urged people to bring their old pots, pans, kettles and percolators to be melted down and turned into airplane parts so Berlin could be bombed more frequently by ever more planes. When the Nazi campaign targeted Russia, funds were raised for the starving and destitute in that country. When the Japanese invaded China, money was raised to help the Chinese. The *Courier*, likely thinking this was a short-term commitment, turned its advertising revenue from government ads into war savings certificates: loyalty to the British Empire was paramount and everyone and every business was expected to pitch in to do their duty.

People's anxiety levels escalated dramatically after the December 7, 1941, Japanese attack on Pearl Harbor. The *Courier* stated that "the people of British Columbia are realizing as they never have before that we are fighting for our very lives... we are in the midst of a final fight for our home, lives, and way of life." With this one act, those who had looked at the early civil defence plans with "tolerant amusement" suddenly realized war was on their very doorstep. A delegation of local Japanese residents appeared before Kelowna City Council less than a week after Pearl Harbor, with a statement: "We, the undersigned Japanese residents of Kelowna and vicinity, wish to express our deep regret at the state of war existing between Canada and Japan and each of us pledges herewith to be a loyal and good citizen of Canada. In presenting this pledge to the authorities of the City we shall be grateful if you and your fellow citizens accept our fidelity and understand our sincere attitude in the awkward position in which we find ourselves." The acting mayor assured the delegation he had every confidence that the Japanese would receive the benefit of the usual British justice and sense of fair play in the future, just as they had in the past.

The 130 men who appeared before council represented about 332 Japanese who were living in the area, half of whom were born in Canada or had become naturalized citizens. The Okanagan was home to the greatest number of people of Japanese descent beyond the west coast, and many had lived in the area for over twenty-five years. A hundred-mile exclusion zone had been established along the Pacific Ocean and all Japanese men between the ages of eighteen and forty-five were deemed a security risk and removed to internment camps in the BC Interior, the Prairies and Ontario. It wasn't long before their wives and children were also removed and interned, often in different camps than their husbands and fathers. Though the local Japanese residents remained in their homes, their world changed: they had to register with the RCMP, they couldn't travel, they had to surrender any firearms and they had to face friends who turned away and the shopkeepers who no longer welcomed their business. Those who tried to enlist were rejected.

Shortly after Pearl Harbor, the *Kelowna Courier* suggested that Japanese residents should be left alone and shown a little sympathy. However, as the "Pearl Harbor Japs" from the coast were rounded up and moved to internment camps in the Interior, the *Courier* and many others changed their minds. The city and its newspaper became known for virulent and hateful statements against any Japanese people who came into the area, for whatever reason. Vitriolic headlines were commonplace and large signs proclaiming "No to Coastal Japs" appeared in store windows and nailed to rural fence posts. When it was impossible to find workers for the orchards and vegetable farms and the BC Fruit Growers' Association (BCFGA) proposed using Japanese internees, city council reluctantly agreed but only if the province guaranteed they would all leave the area once the season was over. When local Japanese farmers arranged for internees to work with them, alarm was raised in case the internees remained in Kelowna for the duration of the war... or worse, after the war. School districts didn't want to pay for internee children to go to school, curfews were strictly enforced and shopping was only allowed on Mondays—and even then, only under the watchful eye of the RCMP.

There was little doubt where Kelowna stood following the Japanese attack on Pearl Harbor in 1941. The Japanese being referred to were those who had been removed from within one hundred miles of the Pacific Coast and sent to internment camps in the Interior. Some were released from the camps to help with the harvest, but they were rarely welcomed to stay longer. | KELOWNA PUBLIC ARCHIVES 784

Though not everyone in town was caught up in the hysteria and paranoia, the majority claimed it was an appropriate response in times of war. Kelowna's British colonial and racist roots were showing. Even when the war was over, the *Courier* reported that when a young Indo-Canadian woman tried to buy a house near a downtown school, neighbours and several prominent organizations signed petitions to stop the sale from going through. "If Orientals settle in the neighbourhood, it would be a starting signal for more Far Eastern natives to move into the residential district, with the result that the area would slowly grow into a Hindu settlement, thereby lowering property values and causing general unpleasantness." In spite of the obstacles and city council's announcement that "we have a town composed of Anglo-Saxons and it should continue so," the young lady persisted and the neighbourhood survived.

Kelowna celebrated the end of the European war in the first week of May 1945. Shops and schools closed as flags and bunting appeared on Bernard Avenue and five thousand gathered in City Park for a Thanksgiving service. Bands played, home guard units marched, Boy Scouts and Legion members sang "Onward Christian Soldiers" and everyone celebrated the "Empire's victory." And after atomic bombs decimated Hiroshima and Nagasaki a few months later, the *Courier* noted that a "joyous but orderly crowd" celebrated Japan's capitulation. With the war over on both fronts, "all Kelowna and his wife and family gathered on Bernard Avenue in the evening and were joined by most of the people in the rural areas." Thousands danced on the street in front of the Royal Anne Hotel as many more watched from the sidelines. Fire sirens were joined by factory whistles and car horns and stores were raided for toilet paper that was turned into streamers for the cars, trucks and bicycles parading up and down the streets. CKOV was on Bernard Avenue with a live broadcast, Chinese residents flew the Chinese flag, armoured vehicles and anti-tank guns were towed, and a flaming gold torch, saved from an early Victory Loan campaign, was symbolically extinguished. Staid Kelowna let loose and celebrated.

The Kelowna and District War Veterans Rehabilitation Committee helped those returning from the war find housing and jobs. The "Women's Problems" subcommittee held teas at the Willow Inn to introduce war brides to Canadian ways. Housing became a major issue and the city offered one hundred lots to Wartime Housing Ltd. for one dollar: two-, three- and four-bedroom houses could be built on a cement pad for about $3,800. Each would be of the latest design with clothes closets, electrical fixtures, indoor bathrooms and a circulating heater. A woodshed was attached for the wood or sawdust that would be used for cooking and heating.

So few building materials had been available during the war that citizens had been encouraged to make do or renovate. Shortages continued even after the war and veterans were given purchasing priority ahead of the general public. As the demand for housing vastly outstripped the supply, even furniture dealers had trouble locating supplies and stoves were almost impossible to find. Since plumbing fixtures could not be produced fast enough to keep up with the countrywide demand, both servicemen and newcomers began building shacks and outside privies on city-owned land.

Wartime houses appeared in Kelowna's north end and near its southern boundary. In keeping with the empire's tradition of rewarding service with land, the government created the Veterans' Land Act (VLA) and bought seventy-five acres from Bankhead Orchards. About thirty houses were built and made available to deserving and needy veterans whose names had been pulled from a hat. Some veterans took advantage of low-interest loans, bought the rest of the land and built their own houses. The VLA hired other veterans to travel the valley giving assistance to new growers, many of whom had bought large acreages in spite of not having any orchard experience.

A SUITABLE MEMORIAL

Kelowna looked for a way to pay tribute and give thanks to both those who served in World War II and those who died during the conflict. Communities across the country were talking of statues and plaques but the idea of a "living memorial," something that would be more useful to citizens, began catching on. Kelowna had struggled with high delinquency rates during the war, and that had been blamed on the departure of most of the community's positive role models and leaders. The young had been left without guidance, had nothing to do and got into trouble with the law as a result. When an ice arena was suggested as a memorial, with a legacy of "developing harmony and happiness for future generations," everyone agreed and began searching for an appropriate site.

The Kelowna Saw Mill, adjacent to the downtown business district, had been sold in 1942 by its early owner, David Lloyd-Jones, to Stanley M. Simpson, owner of the other sawmill in town. Fire destroyed many of the buildings two years later and rather than rebuild, Simpson moved

SAILORS & SONGS
OCT 5
TICKETS $10.00 EACH
CALL 763 9292

Despair and Recovery, 1940–1955

Kelowna Memorial Arena was opened in 1948 in memory of those who served in World War II. It was the first building to be constructed on the new civic centre site (above photo). The arena soon became the home of the Kelowna Packers hockey team, welcomed Canadian Olympic ice dancer Barbara Ann Scott and then, for a number of years, hosted every major event in town. In addition to the ice surface, which continues to be used for much of the year for minor and college hockey, the Okanagan Military Museum has now taken over the lobby and some of the upstairs space for military displays and a library. The distinctive mural portrays all three branches of Canada's armed forces (previous page photo). The mural and the museum are on Ellis Street. | KELOWNA PUBLIC ARCHIVES 2527 / STUART KERNAGHAN, XYPHOTOS.CA its production to his Manhattan Beach operation. When approached by city council in 1944 and asked if he would sell the property to the city for a future civic centre, Simpson agreed, though he insisted on certain conditions. Discussions were initially about the seven and a half inland acres but they soon expanded to include the four and a half acres adjacent to the lake. Citizens approved of the purchase of both parcels by referendum and council agreed to the covenant that Simpson placed on the land. The agreement stated that the land would only be used for civic purposes, that it could never be used for commercial or industrial ventures and that it could never be sold. It was also to be pleasantly landscaped and developed for the use and enjoyment of the citizens of Kelowna. The cost of the land was equal to the amount Simpson paid to have the fire debris and years of sawmill residue cleared from the land: $55,000. The price was substantially below the market value of comparable commercial properties in the area.

It didn't take long for the War Memorial Committee to decide the new civic property was the perfect location for their arena and set about raising funds to pay for the building. It wasn't an easy task, but the first $100,000 of donations and pledges were in hand by January 1, 1946. All available lumber, building supplies and labour were being used to build houses for returning soldiers by that time, so council delayed the project for eighteen months. Costs rose and there was a shortfall of $75,000. Voters approved the increased expenditure by referendum, though some thought council should have been more diligent in calculating the costs. By the fall of 1947, council again asked voters to approve a bylaw for an additional $80,000: this time a few donors asked for refunds. When a further $45,000 was needed, the committee began eliminating some amenities. The 1948 floods caused even more delays when the lake inundated the recently laid foundation. By October that same year, taxpayers were being asked to put up another $50,000 and council was being roundly criticized. Then an arsonist began setting fires and the derelict planing mill directly behind the arena went up in flames. Fire crews let it burn and turned their hoses on the partially finished new building.

The arena's official opening was a sombre event as veterans of both wars marched from the cenotaph to the Memorial Arena on Remembrance Day, November 11, 1948. The invocation called for all to play with generosity, lose gracefully without rancour and be worthy of those in whose memory the arena had been built. The town's first artificial ice rink quickly became the community's winter focal point and home of the

Kelowna City Hall opened in 1951 as the second building on the new civic centre site (top photo). A council chamber was added on the right side of the building, with additional office space added upstairs and to the rear. At various times since the civic centre site was established in 1946, a curling rink, a public health building, a library, an art gallery and a museum have also been located here. Of these, only the museum remains. The Kasugai Gardens, with a somewhat traditional Japanese style, were added in 1987 to commemorate the sister-city friendship between Kelowna and Kasugai, Japan. Its tranquil space is hidden behind city hall, which is located on Water Street (bottom photo). | KELOWNA PUBLIC ARCHIVES 3437 / STUART KERNAGHAN, XYPHOTOS.CA

Kelowna Packers, the city's Okanagan Mainline senior amateur hockey team. When Barbara Ann Scott, the Olympic figure-skating champion, came to town as part of the 1949 *Ice Frolic*, Kelowna "welcomed the world's finest figure skater with all their hearts." The city fathers were apparently so astounded she would perform in Kelowna they bestowed the Freedom of the City on her. A great variety of summer events took over when the ice was removed: wrestling and boxing matches, craft shows, the Royal Lipizzaner Stallions, circuses, symphonies, roller derbies and high school graduations, among others happenings. With seating for two thousand, it was the largest venue in Kelowna for many years.

COMMANDO BAY

Commando Bay isn't in Kelowna, but neither is it very far away, and it was the site of a little-known operation that holds a unique place in Canadian military history. Originally named Dunrobin's Bay after its first pre-emptor, the small bay was renamed after World War II because of the secret activities that took place on its isolated beach and dry upland benches. Commando Bay is now within the boundaries of Okanagan Mountain Park.

As the war in Europe wound down, battles in the South Pacific were intensifying. Deep within the British War Cabinet, an organization known as the Special Operations Executive (SOE) was responsible for training commandos to work behind enemy lines. Most of its operatives were European, and as such were unsuitable for deployment to the Far East. They needed to find Chinese recruits and looked to the British colonies, specifically Canada, for them.

In 1944, a call went out for volunteers. Though many first-generation Chinese men had tried to enlist during the war, few had been selected. The Chinese had been denied voting rights since the late 1800s and many felt enlisting would improve their chance to rectify the injustice. The government in Ottawa thought so too, however, and didn't want to open the door to the possibility. From the twenty-five who volunteered, thirteen were selected for what became known as Operation Oblivion.

There were no roads to Commando Bay, which was chosen because of its isolation and inaccessibility. Supplies and equipment were dropped off at a wharf that had just been built, tents were set up about three hundred yards up the hill above the beach, a cookhouse was added and everyone settled in for the next four months. Recruits were trained in small arms, explosives, sabotage operations, demolition, unarmed combat, and ambush planning and execution. Survival techniques, wireless operation and radio telegraphy were important as well, as part of the mission's goal was to stay in contact from behind enemy lines. The young men worked from dawn to dusk with their only break coming when the commanding officer learned that the Paradise Ranch, their closest neighbour, couldn't find people to pick their peaches and the recruits spent a couple of days helping out.

Demolition training was carried out on the hill above the beach. As their expertise grew, the crew moved along to the mouth of Wild Horse Canyon where they found an abandoned cabin to store their supplies. Was it the cabin left by the Naramata Road building crew? It was originally expected that the recruits would know the Chinese language: most didn't. As often happened with immigrant parents who wanted to ensure their children's success in a new world, most only spoke English. Chinese language instruction was added to the training.

The recruits trained and toughened up during the four intense months, and when it was time to leave they packed up their tents, scoured the area to make sure no live ammunition had been left and departed. Other than the wharf, which soon deteriorated, there were no signs that anyone had ever been at the site. The group returned to Vancouver, went up the coast for underwater training and then headed to Australia for parachute training. Dropped behind enemy lines in Borneo, the men collaborated with local head-hunting tribes and succeeded in driving the Japanese from the area in less than two months. The atomic bombs were dropped not long after, and the Japanese surrendered.

There are no written records of Operation Oblivion. Most of the stories about the secret unit have been lost to time, though a recent video prepared by a daughter of one of the survivors has captured some memories. A reunion of those trained at Commando Bay was held in September 1988: ten of the thirteen soldiers revisited their training site. Among them were businessmen, an aeronautical engineer, a lawyer and an MP. A plaque and some poppy seeds that were scattered along the beach by one of the departing veterans were all that remained of their visit. Chinese Canadians were granted the vote in 1947.

TOO MUCH WATER

Much of Kelowna was built on the flood plain adjacent to Mill and Mission Creeks and Okanagan Lake, and residents learned to live with the often annual reality of high water. Basement pumps were essential for everyone living near any water and when they couldn't keep up with rising levels, live fish settled in for the duration, inches of tadpoles carpeted low-lying fields, mosquitoes were fierce and filling sandbags became an annual rite of spring.

Kelowna was inundated with water every few years, but 1948 was the worst. Relentless rains were compounded by heavy mountain snowpacks and the Okanagan watershed could not contain the runoff when the hot weather arrived. The Fraser River was also in flood and rail, telegraph and telephone lines to the coast were cut. Gasoline couldn't be delivered and had to be rationed for all but essential vehicles; food supplies ran low and officials pleaded with residents not to hoard. Hundreds of railway passengers were stranded in Kamloops when westbound rail lines disappeared under water. The southbound rail line was fortunately still in service, and passengers were diverted to Kelowna, where they were greeted by Red Cross volunteers and given coffee and sandwiches until buses could be arranged to take them to Penticton. Though parts of that road were also under water, they got through to the Penticton airport where Canadian Pacific Airlines and Trans-Canada Airlines became part of the rescue mission. More than 1,200 passengers were flown to Vancouver over a two-day period.

A province-wide plea for funds to help flood victims in the Fraser Valley must have seemed a bit unfair to those in Kelowna struggling with their own catastrophe. Creeks overflowed their banks and flooded acres of low-lying hay and vegetable fields, bridges were washed out and houses alongside the rampaging creeks were bulldozed out of the way instead of being left to collapse into the stream. Some roads were under two feet of water, and everyone gathered to fill sandbags in a sometimes futile effort to keep the rising water out of their homes. City Park was under water and the lower bleachers of the Regatta grandstand were submerged. The city threatened to cut off residents from the already overwhelmed sewage treatment system and told those on septic tanks not to use them: communal outhouses were set up on drier ground. Drinking water had to be boiled, typhoid shots were free to anyone who wanted them and swimming in the lake was forbidden. As lake levels rose, water backed up even farther into creeks and backyards, and gardens five and six blocks from the lake were under two feet of water.

These were also the peak production weeks for making wooden fruit boxes and 1948 was shaping up to be a record crop. S.M. Simpson Ltd., the valley's main box manufacturer, was running seventeen hours a day and producing about eighteen thousand apple boxes during the two shifts. The veneer plant and sawmill were also working at full capacity: closing the plant wasn't an option as no boxes and the loss of five hundred jobs would be a further blow to the community. The sawmill had originally been built on low-lying land but with repeated layers of sawdust and slabs overlaid with loads of gravel the site had been built up over time. High water levels created another challenge, however, as the mill's five boilers were close to being submerged. Makeshift wooden dykes were built and managed to hold back two and a half feet of water though pumps still ran twenty-four hours a day to deal with the seepage. Electric motors, many operated by leather belts, had to be raised on wooden blocks as the men sloshed through floating debris in their high rubber boots.

It took Kelowna many weeks to dry out. Municipal authorities blamed provincial and federal governments for not acting on a 1946 engineer's report that highlighted the urgent need for improved flood control. The Honourable C. D. Howe said works of this type were best left for the next Depression. By 1954, though, a flood-control project created a channel between Okanagan and Skaha Lakes and then straightened the meandering river between Skaha and Osoyoos Lakes. The catastrophic floods of 1948 would never recur.

A GOOD TIME FOR ORCHARDISTS

Okanagan orchardists flourished during the war. Currency restrictions plus embargoes on bananas, citrus fruits and foreign apples all resulted in a strong Canadian demand for valley produce. Customers were so happy to have any fruit they bought what was available in spite of high prices and questionable quality—growers had decided to maximize production by applying enormous amounts of fertilizer, though it was known to reduce the grade and storage capacity of their apples.

More people moved to town after the war, and more land was needed for residential development. Level farmland was seen as the best land to build on even though it was also the most productive and easiest to irrigate. Alternatives had to be found. Valley hillsides had always been difficult to irrigate but when aluminum became available after the war and was found to be both malleable and corrosion resistant, it provided the solution. Soon electric pumps and more efficient sprinkler heads were added to the new aluminum technology and the hillside acres of sandy loam were transformed into productive orchards. Many of the early orchards were torn out and replaced with houses, though an occasional apple or cherry tree was often left behind in the yard. As land prices rose, many acres of grazing lands and hay farms were no longer viable and they too were transformed into subdivisions.

The BC Fruit Growers' Association (BCFGA) decided to get into the juice business just as the Okanagan Fruit Juice Company began production in its new plant. Since the BCFGA had first call on both the culls and the McIntosh crop, the Okanagan Fruit Juice Company decided it couldn't compete and be profitable, and sold its new state-of-the-art plant to the BCFGA. Sun-Rype was the BCFGA's brand name. | SHARRON SIMPSON COLLECTION

When the war ended, so did the protection apple growers had enjoyed during the hostilities, and they were overwhelmed by the tons of culls they were still producing. There were few options other than letting the apples rot, either on the trees or mounded on empty lots or in country ravines. Currency restrictions remained in place in Britain and Okanagan orchardists couldn't access their traditional market. The decision was made to "gift" 1.1 million boxes of apples to Britain to avoid dumping them or overwhelming the Canadian market. The British government hadn't bought apples for three years, and even then it had only been a meagre 434,000 boxes. BC Tree Fruits paid the freight charges to the coast, the shipment went through the Panama Canal and the gift of small-sized McIntosh, Newtowns, Romes, Staymans and Jonathans rescued both the Okanagan growers and the fruit-starved British. Not all growers agreed with

Sun-Rype's "Blue Label" Pure Apple Juice has been the company's signature and most recognized juice for many years. | KELOWNA PUBLIC ARCHIVES CL96

BC Tree Fruits' generosity but when the federal government later came through with a $2 million subsidy, the disgruntled stopped complaining.

There had been earlier attempts to use the culls for vinegar, dehydration and apple juice, though the amounts produced were insignificant. The Okanagan Fruit Juice Company began making a new cloudy (opalescent) apple juice in the Rowcliffe Cannery and this became so successful they decided to build their own state-of-the-art production facility. With local backing and additional technical and financial support from the Hawaiian Dole pineapple family, production got underway in 1946. Their timing couldn't have been worse. Apple growers, through the BCFGA, had just decided to form BC Fruit Processors Ltd. and get into the apple by-products business to help them deal with the overabundance of culls. Since this new company would have first call on the culls as well as the area's McIntosh crop, Okanagan Fruit Juice realized they couldn't compete and sold their facility to the new growers' company.

It was a slow start—the first year they produced 373,000 cases of apple juice and made concentrate for apple butter, vinegar and dehydrated apples, but still only used a small portion of the culls. Business improved with the new modern facility and the company decided to absorb most of the juicing operations from around the valley into the Kelowna plant. The exception was Oliver, where apple juice had first been produced. That operation continued for a few more years until it made better economic sense to use tanker trucks to bring the juice to Kelowna for processing. BC Fruit Processors' brand, Sun-Rype, soon became a familiar name on store shelves.

The canneries, which had been such an important part of the fruit industry, also began to close. Frozen food was gaining in popularity and the nutritional benefits of fresh produce were also being recognized, so the market for canned foods was diminishing. That left peach, cherry and apricot growers with few options beyond the fresh market and they too approached the BCFGA to develop products to utilize their crops. Sun-Rype and the Dominion Experimental Farm in Summerland soon developed pie fillings—apple and cherry were the most popular—along with apple sauce, apple dessert, apricot juice and concentrate, and apple-cot and orange-cot juices.

Always looking for more opportunities to utilize their culls, BC Fruit Processors made the precarious leap into fruit-based alcoholic beverages. With only Growers Wine in Victoria and Calona Wines locally, there wasn't a lot of competition. The Summerland Experimental Farm would ferment a few hundred gallons of apple juice and add pieces of dry ice, by hand, to the get the necessary carbonation. The bottles would then be filled and rushed to the Kelowna liquor store. Provincial liquor laws didn't allow for alcohol advertising or any promotion of alcoholic beverages, but that didn't matter during the Regatta. At any and every opportunity the Regatta announcer "just happened" to mention that a new batch of the wonderful new Okanagan Sparkling Cider was arriving at the local liquor store as he spoke. It didn't take long before the cider was flying off the shelves. However, the company was a bit conflicted about producing alcohol along with its juice and food products and soon sold its inventory and the rights to BC Sparkling Cider to Victoria-based Growers Wine Company.

OTHER THAN ORCHARDS

The war years were also peak production years for S.M. Simpson Ltd. The arsonist's fire that had destroyed much of the plant in 1939 enabled Stan Simpson to order the latest machinery just before war was declared. None would have been available a few months later, though sawmills were essential wartime industries and given mandatory production quotas to support Canada's war effort. Women took on various unconventional jobs as men joined the armed forces, but it was with the understanding that the men would return to their old jobs when the war was over. While sawmill production was an essential service, logging was not, and when the loggers left for war, many sawmills ran short of logs. Mill owners tried to convince the government to use Japanese internees in the woods but they were deemed too great a security risk and permission was denied.

S.M. Simpson Ltd. was dealing with increasing demands from both the local orchard industry and the British Box Board Agency, which ordered "butter boxes" (though their actual use and final destination were classified secrets). One shipment of Simpson boxes was torpedoed in the North Atlantic and the mill received a cable asking them to replace it immediately. Dynamite boxes were built for Canadian Industries Ltd. (CIL) on Vancouver Island and a never-ending line of railcars pulled into the siding beside the box factory. Shook was loaded around the clock before the cars headed to Vancouver and on to the Panama Canal. Dimension lumber was also shipped but the need was so great and so urgent that it often left before it could be dried. The green lumber warped and bent but was still used for army barracks, munitions factories and hangars; orders sometimes read, "Send everything you've got."

The number of new fruit boxes needed each year was determined in the spring when the blossoms set, and box factories planned their

S.M. Simpson Ltd. continued to make a great variety of fruit boxes, veneer containers, berry boxes and grape baskets into the early 1950s. Yet corrugated cardboard boxes had been introduced during the war and had begun to take over a large share of the wooden box market. This display was part of an exhibit showcasing local industry in 1953. It was held in Memorial Arena. | SHARRON SIMPSON COLLECTION production accordingly. When the packinghouses determined they would need 900,000 new boxes for the 1943 crop and the box factory was already working at capacity, the fruit industry began exploring other options. They tried packing apples in paper bags but there was too much bruising and consumers were unhappy. Then it was a mix of corrugated fibre and wood and Simpson's mill provided wooden ends that were wrapped with the heavy paper. It was definitely a temporary solution. The next effort was a corrugated cardboard box but it wasn't rigid enough to be stacked, so the mill had to produce millions of small triangular pieces of wood that would be inserted into each corner of the box so it could be stacked. It too was a temporary fix and much cheaper than the all-wooden boxes. Not all consumers liked the new containers but it was wartime, and everyone had to make sacrifices. Box makers were relieved that an alternative had been found and they could continue their wartime production. They were also certain that business would return to pre-war levels once hostilities had ceased, and were not concerned that the change might signal a different way of doing things in the future.

ARRIVING AND DEPARTING
By Road
The completion of the Hope–Princeton Highway in fall of 1949 was the fulfillment of a hundred-year dream. Criss-crossing the historic fur brigade trails, it was the largest highway project ever undertaken by the province. The new route reduced the distance between Kelowna and Vancouver by one hundred miles and several hours of travel. Though many would have been happy to have it open earlier, unpaved, the decision to complete the eighty-three-mile link between Hope and Princeton as a paved all-weather road was soon welcomed by all.

Accompanied across the "hallowed ground" by a pioneer who had been in the area for fifty-four years, Premier Byron Johnson turned a golden key in the lock and swung open an improvised gate across the 4,200-foot Allison Summit, the new highway's highest elevation. The grand and much anticipated celebration attracted over six thousand of the area's important and curious. Since lunch had been planned for two thousand, the traffic backed up, bumper to bumper, for four or five miles in both directions; some waited over three hours for a police escort to the summit, while the impatient abandoned their cars and buses and walked. Most had not anticipated the elevation and arrived exhausted.

The Hope–Princeton also meant a new kind of highway driving was needed, and people were cautioned to obey the posted speed limits: some of the curves were banked for specific speeds and motorists who ignored the warning signs were "asking for trouble." The warnings were underscored when three people were killed returning home from the ceremony. Over the next few days, mangled radiators and bent fenders reminded drivers that this was no speedway, especially when they encountered heavy frost in the shaded gorges along the "tricky" highway.

The building of the Hope–Princeton Highway was one of the signature events that opened the Okanagan Valley to the rest of the world. Penticton was the first major town encountered by travellers coming from the coast, and by 1951 it had become the valley's largest with a population of 10,517 (1941: 5,777). Kelowna, with its boundaries still constrained, grew to 8,466 (1941: 5,118) while Vernon remained the smallest at 7,778 people (1941: 5,209). Those who can still recall those times remember Penticton, with its beautiful beaches on both Okanagan and Skaha Lakes, being everyone's choice as the valley's best summer party town.

By Water

The Queen of Okanagan Lake took her last trip down the lake in August of 1951. The *Courier* reported that noon-hour crowds had quietly lined Kelowna's beaches to watch as the SS *Sicamous* passed by. A solitary red-and-white checkered CPR flag "fluttered bravely from the forward mast" while the *Pendozi*, *Lequime* and *Lloyd-Jones* diverted from their regular route to circle the "old lady" and sound their whistles in tribute. Cars on shore tooted their farewell and the fire hall bell rang out in respect. The old sternwheeler was being towed from her mooring at Okanagan Landing, where she had been waiting out her uncertain future for twenty years. The *Sicamous*'s top deck had been removed and the sternwheeler had spent its last two years of service carrying freight. It hadn't been a worthy ending for so fine a vessel. The CPR offered the *Sicamous* to both Kelowna and Penticton. Kelowna declined but Penticton finally paid the CPR one dollar for the "tired but proud old lady" in 1949. It was another two years before the now-decrepit vessel was towed to the beachfront on Okanagan Lake. More recently, a dedicated group of volunteers has restored the still-beached *Sicamous*, which is now available for rent, though its financial situation is always precarious. It is part of the Penticton Marine Heritage Park, along with the tug SS *Naramata*.

Two of the Kelowna–Westbank ferries: MV *Lequime* and MV *Pendozi*. Crossing Okanagan Lake was an ongoing problem. When the MV *Pendozi* couldn't meet the demand, the 1947 launch of the second ferry, the MV *Lequime*, eased the pressure for awhile. But when MV *Lloyd-Jones* was added to the fleet in 1950, everyone acknowledged the improvement was only temporary. Talk had turned to a more lasting solution: a modern highway along both sides of Okanagan Lake and a bridge at Kelowna.
| KELOWNA PUBLIC ARCHIVES 6291

By Air

Penticton was not only the largest city in the valley, but the first to have its own runway and airport. The facility was opened for emergency military use in 1941, but it wasn't until 1947 that Canadian Pacific Airlines (CPA) inaugurated the first scheduled service between Vancouver and Calgary via Penticton, Castlegar and Cranbrook. Kelowna residents who wanted to fly out of the valley drove to Penticton to catch a plane. Scheduled flights to the Rutland airfield had been discussed but plans were put on hold during World War II.

Kelowna took the initiative when the war ended and purchased the 320-acre Dickson Ranch in Ellison to be the future site of its airport. It cost the taxpayers twenty thousand dollars. The "Ellison Field" officially opened in August 1949. Many of the 3,500 cars and 10,000 people planning to watch the mayor buzz the airport before cutting the inevitable silk ribbon were stuck in a nine-mile-long traffic jam and never made it to the field. The highlight of the day for those who did arrive was the opportunity

Despair and Recovery, 1940–1955

to see one of CPA's "heavy" planes land on the grass runway—it was a "tribute to the Kelowna airport" flight. Although hopes were raised, CPA didn't start scheduled service into Kelowna for another ten years.

Lobbying for and establishing the Kelowna Airport had been a giant leap of faith. Commercial air travel was in its infancy and very few people had their own planes, and for a few years the Ellison Field risked closure because so little was going on. As planes came and went out of Penticton, L & M Air Service of Vernon flew its first intercity flight in September 1949 to connect Kamloops, Vernon and Kelowna with CPA's scheduled service in Penticton. The daily (except Sundays) flights were aboard a sleek twin-engine plane, an amphibious six-passenger Beechcraft, which landed on the lake at the foot of Bernard Avenue, and dropped off and picked up passengers at L & M's new wharf. The plane would land at Ellison Field during the winter with taxi service provided so passengers could travel the considerable distance to downtown. This was "red letter service," as Vancouver was now only two and a half hours from Kelowna, Toronto was nine hours away, and it only took thirty hours to travel to England. But despite how grand the dream was, it didn't work in reality, and the service was soon cancelled.

Traffic into and out of Kelowna's airport was so light that there was a constant risk of it being abandoned and swallowed up by spreading housing developments. A reprieve arrived in 1951 when Ralph Hermanson brought his Cariboo Air Charter to town and offered charter flights and student instruction. Many local residents learned to fly, with some even buying their own planes, and Mr. Hermanson became the airport manager and a strong advocate for both scheduled service and a paved runway.

CANADA'S GREATEST WATER SHOW

Kelowna's wartime Regattas took on a distinctly patriotic flavour as all profits were sent to the federal treasury to help fight the war. Military themes persisted: the "Victory Regatta," the "On to Victory Regatta," the "Let's Finish It Regatta." Various major-generals were also invited to become the Regatta's honorary commodores. The "On to Victory" Regatta of 1941 invited a team of American majorettes to lead the parade. The Battle of Britain was fresh in everyone's minds and with the US still on the war's sidelines, the empire took precedence. When the young ladies were replaced by a reserve military unit and bumped to the back of the parade, they were so mad they packed up, got on the ferry and headed home. In a huff.

The "Liberty" Regatta in 1943 provided the most spectacular evening program ever staged: a commando attack on a "Nazi" beachhead. Spectators had to be in their seats before shooting began so the local militia could secure the area and no one would get hurt or interfere with the battle. Outside of motion pictures, the locals had never seen anything like it. The attack started shortly after eight o'clock just south of Ogopogo Stadium, the bleachers overlooking the swimming pool. The beach's defence posts were manned by "Nazi" units that had been softened up by "heavy shelling." Under a screen of smoke laid down by "mortar fire," the "invading forces" stormed the beach and captured the pill boxes being defended by the "enemy." Band concerts and acrobats completed the night's entertainment. They were likely anticlimactic.

By the end of the war, rhythmic swimming had become popular and was introduced to Regatta audiences during an evening show. The performance had unfortunately been scheduled so late in the program that it was dark and spectators were left baffled about what the three young ladies were doing in the pool. Things improved the following year when a larger team from Vancouver and Victoria put on a display of "the highest type of swimming that requires much practice and an accurate sense of timing on the part of all participants." Everyone could fortunately see this time, and they were in awe at the intricacies of the water ballet. It wasn't long before Margaret Hutton, a 1934 British Empire Games Canadian backstroke champion, arrived in town to teach ornamental swimming to the area's young ladies. This was quite a coup for the Regatta as Margaret had moved from competitive swimming to Hollywood, where she had choreographed a water ballet for the movie *Pagan Love Song*. She had also taught film stars Esther Williams and Eleanor Holm how to perform. Her rhythmic swimming productions—with their specially designed lighting, paddleboards and swimming costumes—became the centrepiece of the Regatta's elaborate evening programs.

The Kelowna Regatta was consumed by the war and all things related to it. Burning Hitler in effigy added to the patriotic message about ridding the world of evil. | KELOWNA PUBLIC ARCHIVES 662

It wasn't long before the Regatta's queen became known as the Lady of the Lake. (As the event moved away from the lake, the title became Miss Kelowna Lady of the Lake.) In 1944, a well-protected Lady of the Lake was joined on stage by various military personnel for the reading of a commemorative roll call of local citizens who were serving overseas. | KELOWNA PUBLIC ARCHIVES 669

The Kelowna International Regatta grew into a five-day celebration. Junior boys and girls and senior men and ladies came from Vancouver, Victoria and Ocean Falls, up the coast, as well as from Washington and California, to compete in freestyle, backstroke and breaststroke events and medley relays. War canoes raced while three-metre diving competitions were interspersed with boats racing with their "pepped up" motors. A new ballroom, dining room, lounge and grandstand were built. A diving plank was added to the wooden diving tower in 1945 to allow Dr. George Athans—the British Empire Games springboard diving champion who had come to Kelowna to practise medicine—to perform at his best, though it was noted that few would actually dive from that extraordinary height. The board was replaced with a steel Olympic standard ten-metre diving tower in 1951 when there were few others like it in North America, and it was named after Dr. Athans. Though terrified, every kid in town clambered up the ladders and launched themselves into space: it became a summer right of passage. Athans convinced his friend, Dr. Sammy Lee from San Francisco, the Olympic high tower diving champion, to join him for an exhibition in 1953. The crowd was awestruck.

Being "midway" between Seattle and Detroit, the Kelowna Regatta was on the World's Fastest Power Boat circuit. The tour's hydroplanes—*Slo-Mo-Shun IV* and V, *Miss Seattle, Miss Fury* and *Breathless*—thrilled thousands of spectators, including those attending the International Regatta, at speeds of up to two hundred miles per hour. The curious could wander the pits along Hot Sands Beach and watch the races throughout the day.

These were the legendary glory days of the Kelowna International Regatta. Athletes came to compete and everyone else came to party. The Bank of Montreal hosted an elegant garden party at Hochelaga, the home of their local manager; the Lieutenant Governor declared a temporary Government House on the lakeshore in Okanagan Mission and hosted the most prestigious garden party ever held in Kelowna. Boaters partied at the Kelowna Yacht Club, visiting military brass were entertained at the armoury and other noteworthy out-of-towners were hosted for morning coffee and a fashion show. Teen Town had a wiener roast at the beach and, at a time when it truly mattered, the Lady of the Lake hosted visiting beauty queens and their princesses from throughout the province and Washington state. Private railcars were shunted onto sidings in the north end so visiting CN and CP vice-presidents could entertain visitors during the event. The Kelowna Little Theatre involved the whole community in staging ever grander evening programs, while visiting bands began playing early in the morning and would continue well into the evening. The Lady of the Lake Ball was held at the much-decorated Memorial Arena, though it was only one of many dances going on around town. When about eight thousand people lived in Kelowna,

The Regatta evening performances featured choreographed shows in the water and on stage. Paddleboard and rhythmic swimming presentations were a highlight, including this tribute to Kelowna's fiftieth anniversary with its small replica of the large cake that sat at the foot of Bernard Avenue for the year. | KELOWNA PUBLIC ARCHIVE 2341

it was not uncommon for one hundred thousand visitors to arrive in town to celebrate and party during the four- or five-day Regatta.

The whole of Kelowna gravitated to the Kelowna Aquatic Club in the summer. Lifeguards taught swimming lessons along Cold Sands Beach (the beach facing north, which has since been washed away) and the full sun of Hot Sands Beach attracted the bikini-clad sun seekers. Kids had to be able to swim fifty yards, unaided and without stopping, before they were allowed on the dock and in the big pool. They came with their friends, stayed for the day, brought their own lunch or bought fish and chips, and finally drifted home late in the afternoon. Parents knew their children had gone to the Aquatic, where lifeguards would keep an eye on them, and didn't worry. They knew their kids would head home when they were tired and then likely do it all over again the next day. Kelowna was a great place to grow up in.

The International Regatta was followed by the Junior Regatta, in which locals competed and the Man of the Lake was chosen. Though he had few perks and no official functions, the event gave the young men who had spent the summer racing shells and war canoes a chance for a moment in the limelight. Locals also competed every Tuesday

Art Jones, the "Silver Fox" of the local racing circuit, was still in the cockpit at seventy-five. He built and owned a succession of hydroplanes and needed a large house to display all his trophies. One of his champions was *Miss Kelowna*, the fastest boat on Okanagan Lake at the time. He was fearless and made "many a younger man pale at his carefree spirit." | KELOWNA PUBLIC ARCHIVES 4008

The Kelowna Aquatic Club's second diving tower. It became the summer's rite of passage to climb to the top and jump off. Some had to climb back down but the really brave launched themselves into space. | KELOWNA PUBLIC ARCHIVES 3963

The Kelowna Aquatic Club was the centrepiece of Kelowna's summer. Not only was it home to the Kelowna International Regatta, but it was also every child's summer hangout. Capacity crowds came for the four or five days of Regatta, families and friends gathered for weekly Aquacades, children learned to swim, parents danced in the pavilion, and ladies came for tea on the veranda. | KELOWNA PUBLIC ARCHIVES 2305

Despair and Recovery, 1940–1955

Whatever works—including waterskiing behind a float plane. It was all an adventure! | KELOWNA PUBLIC ARCHIVES 2397

night during July and August in the Aquacades, or mini-regattas, in events that were similar to those held during the International Regatta. At times, two thousand spectators would gather in the stands enjoying the warmth fade from the day as they watched their children compete. Those who were good enough joined the Ogopogo Summer Swim Club and trained to represent Kelowna and compete in other regattas. Youngsters swam, war canoe teams raced the half mile between the ferry dock and the finish line in front of the grandstand, and the audience yelled as youngsters tried to paddle their apple boxes to the finish line before the unwieldy crafts sank.

Waterskiing was also gaining in popularity by the late 1940s. Local athletes practised long and hard to complete the amazing 180- and 360-degree turns and then stay upright as they headed over the jump anchored in front of the grandstand. Adults came for lunch or tea on the veranda overlooking the pool and diving platform, danced to the music of Pettman's Imperials at the Aquatic Ballroom or celebrated special occasions with Mart Kenney and his Western Gentlemen. Teen Town organized weekly dances in City Park for both local and visiting teens. Everyone gravitated to City Park and the Aquatic Club in the summer. The Regatta's slogan—"No matter where you live, if the place is good enough to live in, it's good enough to be proud of and to work for"— mirrored the community at the time: everyone was engaged, everyone was involved and everyone had fun. These were remarkable years for those who had the good fortune to live in Kelowna.

NEIGHBOURING COMMUNITIES

Okanagan Mission

Aside from the turmoil of young people departing for war, the Mission community had remained relatively unchanged and was still defined by its earlier British roots. More newcomers arrived to clear the hillsides and plant the recently introduced dwarf fruit trees. The community hall— the Red Barn—became the gathering place for badminton, tennis, Boy

The Eldorado Arms took on new life when it was renovated and upgraded. It remained a popular gathering spot for several more years. | COURTESY OF JENNIFER HINDLE

Scouts and Girl Guides, while the Eldorado Arms added a few attractive cottages for the guests who came to enjoyed the rural setting and the bit of Britain that still remained.

However, change was on the way for the Mission. The old Bellevue Hotel was finally demolished in 1954; though it hadn't been used for years, its decline mirrored the end of the Okanagan Mission townsite. The post office and general store remained but people were more mobile and the community no longer needed its own commercial centre. The *Courier* reported that everyone was "up in arms over the appalling condition of the highway between Kelowna and Okanagan Mission." Petitions circulated asking the Department of Public Works to finish the road to Kelowna and pave it—loose gravel had been left sitting on the surface, ruts were six to twelve inches deep, windshields were being broken and driving was hazardous.

Rutland

Rutland was rural and the majority of its citizens wanted it to remain that way. When the subject of incorporation came up at a community meeting in 1948, "spirited and impromptu speeches" resulted in a convincing vote to leave things as they were. Citizens nonetheless wanted some of the amenities of a town and in 1948 agreed to build a new junior and senior high school for students from the surrounding rural areas.

The biggest issue was whether Rutland's airport would prevail over the upstart Kelowna proposal. Various air vice marshals visited the valley and said the surrounding mountains were a major impediment to any landing field. They did, however, concede that amphibious air service might be a good alternative. Short-haul flights didn't make economic sense, yet perhaps shipping fruit by air would be viable. Cargo planes would have to be developed unless air force Lancasters could be converted, but the downside of the large planes was that longer runways would be needed. Glider trains might be an option… but again, only for long-haul flights.

All this postwar conjecture did nothing to quell the enthusiasm of members of the Rutland branch of the BCFGA, who insisted a local airfield would better serve their orchardists. They doubted reports about problems with updrafts and down drafts, and with Gopher Creek nearby there was plenty of water to irrigate the grass runway. Prospects brightened when the Rutland field was given a temporary federal operating licence for light aircraft, though it was conditional upon certain improvements being made. Prevailing winds would require two landing strips, one of which would have to be built across Belgo Road; loose rocks had to be removed from the runway, and nearby trees had to be removed. The utility pole at the end of one runway would also have to be removed, and a wind indicator, a telephone and a refuelling facility added.

The field was being used sporadically but things picked up when two former RCAF instructors arrived with plans to form a flying club, train student pilots and establish an "airpark" for tourists. They were certain the existing Rutland field could handle the traffic better than Kelowna's Ellison Field, as the town would likely have to extend its runway and buy expensive farmland to do so. The Kelowna Aviation Council pleaded for unity. The federal licensing agency suggested one airfield was adequate and the two communities should try to work out their differences. Rutland put up a good fight, but in the end Kelowna's Ellison Field prevailed. Rutland's proposed airfield was eventually subdivided for residential development and parks.

Glenmore

Glenmore remained rural during this period but its southern boundary was starting to look more like a Kelowna suburb. The hayfields near the city limits could easily be developed but the Pridham family's 113-acre apple orchard became the first large orchard on the valley floor to be subdivided. A residential area was laid out with space for a future "high class shopping district." Although it took a few more years to become a reality, the Capri Shopping Centre became Kelowna's first, though many questioned the wisdom of the development being so far out of town. Adding the Capri Hotel was even riskier. The centre was developed by the Capozzi family, on the Pridham orchard property, hence the name: Capri. However, the surrounding communities had little infrastructure and the only way the new development could proceed was if Kelowna provided water and sewage services. The need to extend Kelowna's boundaries soon became a hot topic of discussion.

BENNETT TAKES OVER

Kelowna continued to be represented in Victoria by W.A.C. Bennett, but after sitting in the legislature for a decade, the self-styled "man of action" felt he had accomplished little. Rather than quit in frustration, Bennett crossed the floor and sat as an independent. Many thought his political life was over: he rejected the mainline political parties and they rejected him. He had become a nuisance.

The Social Credit Party had emerged in Alberta during the Depression. In spite of its unconventional and untried monetary policies, and a platform based on solidly Christian values, it had provided the province with a strong and stable government. When the party moved to BC, it did so without a leader and had little to hold it together. Although Bennett joined the BC Social Credit Party in 1951, he still wasn't sure this would be his long-term political home and he wasn't interested in being the party leader. The two mainline parties had agreed to implement the single transferable vote system for the 1952 election: electors were to choose their favourite candidate as number one, their next favourite as number two and their least favourite as number three. The Liberals and Conservatives were confident their parties would be voters' first and second choices, and they would continue to run the province. When the CCF won the popular vote and the Social Credit (Socred) Party was most voters' second choice, it was a shock. In the midst of the uncertainty, the Social Credit Party held their leadership convention and W.A.C. Bennett officially became their leader. And when the final count was announced, the BC Social Credit Party had won nineteen seats and the CCF eighteen, while the Liberals had six and the Conservatives four.

Though the Socreds were six seats short of a majority, Bennett rejected another coalition, manoeuvred and wrangled, and convinced a baffled Lieutenant Governor that he was rightfully the province's next premier. On August 1, 1952, about seven weeks after the election, W.A.C. Bennett assumed the office and became BC's first Social Credit premier. Bennett was a populist and readily connected with ordinary people and his fellow small businessmen more than with the business and social elites in Vancouver and Victoria. Social Credit's popularity engulfed the province, Liberals and Conservatives were wiped out, and the single transferable vote system was soon eliminated. Bennett became the unique politician who not only had a vision of greatness for his province, but was also able to articulate it and capture the public's imagination in the process. Bennett set the stage for a period of unparallelled growth in BC.

MOVING ON

Kelowna's golden jubilee, its fiftieth birthday celebration, was held early in May 1955. The *Courier* printed 13,000 copies of its eleven-section, eighty-eight-page *Golden Jubilee Edition*, though only 4,500 were needed for its normal circulation. Pre-publication sales were so brisk that the papers were sold out well before the actual celebrations; the *Courier* apologized—it had no idea there would be such demand. Everyone was involved in the celebrations and businesses took out full-page ads to let readers know how much they had contributed to Kelowna's success during the past fifty years. The special edition featured year-by-year highlights along with pages filled with views of Kelowna in 1905 and then again in 1955: photos of the pioneer Lequime family were on one page while the photos of other pioneers, including Laurence, Christien, Postill, Brent, Mrs. Saucier and Dan Gallagher, were on another. A copy of the 1905 fire map identified the businesses along Bernard Avenue when only five hundred people lived in town, and told of how the volunteer fire brigade managed with a hand engine and four hundred feet of hose. Pictures of schools and churches, orchards, sheep and onion fields filled other pages. It offered readers a chance to look back at Kelowna's history as well as marvel at how much things had changed.

The City of Kelowna's Armorial Bearings

The shield, with wavy blue lines on white at the base, depicts Okanagan Lake. From it rise three triangular spires, representing mountains; above these are two apples of gold. A wreath supports a bearing apple tree. At the base of the tree, the crosscut saw is emblematic of the lumber industry and early pioneers. The supporters on either side of the shield are a grizzly bear, indicating the derivation of the city's name, and a seahorse, which in heraldry is the closest approximation of the Ogopogo. The motto, "Fruitful in Unity," alludes to Kelowna's steady progress, largely attributable to its fruit industry and its community-mindedness and co-operative citizens. The mayor's chain of office was a jubilee anniversary gift from the residents and businesses that had been part of the community for fifty years. | COURTESY OF THE CITY OF KELOWNA

Over four thousand people gathered in City Park on a Sunday afternoon for the dedication of the Jubilee Bowl, the city's fiftieth anniversary tribute to its founders and the old-timers who had played such an important role in the city's development. The stage was located in City Park near the beach; the concrete seating, which was added later, is all that remains at the site today. The facility was torn down in the late 1990s. | KELOWNA PUBLIC ARCHIVES 912

Okanagan Investments, the successor to the 1909 Okanagan Loan and Investment Company, marked the jubilee by commissioning the city's armorial bearings from the College of Heralds of Great Britain. The city had thought about having a coat of arms designed at various times, but never had the money to do so. The *Courier* likened the issue to "a woman desiring a diamond wedding ring but willing to wear the old plain one until the family finances could afford the one she desired." The investment company made sure the correct and appropriate armorial bearings were designed, though the College of Heralds was likely perplexed by the insistence that a mythical sea monster needed to be included.

A brief ceremony was held in the Paramount Theatre on May 5, the actual date of Kelowna's incorporation, when Mayor Ladd accepted the ceremonial regalia of office as a gift on behalf of the city. Few other communities of this size could boast such distinguished symbols of office, and certainly none in the valley. Only those who had lived in the city for fifty years or more, or represented businesses that had been in Kelowna for as long, were allowed to contribute funds to pay for the finery. The initial plan was to have the chain of office made of brass but the response was so "hearty" that the decision was revised to silver plated, and then real silver, then gold plated. As generous citizens donated even more money, the final chain was made of fourteen-karat gold. The cost was $1,500 but since $2,000 had been raised from the 122 donors, the balance was spent on the mayor's official robes of office. They were to be patterned after those of the mayor of Vancouver and it took some time before the committee found a skilled garment maker who knew how to make the short slashed sleeves that would fall back to reveal the white kid gauntlets. A cloak and tri-cornered hat completed the ensemble.

About fifteen thousand people gathered along Bernard Avenue over an hour before the mile-long "50 Years of Progress Parade" got underway. With the Canadian Legion Pipe Band leading the way and the mayor in his new robes of office following, Kelowna's history unfolded. Members of the Kelowna Riding Club, dressed in elaborate Native costumes, were followed by fur traders, gold miners, Father Pandosy, cow punchers and polo players. Many floats showcased the community's recreational opportunities and the Lady of the Lake added a touch of class, while a float with a replica of the recently proposed Okanagan Lake Bridge caused great excitement. Lumberjacks carried logs and squirted the crowd with their modern firefighting equipment; fruit salesmen pushed wheelbarrows loaded with apples; costumed Japanese residents featured old-time transportation; and apple packing techniques and the new mosquito control truck drew great applause from spectators. The Chinese community's float depicted their progress from coolies to cap-and-gowned college graduates. Volunteer firefighters brought the parade to a close with their old hose and reel equipment and their new modern steam pumper trucks.

Mayor Dick Parkinson wearing the official robe and chain of office. The kid gauntlets and tri-cornered hat rest beside him. After the first flurry of excitement about the new regalia, few mayors were prepared to wear either the hat or the gloves. The chain continues to be used for ceremonial occasions today, but the cloak has been replaced with another, and the tri-cornered hat and the gauntlets have disappeared.
KELOWNA PUBLIC ARCHIVES 870

Old-timers were honoured at a civic banquet later that day and two ladies who had each lived in the area for eighty years cut the cake. The cake was a replica of the twenty-seven-foot-high plywood cake on display at the end of Bernard Avenue. With the wonders of remote technology, another of the old-timers at the banquet flicked a switch to light the neon candles on the downtown cake. The evening wrapped up with the *Gay Nineties Review* at Memorial Arena. At a time when nine thousand people lived in Kelowna, about eigth thousand jammed into the building for the 8:30 presentation while another five thousand attended the 10:30 performance. Between shows, everyone joined the old-timers as they took over the floor and danced their collective hearts out. Kelowna gloried in its fifty years of progress and its citizens unabashedly celebrated their wonderful community, its unmatched lifestyle and its limitless opportunities. It had been quite a week… and quite an amazing fifty years.

The candles on Kelowna's fiftieth anniversary cake were lit on May 5, 1955, and remained "on" for the rest of the year. The cake, complete with its good-luck horseshoe, was ensconced at the foot of Bernard Avenue. Garlands were added for the Christmas season. | KELOWNA PUBLIC ARCHIVES 7889

The Kelowna Board of Trade published a new promotional brochure in 1949. Photos showed a wide and busy Bernard Avenue and told of the gracious lifestyle led in the elegant homes scattered along the lakeshore. Other pictures showed a community with all the amenities prospective residents could possibly want: a new hospital, new schools and an abundance of sports and recreation opportunities. Kelowna was "the Heart of the Okanagan… where people lived by choice…'neath the rays of a benevolent and almost constant sun." Readers were invited to make Kelowna their home, and during the years that followed many accepted the invitation.

CHAPTER SIX:

Kelowna Grows Up— The Tumultuous Years, 1955–1975

The next few decades were tumultuous in many parts of the world: there was the Cuban missile crisis, the Vietnam War, the Berlin Wall and, in Canada, the Quebec crisis. BC celebrated its centennial and the Social Credit Party defined provincial politics with Kelowna's MLA, Premier W.A.C. Bennett, as its leader. The province opened for business as new highways, bridges, railroads and mega power projects were built: BC stopped being the "blight on Confederation," as that earlier Royal Commission had labelled it. About nine thousand people lived in Kelowna in the mid-1950s, though that number would double over the next twenty years and the community would be challenged to keep up with the growth.

Kelowna was also modernizing and updating its image. Apartment buildings began replacing the stately old houses along Pandosy Street. Hochelaga, the spacious home of the Bank of Montreal's manager, was torn down and replaced with a four-storey building of the same name. Dr. Knox's elegant home, just down the street, was also replaced by apartments. The 1930s art deco post office was no longer large enough, and before the community understood that such buildings were an important part of its heritage the imposing white stucco building, with its shiny marble floors and bronze wicket grates, was demolished.

In the early days, Kelowna made do with makeshift courtrooms over bakeries, in CKOV's old studios, in a converted house just off Bernard Avenue and in city hall committee rooms. The mayor led a delegation to Victoria in 1950 demanding that adequate court and police facilities be

Kelowna Post Office. Kelowna's art deco post office was built on Bernard Avenue during the 1930s. It was demolished forty years later before the city recognized its heritage value. | KELOWNA PUBLIC ARCHIVES 3448

provided for the city. Four years later—and after considerable negotiation with S.M. Simpson to get his agreement to put the provincial building on the civic centre lands—Kelowna's new court house opened in 1955. The L-shaped building occupied the lakefront across from city hall until it was torn down in 2001; the property is now part of Stuart Park. As part of the negotiations to build on city property and acquire the court house site, the province exchanged land near what is now Kerry Park along with the promise to build a double ferry strip at the foot of Mill Street (now Queensway) and a seawall along the shoreline to accommodate the new Kelowna Yacht Club. A narrow boat launch and a parking lot still occupy the old ferry wharf site, the seawall is part of the walkway joining City Park with Stuart Park and the yacht club remains in its original location, though they have bought the property immediately to the north from the city, and will be relocating their clubhouse.

Convincing the province that Kelowna needed its own court house was a long and challenging process. Its genesis dates back to 1948, when BC's chief justice, Wendell Farris, came to town to officiate at a hearing. The courtrooms were then on the third floor of the old Casorso Block on Bernard Avenue. There was no elevator and the judge had to walk up three flights of steep stairs to preside. He was so exhausted and so mad he declared the Supreme Court would no longer preside in Kelowna, until the community provided facilities befitting the dignity of his court. It took seven years of hearings in the Vernon Court House before the court would return to Kelowna.

Kelowna General Hospital became so overcrowded that single rooms become doubles and four-bed wards became five- and six-bed wards. Closets were transformed into offices, buildings that should have been torn down were renovated and psychiatric services and physiotherapy were offered for the first time. Practical nurses and lab technicians were being trained as a great variety of specialists joined the staff. After much

Kelowna Court House when it opened in 1955. The building, on the lakeshore across from Kelowna City Hall, was demolished in 2001. | KELOWNA PUBLIC ARCHIVES 8071

deliberation, officials also decided the elderly were entitled to specialized care, and since many were occupying the acute care beds so badly needed by really sick patients, it made sense to build a facility just for seniors. Kelowna's first extended care unit opened in 1970 and signalled a major change in the treatment of the elderly. It wasn't long before a fourteen-acre orchard and greenhouse operation was purchased, just a few blocks east of the hospital, which would become the Cottonwoods Extended Care facility.

Early Kelowna had been small and compact, and city council never begrudged spending money for education. Schools in town were overflowing, and as people moved beyond the downtown core the new neighbourhoods needed their own facilities, including junior and senior high schools in Rutland, Glenmore and Okanagan Mission. The nature of education changed as well, as the province took over both school funding and curriculum planning.

KELOWNA COMMUNITY THEATRE

Kelowna's cultural opportunities also improved in the early 1960s. A small group of like-minded citizens spearheaded a fundraising campaign to build a community theatre. The Empress Theatre on Bernard Avenue had been built in 1919 and had served the town well. A number of tenants had used the building, including a bank, before it was renovated to fill in for the burned-out opera house and host the Gilbert and Sullivan shows that toured the Okanagan. Yet its basement dressing rooms were so small and so inadequate for those performances that the forty or fifty performers had to expand to the back rooms of Chapin's Café next store. Famous Players took over the building in 1930 and brought movies to town. A matinee ticket to see the likes of Tarzan, Charlie Chaplin and the Wizard of Oz on film cost fifteen cents. The theatre was also used by community groups, including the fruit growers and their often raucous meetings, even once the new Paramount Theatre was opened in 1949. Though Kelowna relished the luxury of the two theatres, the Empress stopped being a theatre in 1957. The cultural vacuum was immediate.

The citizens' committee set out to raise $35,000 of the $80,000 needed to build a new theatre. The city promised funds, but only if the community came up with the initial amount. The balance of the money would come from a Winter Works program. Many were vocal in their support of the arts and various theatre groups emptied their bank accounts, but the campaign didn't reach its goal. A second campaign wasn't much more successful, but taking a leap of faith the committee decided to build anyway. S.M. Simpson Ltd. owned the lumber yard across from city hall and sold a portion of it to the city at a "very nominal price." The sod was officially turned, the stage and the balcony were deleted from the plans and the building went up, with the community pitching in. The stage was built later by local carpenters who volunteered their time, civic employees did the landscaping in the evenings, truckers hauled fill and topsoil to the site at no cost, the town's painters painted and school janitors cleaned and installed the seats. The Kelowna Little Theatre bought 250 seats from the old Empress Theatre, and another 400 were donated by Famous Players and R.J. and Bill Bennett, who had bought the old building. Lighting fixtures were also salvaged from the Empress, along with some carpeting and an old piano. It truly was a community theatre.

The official opening was a grand event. Tickets were a "very reasonable" ten dollars each and Teresa Stratas, the vivacious twenty-four-year-old Metropolitan Opera star who was making her mark at "music's dizzying heights," reduced her customary fee for the concert. She declared she did so for "all Canadians and for this theatre." Miss Stratas had previously performed at the 1960 Regatta evening show and was fondly remembered. Citizens were elated: it wasn't often that a concert of this calibre was available without travelling to much larger centres. If there had been a curtain to raise, the committee would have raised it, but the theatre was still short of a few finishing touches. Some of the wiring hadn't been completed, the heating hadn't been

Kelowna Community Theatre (above photo) was built in the early 1960s by the community when the Empress Theatre, the town's only other performance space, was closed. The new theatre has showcased local and visiting performers ever since (next page photo). Now within Kelowna's newly created cultural corridor, its newest neighbour is the five-storey brick provincial court house just down the street. Both are located on Water Street. | KELOWNA PUBLIC ARCHIVES 3464 / STUART KERNAGHAN, XYPHOTOS.CA

installed and the dressing rooms were marginal, as were the stage fittings. The Royal Winnipeg Ballet came to the rescue and loaned the theatre a blue and black velvet backdrop, which was hung to create a stage for the performance.

Students attended a special matinee but it was the gala evening performance that was sure to be remembered. Over eight hundred attended—"the cream of Kelowna's society"—many of whom had been entertained at one of several private dinner parties that added to the important occasion. The high school band serenaded as car after car of glamorously gowned women and their escorts arrived as dusk settled on the September night. The entrance had been framed with flowers and Mayor Parkinson, escorted by the Legion Pipe Band, entered the lobby wearing his chain of office and ceremonial robes to officially receive the key to the theatre. It was surely the most glamorous event in the city's history.

The Kelowna Story: An Okanagan History

209   Kelowna Grows Up—The Tumultuous Years, 1955–1975

QUONG'S—A FAVOURITE

Other than the Royal Anne Hotel, there were few elegant places to eat in Kelowna. There were various Chinese restaurants, including the Golden Pheasant and the Green Lantern, but the City Park Café—or Quong's, as most people called it—was in a league by itself. It likely had its origins in early Chinatown, maybe 1906, and was just down the street from the Dart Coon Club, the Chinese Masonic Hall. Opinions varied about those early years and whether the café was a quiet, gracious eating place or a brawling, opium-infested dive. Several members of the Quong family ran the restaurant at various times and while the rest of Kelowna closed their doors at 9:00 p.m., Quong's stayed open as long as there were customers. Sometimes those arriving for breakfast met those departing at the end of their evening. The T-bone steaks were fried directly on the top of the cast-iron wood and sawdust stove. They were the best in town. The menu had a selection, but people only ever talked about the steaks.

The café became Kelowna's late-night social hub during the 1940s and through the 1950s, especially for New Year's Eve and during the Christmas holidays. Anyone and everyone in town for Regatta would eventually show up at the café. Election nights drew every candidate and all their supporters. No one would call the police because most of them were at the party too. Quong had a sixth sense about his guests and if he figured they were likely to become a bit rowdy, he marched them straight through the restaurant to the Blue Room. It was blue because of the kalsomine paint; a single light bulb dangled from the ceiling and one long oilcloth-covered table ran down the centre of the room. The chairs were mismatched and if there weren't enough, large pieces of log were pulled up to the table. Matching chairs didn't matter because they rarely lasted long. Booze was usually smuggled in but if you arrived with none, a pot of "tea" could be arranged.

The more respectable front part of the restaurant had booths for privacy with curtains that could be closed or left open depending upon how much you wanted to remain in or out of the public eye. They weren't very effective as patrons were known to stand on chairs and just peer over. If a party got going, a couple of shoulders against the wall of the booth would usually demolish it. Quong was always unperturbed if an unexpected crowd arrived, as helpers and cooks just showed up and partiers never hesitated to pitch in and help in the kitchen. Rumours flew about the upstairs rooms where teens might sleep off too much party or about the man who frantically tore down the stairs only inches in front of a screaming woman brandishing a meat cleaver. A fan-tan game ran constantly in the back room. No one worried about a police raid: three of the officers were among the best players.

Quong's closed in 1964. It was the end of an era and the end of an institution. Over fifty of the town's leading businessmen, politicians and police presented Wan Quong, the last of the Quong family to run the café, with a gold engraved watch.

W.A.C. CAPTURES CENTRE STAGE

W.A.C. Bennett was full of optimism and convinced that anything was possible with proper planning. Long a student of finance, he felt obligated to wisely manage taxpayers' dollars and became his own minister of finance. The Canadian economy was strong during his years in office, but BC's economy was booming. Highways, tunnels and bridges were built, as was a railway to the north (the Pacific Great Eastern, and subsequently BC Rail), and the population grew faster than anywhere else in the country. Foreign capital flooded into the province, everyone was working and the standard of living kept improving. This new economy needed an educated and skilled workforce and both Simon Fraser University and the University of Victoria were created, as were a number of technical colleges. Bennett was a staunch defender of free enterprise but he had no hesitation about stepping in if the private sector didn't deliver.

Bennett always talked about balanced budgets and his "pay as you go" mantra infused his politics from the beginning. The province's direct debt was eliminated after

Premier W.A.C. Bennett with the queen mother and Canada's Governor General, Roland Michener. Though most comfortable on any main street in any BC town, Premier Bennett could also hobnob with the world's most famous. | KELOWNA PUBLIC ARCHIVES 3174

Social Credit had been in office for just seven years. Even though many suggested that was accomplished by fancy bookkeeping or handing the debt off to a variety of Crown corporations, Bennett decided to celebrate.

It was an exuberant party. Armoured cars transported $70 million of cancelled bonds to Kelowna in the summer of 1959, piled them onto a floating barge and dragged them out into Okanagan Lake. Hundreds of dignitaries arrived in town, cabinet ministers were delirious, townsfolk rejoiced, media from around the country converged and thousands of schoolchildren sang "Happy Birthday" to their Mr. Bennett. As the sun began to set, the premier and his cabinet clambered aboard a flotilla of boats and headed out onto the darkening lake. The bonds, having been soaked with gasoline and secured with chicken wire, were waiting. At the appointed hour, Bennett fired a flaming arrow toward the barge. Some suggested the arrow reached its target but bounced off and fell in the lake. It didn't really matter. Nothing was left to chance as an out-of-sight RCMP officer took out his lighter and lit the fire from the back side of the barge. Thousands celebrated for hours, and the next day's newspaper shared photographs of the party with its readers while its headlines told of BC's much envied debt-free status. Everyone, including the premier, had wonderful time.

The celebration marked the midpoint of Bennett's term in office. The first Home Owner Grant was introduced at this time, along with provincial parity bonds—the precursor to Canada Savings Bonds—as a way to generate the capital needed to fund future development. A modern transportation system was in place but Bennett recognized that a cheap, plentiful source of energy was needed to fuel future growth. The Two Rivers plan soon emerged to develop hydroelectric dams on the Columbia and Peace Rivers. Partnerships were formed, and cross-border negotiations were lengthy and mired in red tape. BC Electric, the distributor of the bulk of the province's power, refused to commit to buy the power generated by the Peace project, and Bennett was furious. The company's board of directors refused to change their position, and since they were controlled by Ottawa, Bennett was even angrier. He took over the company on the day following the death of its well-respected president, "Dal" Grauer, and formed BC Hydro as a new Crown corporation.

The W.A.C. Bennett Dam on the Peace River was completed in 1968. It was the largest earth-filled structure ever built at the time and the only public works project built by his government to bear the premier's name.

The Bennett Clock was donated by the grateful citizens of Kelowna in memory of William Andrew Cecil Bennett, and dedicated in May 1981. It recognized Bennett's public service as an MLA for the area as well as his time as premier of BC. The seven steps represent the number of terms W.A.C. was re-elected as premier, and the twenty spires commemorate each year he served. Though silent for many years, the chimes of the carillon can now be heard. The clock is at the foot of Pandosy Street between Kelowna City Hall and the Kelowna Heritage Museum. | STUART KERNAGHAN, XYPHOTOS.CA

BC Hydro went on to build a number of dams and generating stations on the Columbia River, including the Mica and Revelstoke Dams. Bennett negotiated treaties with the US government that he felt served BC well, though his involvement didn't endear him to the federal government: he knew that his job was to look after his province, and if other levels of government didn't like it, that was their problem.

W.A.C. generally let his cabinet members run their own ministries and focussed his energies on building a bigger and ever-grander BC.

His leadership was unchallenged during his tenure and the forty-seven percent of the popular vote his party received in 1969 was unprecedented. He had established a pattern of calling elections every three years, and in 1972 no one, least of all Bennett himself, expected his time in office would be over. Everyone was in shock: *Le Monde* in Paris commented, as did the *Guardian* in Britain. The New Democratic Party (NDP) the successor to the CCF, took thirty-eight seats, the Liberals five and the Conservatives two, which left the Social Credit Party with ten. Eleven senior cabinet ministers lost their seats, though Bennett himself won his eleventh straight constituency election.

Though there had been no talk of retirement, Bennett was seventy-two years old. He had been in power longer than any other political leader in North America. Was he suddenly out of touch with voters? BC had become "Lotus Land," and perhaps people wanted still more and didn't think he could go on delivering. The NDP, under the leadership of the charismatic Dave Barrett, campaigned on the slogan "It's time for a change." Voters apparently agreed. Bennett had long campaigned to keep "the socialist hoards away from the province's gates," but organized labour had influenced voters. With ineffective Liberal and Conservative parties, the province had become polarized into two feuding political regimes. BC has a habit of voting out rather than voting in, and maybe it was just time for a change.

W.A.C. Bennett was unquestionably a larger-than-life politician. He provided inspired leadership, which propelled his province to become bigger and richer and more confident than most people could ever have imagined. W.A.C. would have rather died in office. He said he could take "hecklers, brickbats and criticism better than the praise" he received at the end. He led the Social Credit Party in Opposition for ten months though he rarely appeared in the legislature.

Bennett hadn't planned for his son, Bill, to take over his party and didn't endorse him when he ran for the leadership. When Bill became the new Socred leader, W.A.C. wasn't happy with the minor and behind-the-scenes roll he was assigned. The senior Bennett died in his sleep in 1979; he was seventy-eight years old. Funeral services were held in Vancouver and in Kelowna, where over a thousand people crowded into and around the First United Church and lined the nearby streets. The coffin was draped with the sun-emblazoned provincial flag, the flag that had been created when W.A.C. was in office, and flanked by bagpipers and an RCMP honour guard. It was truly the end of an era.

THE UNEXPECTED

During these years, Kelowna was astounded to find itself dealing with several random fires and numerous incidents of unprecedented violence. Just after St. Theresa's Catholic Church in Rutland opened in 1949, it was destroyed by arson. Two nearby rural schools and large stacks of wooden boxes, awaiting the harvest, also went up in flames. A Doukhobor family living in the area was able to escape before their home and barns were torched. Though it had been quiet in the Okanagan during the early 1950s, a section of the Kettle Valley Railway near McCulloch, close to Kelowna, had been blown up just as plans got underway for the official opening of the new Okanagan Lake Bridge. With the impending arrival of both Premier Bennett and Princess Margaret, all symbols of authority seemed to come under attack.

A month before the bridge was to open in June 1958, a bomb exploded in the beer parlour of the Willow Inn Hotel. The police arrived to find a gaping hole in the wall of the men's washroom, the door hanging by a hinge, the ceiling and support beams shattered, and the night watchman emerging from the dust. Another bomb was discovered before it exploded in the beer parlour of the Allison Hotel in Vernon, a power pole was blown up near Armstrong and a third bomb was discovered on the MV *Lequime* ferry. The deckhand who discovered the bomb in the back of a toilet was so startled he threw it overboard. He subsequently confirmed it looked much like the bomb found at the Allison Hotel—a sealed glass jar containing dynamite and nitroglycerine that had been wired to a cheap pocket watch.

During the late 1800s and early 1900s, thousands of Russian Doukhobors had fled religious persecution and resettled in Canada. Most homesteaded on the Prairies but some found the climate too harsh, and between 1908 and 1912 many resettled in the Kootenays, in southeastern British Columbia. Most were peaceful but a small radical group, the Sons of Freedom, protested any government involvement in their lives. They took their children out of school, burned their own homes and barns, bombed government buildings, railway bridges and tracks, schools, transmission towers, pipelines and churches, and then, young and old alike, confounded other British Columbians by parading about in the nude. The impact and cost of the damages were enormous and even the CPR was forced to reduce the frequency of its train service through the area and restrict all travel to daylight hours. The federal government offered $25,000 rewards for information leading to convictions but the community was tight-knit and fearful, and the money was never claimed. While most of the havoc was created in the Kootenays, Doukhobors were skilled farm workers and many gravitated to the Okanagan to work in the orchards.

People rarely seemed to be the target of these attacks; bombs were usually set to go off when few were likely to be around. The threat to Princess Margaret's safety seemed manageable. The *Courier* reported that Kelowna was "stiff with RCMP," some of whom were wearing red serge while others were in plain clothes, though all carried guns. Roadblocks were set up to check all cars coming into town: guards rode the ferries and frogmen—scuba divers—scoured the bridge pontoons. (In spite of these precautions, two cars, each carrying three young Doukhobor men, would force their way into the royal procession in both Vernon and Kelowna. The RCMP intercepted, no explosives were found and the intruders were ordered to leave town.)

A mobile bomb factory was discovered less than a month later near an abandoned ranch at McKinley Landing, about eleven miles north of Kelowna. It had likely been there for some time, but in August 1958 police discovered ten powerful sticks of dynamite strewn in an arc over the hillside. Pieces of a badly damaged car were found along with the scattered remains of a twenty-year-old male. The car had likely been a temporary home for the two young men before the bomb they were working on exploded prematurely. The other man had managed to burrow under the wreckage and survive burns, lacerations, blindness and exposure for three days until he was discovered.

Doukhobor leaders soon ordered the remaining Freedomites to leave the Okanagan and return to the Kootenays. Though there were few other incidents in Kelowna, bombings, arson and the nude parades continued elsewhere in the province for several more years. Doukhobor parents eventually promised to send their children to school and the youngsters were released from an internment camp in New Denver. A fireproof jail was built at Agassiz to house the arsonists and many family members left the Kootenays to be near them. Though attempts were made to negotiate the group's return to Russia or even to South America, nothing ever materialized. Their leaders were often seen as self-serving and manipulative, and followers paid a very heavy price for the very few, if any, benefits that came their way.

OF UNKNOWN ORIGIN

Though the Doukhobors had left the Okanagan, fire continued to be a recurring menace over the next several years. Most packinghouses were built with massive wooden beams that supported broad wooden floors where wooden fruit boxes were assembled and stored. Though the outside walls were corrugated iron or aluminum sheathing, they melted or collapsed during fires and did little to stop flames from spreading.

Glenmore's Cascade Co-op fire in June 1960 was the first in what became a succession of packinghouse fires. The previous five or six years had seen few fires and while it was determined that this fire was caused by a dropped cigarette, the timing was curious. The plant was just gearing up for the apple harvest so boxes were stacked everywhere and all had been treated with fire-friendly wood preservative. Tanks of compressed ammonia had also been stored in the building and, as they exploded, hundreds of spectators gathered and then took to the surrounding hillsides for a better view. The sawdust insulation in the walls added more fuel to the flames. The nearest hydrant was five hundred yards away, and although a nearby irrigation ditch was dammed and the water pumped, residents were asked to turn off their sprinklers to boost the water pressure. Forest service fire-suppression crews arrived in case embers flew to the nearby hillsides.

In March of the following year, a raging inferno destroyed three KGE warehouses near downtown. Fire crews scrambled and managed to save the two adjoining buildings. It was a million-dollar blaze and firefighters arrived from Vernon, Rutland and Westbank to join Kelowna's volunteer brigade. Along with the apple-grading equipment, over 100,000 cardboard boxes and several thousand cans of apple juice, apple pie filling and apricot concentrate stored in the building were also destroyed. The winds were light when a locomotive was brought to the area to help the firefighters: a cable was attached to the engine and wrapped around one of the covered walkways connecting the buildings to try to stop the fire from spreading. The first walkway tumbled to the ground but attempts to remove others were less successful as the cable kept breaking. The remaining three walkways became funnels for the flames spreading from one building to the next. Three- and four-storey walls collapsed, sending towers of flaming embers over the area. As the *Courier* noted, "cans of apple juice were popping merrily" from the heat.

City council had approved the purchase of the latest hydraulic ladder truck and a new pumper truck the night before the inferno. It wouldn't arrive in town for another four and a half months, and the firemen had little alternative but to fight this fire with a fifty-five-foot extension ladder. It was so unwieldy that it took six men to manoeuvre it into place, and it had to be moved at least ten times during the evening, in order to be able to tackle the flames from every possible angle.

Two weeks later, the *Courier* headline declared "FIRE BUG FEARED" as a second fire destroyed another KGE warehouse and the neighbouring Occidental Fruit Company cold storage plant. It was later revealed that in the two weeks between the fires, charred newspapers had been discovered in another KGE plant but had been extinguished before the fire had spread. The RCMP and the provincial fire marshal decided this was no mere coincidence; this time losses exceeded $600,000. Fire crews came from Rutland, Westbank and Summerland and had to deal with dangling overhead power lines that serviced the city's reservoir pump. If they were cut by the fire, the crews would lose all electricity, the pump would stop working and they would have no water to continue fighting the blaze. It was a potential disaster. Cyanide gases from burning fertilizer were a huge threat as was the risk of exploding ammonia storage tanks. An estimated four thousand people came to watch, spilling over the railway tracks as engineers shunted cars away from the flames, and then perched on the top of the cars for a better view. Along with the buildings, Sun-Rype lost about fifteen thousand cases of apricot concentrate, three thousand cases of pie filling, barrels of prune juice concentrate and thousands of cartons.

Vernon was also hit twice during the same time, as fire destroyed a large pile of empty boxes stacked on the railway platform adjacent to the packinghouse: only a cement wall had stopped the flames from destroying the building. Fruit industry buildings were also destroyed in Winfield and Summerland. Though there was no proof of arson, there were too many coincidences: there had been no packinghouse fires for years and now there were several; only the fruit industry was targeted; most fires occurred on Monday nights when there was little wind; and all were well established when discovered.

If these fires had been intentionally set, the fire bug took some time off... perhaps there was too much attention... but five months later, the *Courier*'s headline declared, "Occidental Struck Again in $350,000 Holocaust." It was a further blow to the industry, the city and the company, which was still rebuilding its packing plant and the cold storage area destroyed just months before. The timing was even more suspicious as the apple harvest was only a few weeks away. The night watchman had made his rounds, gone into the compressor room for a few minutes, and emerged to find fires burning in several places. The older part of the dry wooden building covered a half a block and the explosions and fires seemed to light everywhere at once. The sawdust insulation burst into flame and crowds gathered again to watch as the flames shot two hundred feet into the air.

Again, no one could prove arson, but everyone speculated about the coincidences and then added a consistently full moon to the equation. Total losses exceeded $2 million; packing plants in the North Okanagan banded together, worked around the clock, and dealt with that year's apple harvest. The Occidental's tomato packing line moved to the Canadian Canners plant, processing continued and everyone struggled with increasing insurance rates. The whole community was on edge: other businesses increased their fire patrols and city council had no difficulty justifying the expensive new firefighting equipment they had just ordered. Arson or not, the packinghouses and warehouses had been built at a time when wood and sawdust were the only materials available: neither gave any protection against fire and sprinkler systems had not yet been introduced. Most of Kelowna's early packinghouse history was destroyed in a very short span of time.

GROWTH, REGARDLESS

Like many other farming communities after World War II, Kelowna needed room to grow. Still confined by its original boundaries, the city quickly ran out of land and surrounding orchards lured new housing developments and new industry. The health risks of malfunctioning septic systems and the risk of losing a growing tax base sent city council scrambling to gather adjacent neighbourhoods into its boundaries. Glenmore agreed to unincorporate in 1960 and its southern properties, including the Kelowna Golf Club and the cemetery, amalgamated with the city. The new Capri Shopping Centre and its "swank" new sixty-room hotel also became part of Kelowna. The surrounding residential development soon followed and Harvey Avenue, leading from the new Okanagan Lake Bridge, was straightened and redirected through the old Pridham orchard.

Not every neighbourhood wanted to become part of a greater Kelowna, however. Even promises of chlorinated water, sewer systems and better fire protection didn't entice some. The residents of the old Guisachan farm threatened legal action if they were forced to amalgamate.

It took four years of meetings between Kelowna and its neighbours, plus polling and referenda, before the next amalgamation took place. By the mid-1950s, when that happened, the city's land base doubled and another 2,500 people pushed the population of Kelowna to 9,181. City council declared a five-year moratorium on further expansion… and then adjacent neighbourhoods began clamouring to be let in.

A few smaller boundary extensions occurred between 1960 and 1970, but when Orchard Park Shopping Centre opened in 1971, it was outside the city. The centre's sewage had to be trucked across the lake to Westbank for disposal. When the businesses asked to have the boundaries extended so they could hook up to Kelowna's sewage treatment facilities, residents objected. Ten percent of Kelowna's voters signed a counter-petition, forced a referendum and stopped the boundary extension. The shopping centre's neighbours didn't want to lose their rural status but Orchard Park was so desperate the owners applied directly to the new NDP Minister of Municipal Affairs. He approved, Kelowna's citizens weren't asked and the rural neighbours were furious. Orchard Park Shopping Centre became part of Kelowna in March 1973 and arrangements were soon made for sewer and water lines to be extended to the complex.

Kelowna and the province had been discussing other boundary extensions but there was no indication what, when or if any changes might be made. Then, just seven weeks after Orchard Park became part of the city, the province announced that a new municipality was being formed: Kelowna's boundaries would be dissolved and a new city would be formed to encompass the suburbs of Okanagan Mission, Rutland and Glenmore and all the land in between. The new city would also be called Kelowna but would now cover eighty-two square miles with about 51,000 residents. In 1971, the old city had been eight square miles with a population of just over 19,000. It was a quite a change.

Rutland was "shocked and disgusted" and declared democracy dead. Some saw the change as inevitable and knew that if asked, the citizens would never have agreed. Others thought it wise and necessary and the only way to deal with the water and sewage issues plaguing the area.

FARM, ANYONE?

Many farmers felt they could make more money selling their land for houses than they could by farming it. Others were relying on their land to fund their retirement. The New Democratic Party had defeated Bennett's Social Credit Party only a few months before but lost little time in bringing in legislation to preserve what it saw as the province's fast-disappearing farmland. The NDP soon proposed Agriculture Land Use legislation, which restricted development on agricultural land.

Farmers were furious but so were real estate speculators: farmers didn't think they should bear the brunt of preserving the province's farmland, while speculators felt they should be able to develop anywhere. It was a curious partnership as orchardists and speculators both joined a raucous protest on the grounds of the legislature in Victoria. The NDP proposed the government purchase the development rights from the farmers with a lump sum payout. Though many agreed, the government then decided the option was too expensive and replaced it with a farm subsidy program. With many amendments, the Agriculture Land Reserve (ALR) legislation finally passed in April 1973.

Growers in the Okanagan were vocal and angry... the legislation was "dictatorial" and "totally unacceptable." They divided into two camps: those who wanted to outright quit and those who wanted to continue but retain the right to dispose of their land any way they wished. Most were struggling financially and this was just "another nail in their coffin." If the government needed their land, they should darn well pay for it. Some felt farm work was paying less than unemployment insurance or welfare, and if that was the case they'd stop repaying their loans. Then an elderly Benvoulin farmer reminded everyone that "future generations will curse you if you subdivide good farm land." Some of the original ALR land was in frost pockets, or had poor soil, or steep hillsides, and sometimes the designation was lifted or changed. Agriculture still occupies almost half of Kelowna's land base, and in spite of periodic challenges, few would argue today for the total removal of the ALR classification.

"Fruitleggers" began to multiply. Low returns had been plaguing orchardists for years and the battle over collective marketing was always simmering. The independents didn't want to flaunt their opposition so they quietly stripped the back seats out of their cars, loaded them with boxes of fruit and smuggled the fruit out of the valley to Vancouver and Calgary. (There were few fruit stands or farmers' markets at the time.) Fruit inspectors patrolled the highways but had little authority to seize the cargo. A bit of immunity went a long way and the independents became bolder and sent their fruit out of the Okanagan in convoys of pickup trucks. The RCMP was called in to stop them but didn't want to get involved. The public were sympathetic, too, and it became a public relations nightmare the collective marketers couldn't win. The long-standing disagreement between the fierce independents and those who felt collective marketing was the orchardists' best option ended in a standoff.

The irrigation flumes, trestles and siphons that had criss-crossed the valley landscape for many years began vanishing in the 1960s. Over time, much had been replaced or rebuilt or improved upon but the systems were becoming increasingly expensive to maintain. The Agriculture and Rural Development Act provided funds and most of the irrigation went underground. While open ditches can still be found in Glenmore and in some parts of Okanagan Mission, most water is now carried to the orchards by pipe for spray irrigation.

WE NEED AN EDUCATION

A few years after W.A.C. Bennett became premier, he embarked on a program to ensure BC had the educated workforce necessary for the province to thrive and flourish into the future. The decision showed great foresight and wisdom on the part of a leader who had not had the opportunity for such an education himself. The only opportunity in the province to get a higher education at the time was University of BC (UBC) in Vancouver. An announcement was made in 1960 to create a new BC Vocational School (soon to become the BC Institute of Technology—BCIT) and the University of Victoria, and Simon Fraser University was also under construction three years later. Located in the Lower Mainland and on Vancouver Island, they were beyond the reach of people who lived in the Interior and more remote communities. For many, the option of staying home to complete grade thirteen, first-year university, at their high school was a better choice while others chose to go directly to UBC after grade twelve.

Okanagan residents began lobbying for a junior college but had to settle for the BC Vocational School, which opened a Kelowna campus on KLO Road in September 1963. The school offered pre-employment and pre-apprenticeship training in a number of trades as well as practical nursing and commercial training. Prospective students were likely those who had left school early, wanted to be involved with apprenticeship programs or planned to move directly into the job market. Residents had aspirations beyond a technical school, however, and kept lobbying for a college. Old valley rivalries surfaced immediately and Vernon, Kelowna and Penticton all declared the college should be in their town. A committee of representatives from ten school districts, from Revelstoke to Osoyoos, was formed in 1964. An independent study was undertaken the following year to recommend curriculum, cost sharing and a location: sixty-five acres of the Westbank Indian Reserve overlooking Okanagan Lake. Not thinking there could be a problem, the committee signed a preliminary ninety-nine-year lease agreement. Early designs showed low white buildings nestled into the hillside with a stunning view across the lake… to Kelowna. Penticton withdrew support.

Vernon declared that the centre of the region had moved northward as a result of Penticton's withdrawal and was adamant that the college should be built in their community. A referendum was held the following year to confirm everyone supported the consultant's recommendations, including the campus across the lake from Kelowna. Only twelve percent of Vernon's voters supported the recommendations and the proposal died. The committee remained undaunted and looked for ways to establish a college without having to go to referendum and rely on parochial voters.

Okanagan College became a reality in 1968, two years after the referendum. Since grade thirteen was paid for by the province, it was decided that the 165 students at Kelowna Senior Secondary, 72 at Salmon Arm Senior Secondary and 143 in Vernon would transfer to the college, with locations in each of the towns, and become the first class of the new institution's two-year university transfer program. Full-time tuition was one hundred dollars per term per student. Everyone was suspicious and certain that it was only a matter of time before all programs would be consolidated in Kelowna. The committee knew another referendum wouldn't survive the entrenched valley rivalries and the idea of a multi-campus college emerged.

Okanagan College in Kelowna started as two portables on the BC Vocational School's KLO site in 1970: one was divided into classrooms while the other contained laboratories. They burned down a few months later. The following year, the BC Vocational School and Okanagan College in Kelowna become a single entity and staked out the KLO campus as their headquarters. Now both Vernon and Salmon Arm were convinced their programs would be closed so their funds could be diverted to enhancing the Kelowna campus. Penticton citizens decided they were losing out in spite of the turmoil and voted to join the Okanagan College system in 1974. Ten years after becoming a reality on paper, Okanagan College was still only offering the first year of a two-year diploma program and vocational students had to transfer to Vancouver and BCIT for their second year. Tenacity, vision and hard work prevailed but in the first ten years Okanagan College sometimes had little else going for it.

WE ALL MUST ADAPT

Sun-Rype was utilizing most of the Okanagan Valley's apple crop but when other juice makers began intruding into its traditional market, the company had to take a hard look at its product lines. Citrus juices had been a major competitor from the outset, but when staff recommended the company expand into these products, the members of the board, all apple growers, were horrified. They eventually agreed, however, and expanded the company's product line, for the first time sourcing raw material from beyond the Okanagan.

As competition grew, Sun-Rype also had to rethink its relationship with the Summerland Experimental Farm. The federal research station and Sun-Rype had partnered on a number of new products: the station would develop the products, fine-tune the processing, and then make them available to whoever wished to go into commercial production. Sun-Rype had been developing its new products in partnership with the research centre since its inception but with the increasingly competitive marketplace, new products and unique processing methods became vitally important. Sun-Rype moved its product research in-house in the early 1960s.

Agriculture and the industries that supported it, including the sawmill, pretty well defined the community in the 1950s and 1960s. There was so little going on, in fact, that a federal program identified Kelowna as being one of Western Canada's most vulnerable and underperforming areas. Money followed in hopes of getting private companies to move their operations to Kelowna. Some did, including White Star Trucks, Westmill Carpet and the American Can Company. Since Sun-Rype packed all its juices and pie fillings in cans at the time, and can costs were becoming an increasing part of the overhead, it explored the possibility of setting up its own manufacturing plant. Money was tight but with the federal incentive dollars in hand, it approached American Can about building a plant in Kelowna. The company had been shipping cans to Sun-Rype from its Vancouver plant for years and didn't want to lose a good customer. American Can purchased land just north of the juice plant and connected the two operations with a conveyor line across the intervening road.

The arrangement lasted for a few years until the cans began to cost more than the juice they contained, and Sun-Rype again began searching for more cost-effective containers. Tetra Brik, a Swedish innovation, was being introduced to North America about this time; Sun-Rype revised

Cans for Sun-Rype's juice and pie fillings were shipped by rail from the American Can Company's plant in Vancouver. The railcars were shunted onto the siding where the cans were unloaded with a specially devised six-pronged fork and transferred by conveyor to the company's warehouse. | KELOWNA PUBLIC ARCHIVES 4864

its juicing process, tested the marketplace and devised new labels, then installed a Tetra Brik packing line in the Kelowna plant. The new containers were wildly successful and the company had to fall back on its canning line for a few months to keep up with the increasing demand. The American Can Company continued to supply other BC and Alberta customers from the Kelowna plant for a few more years before closing shop and consolidating operations back in Vancouver.

BULK BINS for FRUIT and VEGETABLES
★ Harvesting
★ Transportation
★ Storage

Designed for Strength, Durability and Convenience

- Cut-to-size Waterproof-glue Plywood
- Cut-to-size Wood Parts
- Hardware and Glue
  -supplied for your assembly

Technical advice and service provided
to assist you with your requirements

DETAIL OF CORNER BOLTING

Tested and Proven
OVER 60,000
in successful use!

S. M. SIMPSON LIMITED
Supplier of Quality FRUIT and VEGETABLE CONTAINERS
BOX SHOOK   VENEER CONTAINERS   BULK BINS
P.O. Box 220   KELOWNA, B.C.   PO 2-3411

An advertisement for early bulk bins, which notes that there were "over 60,000 in successful use!" There are now many millions in use worldwide.

The fruit industry never fully returned to wooden boxes after the war. Experiments with various styles and combinations of wood and cardboard continued, adaptations were made and new materials introduced, and cardboard gradually pushed the traditional wooden boxes to the sidelines. The new packaging was a blow to the valley's box makers and most simply closed shop and went onto other things.

S.M. Simpson Ltd. was the exception. After considering a variety of options, the company announced the construction of a new plywood plant at its Manhattan Beach location. The land was still plagued by high water tables but layers of sawdust, slabs and shavings overlaid with gravel had made it workable. The new plywood plant created more challenges as over 3,500 pilings were driven twenty to forty feet into the ground, which left four feet above ground to support the floor. Premier Bennett officially opened S & K Plywood in May 1957 during one of his visits to inspect the progress on the new Okanagan Lake Bridge. The unsanded spruce plywood the plant produced was used by the construction business until an opportunity appeared that enabled the company to get back into the fruit business.

When staff from the Summerland Research Station visited New Zealand in 1954, they discovered a shallow apple bin made from lumber, linoleum and war surplus bomber tires that was being used in the orchards. It was efficient, the apples required less handling and it required less manpower. They were quickly convinced the system, with some adaptations, could work in the Okanagan. An industry committee soon agreed on the dimensions for the new bulk bin, which held the equivalent of twenty-five boxes of apples and only required orchardists to add a fork to the front of their tractors to lift the bins onto the truck deck. Once the apples were delivered to the packinghouse, the bins could be returned to the orchard and used again, and again.

Bulk bins are distributed throughout the valley's apple and pear orchards just prior to picking. The crews descend on the orchards, strap on picking bags, fill them and empty them into the bins, which hold the equivalent of twenty-five of the older bushel apple boxes. Once the bins have been filled, they are collected by a tractor fitted with a forklift, and loaded onto a truck for delivery to the packinghouse. Once there, the bins are immersed in water so the apples can float out and onto a conveyor belt for grading. | SHARRON SIMPSON COLLECTION

It didn't take long for Simpson's to start building the bins from plywood. When the apples were bruising as they were dumped onto the packinghouse conveyor belt, a system was devised to submerge the bins in water; the apples would float out and water currents would carry them to conveyor belts for grading and packing. S.M. Simpson Ltd. was awarded a patent for the new bin in 1960, as growers from Osoyoos to Vernon and then Washington state converted to the new system.

An export market soon developed, when Simpson's established a production facility in England. The bins were initially sent from Kelowna unassembled, but when a strike at the Kelowna mill shut off supplies, the company sent sheets of plywood to be cut and assembled on site. The English subsidiary supplied seventy percent of the United Kingdom market by 1967. The bins moved on to Europe as well, where they were adapted to meet other countries' needs, and then on to South Africa and South America.

Bulk bins have been an integral part of the Okanagan fruit business for half a century now and the apple boxes they replaced are collectors' items. The bins have been adapted for many other products: smaller sizes are used for soft fruits, grapes, vegetables, frozen food, fish and seeds. Manufacturing companies use the bins for shipping parts; others use them for storage or even coffins. Some are now plastic. From the germ of an idea that was transplanted from one side of the world to the other, the bulk orchard containers that were reconfigured and fine-tuned in Kelowna have now spread around the world.

In the never-ending cycle of boom and bust, S.M. Simpson Ltd. was bought by the American multinational Crown Zellerbach (CZ) in 1965. In the intervening years several more companies have owned the Kelowna mill though they too are no longer in business. In 2004 Tolko Industries Ltd., a Canadian-owned specialty forest company based in Vernon, bought the original Manhattan Beach sawmill and plywood plant. Its products have changed, as has the plant itself, which is now surrounded by a much-changed and expanded city. In spite of occasional speculation about its demise, the sawmill built by Stan Simpson in the early 1930s, the valley's largest year-round employer at the time, continues to be one of Kelowna's major businesses.

Shortly before his death in 1959, the City of Kelowna honoured Stanley M. Simpson, the mill's founder, by awarding him the Freedom of the City for his contribution to his adopted community.

FINALLY: OKANAGAN LAKE BRIDGE

Many early residents thought the idea of a bridge across Okanagan Lake was preposterous: it was too great a distance and would cost far too much. Yet as more people moved to the valley and tourism became a reality, the ferries were seen as an irritant and an obstacle to the free flow of both cars and goods. With the arrival of the Cold War in the 1950s and related talk of World War III, a bridge across Okanagan Lake was seen as a "missing link" in the free flow of traffic between California and the Alaska Highway. Other valley communities were canvassed to see if they supported the idea. The usual rivalries came to the fore and Penticton's mayor never did come on side. Naramata residents were furious at the prospect of their long-hoped-for road along the east side of the lake being usurped by a bridge. The premier assured them their road would be built… when increased traffic warranted it.

With the arrival of Social Credit and their mandate to get BC moving, bridges were already being built in other parts of the province. It took awhile to convince the government the Okanagan Valley really needed a bridge… or perhaps the premier didn't want to be seen favouring his home town. Though locals had been advocating for free ferry passage for some time, they didn't seem averse to a toll bridge. While a previous government had toyed with the idea of a bridge and had gone so far as to design a twin-towered suspension bridge rivalling Vancouver's Lions Gate, there was no money to build it. When Social Credit came to power, they redesigned the bridge into a causeway, pontoon and lift span alternative. Tenders were called in December 1955 for the less glamorous and less expensive bridge, which was also more suited to the shifting sand on the bottom of Okanagan Lake. Everyone was certain the new Okanagan Lake Bridge was the solution to the traffic problems that had plagued the valley from the time the first settlers arrived.

Most of the equipment needed to build the bridge was brought by train from Vancouver: a concrete plant, a pile driver, the prefabricated steelwork and a tug. A construction camp was set up on the old railway lands (now Waterfront Park); a graving dock was dredged and fitted with eighteen-foot timber doors for the construction of twenty-four concrete pontoons. Each pontoon weighed seventy tons, at two hundred feet long and fifty feet wide. The pontoons were attached to the road deck with steel cables that had been embedded twenty-five to thirty-five feet into the lake bottom. The pontoons were floated to the bridge site, earthen

Early plans for the first Okanagan Lake Bridge were for a structure that looked like the Lions Gate Bridge in Vancouver. Engineering studies subsequently proved the design unworkable and it was replaced with a floating bridge. The community embraced the early design and built a float to celebrate its impending arrival. | KELOWNA PUBLIC ARCHIVES 2346 causeways built—1,400 feet from the west and 300 feet from the east. City Park had to be reconfigured and many were certain the park would be ruined. Japanese Canadians donated ornamental cherry trees, an addition was made to the existing grandstand and a new park entrance and paved roads convinced the skeptics the park would survive. An operator sat in the bridge control room halfway up the east tower to raise the 260 foot vertical span and give 60 feet of vertical clearance to the barges and rigid-masted sailboats.

People in Kelowna were almost as excited about Princess Margaret coming to town as they were about the bridge. This was the princess's first trip to Canada; she was twenty-seven, beautiful and very royal. The front page of the *Daily Courier's* sixty-page *Souvenir Bridge Edition* featured Margaret on the top half with a photo of the new bridge relegated to the lower half. A temporary Government House was again created in Okanagan Mission: it was panelled throughout with BC cedar; all rooms overlooked the lake; the living room had turquoise walls with a dark-beamed ceiling and a coffee table surfaced in white tile. The sun-dappled lawn went down to a wharf decorated with centennial bunting (this was also BC's one hundredth anniversary), and "the water was clear, with a bottom of sand and gravel that the Princess need never touch." Every minute detail was revealed. The power in the house went out at one point, sending the resident RCMP officers into panic mode until they realized the extra communications equipment installed for the occasion had overloaded the circuits.

Kelowna gave Princess Margaret an "ardent and zealous welcome." Over five thousand schoolchildren packed into the Aquatic's Ogopogo Stadium the night the princess arrived and alighted from an amphibious Mallard aircraft belonging to Pacific Western Airlines. Premier Bennett greeted her, and the crowd broke into a rousing rendition of "God Save the Queen" and those who had the privilege of meeting her—and there were many—"felt momentarily transported to a wonderland." The welcome lasted twenty minutes. The local rumour mill was working well as word spread that Captain Peter Townsend, the princess's unsuitable love interest at the time, had quietly arrived in town to meet her.

Businesses along the royal travel route were encouraged to decorate their storefronts and citizens were told to display flags. All stores were closed during the opening ceremonies, though restaurants and women's church groups sold box lunches for spectators to take to the park. The bridge opened for traffic an hour and a half after the official ceremony

HRH Princess Margaret cuts the ribbon to officially open the new Okanagan Lake Bridge at 12:27 p.m. on July 19, 1958. The thousands who gathered in the brilliant sunshine were awestruck as the princess appeared with Premier W.A.C. Bennett and Minister of Highways Phil Gaglardi. She was wearing a yellow silk surah suit with an overblouse of sheer lime yellow and white, and a white cloche hat softly draped to the right. The *Courier* added she also wore a diamond dogwood pin, lime yellow shoes and elbow-length white gloves with a gold bracelet and pearls. HRH was given a pyramidal form of the wire cable used to anchor the pontoons as a memento of the occasion. | **KELOWNA PUBLIC ARCHIVES 17**

but the toll booths didn't open until midnight the following day. The MV *Lloyd-Jones*, the most recent addition to the Okanagan ferry fleet, sailed past the new bridge in tribute on Saturday at four p.m. with 190 dignitaries on board. The captain sounded a salute and the lift span operator responded. It was the end of an era and the long, proud and often fractious history of the Okanagan Lake ferries.

Those who remember living with the ferries have many stories about racing down the west side hill, with car horn blaring, in hopes the captain would hold the last sailing of the night for arrival. Others remember waiting for hours on holiday weekends for the next ferry only to miss getting on board by one car. Sometimes the ferries transported hazardous material but that was usually late at night and no one else was allowed on board. Other times sheep filled the entire deck, on the way to their summer pasture, and then no one else *wanted* to be on board. There was also the occasional well-orchestrated getaway that left the unsuspecting stranded on one side or the other. There were many efforts to keep a channel open when the lake froze but when that wasn't possible, sailings were cancelled. The ferries remain a colourful and charming part of Kelowna's history and speak of a slower time—which was, in the end, what people complained about most.

A BC Toll Highways and Bridges Authority had been created by the Bennett government to raise money to pay for the construction of the province's new bridges and highways. The debt was to be paid off by the tolls collected on Okanagan Lake Bridge, among others. A single trip for most vehicles was fifty cents a crossing or, for commuters, fifteen trips a week for $1.50. Trucks paid from seventy-five cents to $2.00, depending on the size. The tolls remained in place for five years until Premier Bennett suddenly announced their removal on April 1, 1963. The only official ceremony marking the end of the tolls was held in Kelowna where the mayor announced, apparently with a straight face, that "there are no politics involved in this occasion." Bridge decorations soon arrived from Victoria to mark the non-event. Traffic was halted from both the east and the west so senior civic officials from all over the valley could join the premier on the bridge for the brief ceremony. A no-host luncheon followed with Kelowna's mayor encouraging every valley community to attend "to show their appreciation to Premier Bennett for what has turned out to be a major economic factor in the present health of the Okanagan."

Raising the Okanagan Lake Bridge lift span for the *MV Fintry*. The City of Kelowna bought the *MV Pendozi* for one dollar when it was decommissioned, with plans to find a suitable owner. The boat sank in twenty feet of water on January 1, 1965; the city engineer suspected foul play. Once the boat was refloated, the Westbank Yacht Club became the "suitable owner" and the old ferry became their clubhouse. The *MV Lequime* was transformed into the *Fintry Queen*, which remains docked in Kelowna. The third Okanagan Lake ferry, the *MV Lloyd-Jones*, is thought to be registered in the Dominican Republic under a different name. | COURTESY OF JERRY VANSOM

The Kelowna Story: An Okanagan History

Okanagan Lake Bridge—1958. A grateful Kelowna wanted to name their new bridge after Premier Bennett, their MLA, in recognition of his efforts to make it become a reality. He declined the honour. | KELOWNA PUBLIC ARCHIVES 4475

ONE DISASTER AFTER ANOTHER

The Kelowna International Regatta continued, though the organizing committee sometimes struggled to maintain the momentum and attract headline acts for the evening shows while keeping it a family event. However, all of the things that could possibly go wrong came together in 1969. Two young boys were seen playing with matches under the 4,400-seat wooden Ogopogo Stadium in mid-June. Soon flames spread up and along the seats, engulfing the pavilion's restaurant—including the plate of sandwiches ready for an afternoon event—the dance and banquet hall, the change rooms and the boat storage. Staff raced through the building to make sure no one was inside and then headed underneath and tossed racing shells, oars and Regatta night show decorations into the lake.

The Aquatic's facilities were the most widely used in the city and the loss was not only a blow to "Canada's Greatest Water Show" but also to the generations of Kelowna residents whose lives centred around City Park and the Aquatic. Children had taken swimming lessons and then spent most of their summers in Ogopogo Pool; they had participated in weekly Aquacades, and competed and performed in the Regatta. Some had gone on to become Lady of the Lake candidates while others earned their Red Cross Bronze Medallions and became lifeguards. Many of their parents had done the same and then danced in the ballroom and attended community banquets at the only suitable facility in town. The Aquatic fire ended an era that had shaped the lives and friendships of generations of residents and visitors alike.

The community rallied and nothing was cancelled for that year's Regatta. Tommy Hunter headlined the night shows for spectators who sat on temporary bleachers and gathered to watch the manoeuvres of the crack US Navy Blue Angels precision flying team. The team had managed the short airport runway but found the mountains made their formations a bit tighter than usual, and held a practice in the afternoon to make any last minute adjustments. One pilot found himself a little higher and a little behind in one of their formations and cut in his afterburner to catch up. The plane exceeded the speed of sound, though only momentarily, and blew out seventy-five percent of the windows in an eight-block area of downtown. Six people were injured, though none seriously. Plywood was slapped over the gaping holes in the office and shop windows and the Regatta Parade carried on as scheduled a few hours later. NATO paid for the repairs.

Kelowna's Aquatic Centre (left photo) was the town's most popular summer gathering place as well as home to the famous Kelowna International Regatta. Generations of families learned to swim, competed (and watched others compete), lunched on the dining room veranda and danced to the Pettman Imperials. The in-lake pool, diving towers and 4,400-seat Ogopogo Stadium burned to the ground in June 1969 (bottom photo). Thousands watched in awe as the intense heat peeled the paint off nearby cars and destroyed Kelowna's centrepiece. The loss changed the Regatta and moved many events and people away from the lakeshore and to other facilities. | KELOWNA PUBLIC ARCHIVES 1854, 4166

The Ogopogo's image had not changed much by the early 1950s and the monster appeared on signs and postcards to promote the area. | KELOWNA PUBLIC ARCHIVES 1894, 4828

KELOWNA, B.C. 1955

The third in the Regatta's trio of disasters got very little press—perhaps the event organizers felt jinxed and didn't want to talk about it. The Kamloops Sky Diving Club had been performing during the Regatta until one of their divers missed the targeted landing area and ended up wedged in the lane behind the Bernard Avenue stores. Little mention was ever made of the incident, and whether a death occurred or not seems to be lost to time, though a rumour persists.

Kelowna was growing and by the late 1960s had already recognized the need for more recreation opportunities. A massive report highlighting the need for an indoor pool, a community centre, a seniors' building and acres of playing fields had been released only a month before the Aquatic fire. It lurked in the background as the community struggled to deal with the loss of their Aquatic Centre and discussed what to do with the $300,000 insurance settlement. Those who wanted to rebuild also wanted a huge swimming pool, a much larger yet also portable grandstand, more restaurants and a dance floor. Others wanted it to become the town's convention centre. Some wanted the new facility to be in City Park; others didn't. It took many many meetings and endless discussions before the decision was made to add the Aquatic insurance dollars to other municipal funds and create the multipurpose midtown Parkinson Recreation Centre. The centre was named after Dick Parkinson, "Mr. Regatta" to many and later the mayor, in recognition of his contributions to the community. The decision remains contentious among those who lived in Kelowna at the time and grew up at the Aquatic. Yet the rec centre's indoor pools, various multipurpose rooms and outdoor playing fields have evolved over the intervening years and are still much used.

Gradually, the Regatta drifted away from its focus on the lake and its traditional activities were replaced with soccer tournaments, wrist-wrestling championships and a lumberjack show. A craft show was held in the arena, which was later transformed into a casino. An agricultural show was held in City Park along with a Bavarian beer garden; a volleyball tournament was followed by a bathing suit contest and a bathtub race to Penticton. The new Regatta paid less attention to the water and lost some of its family focus. Residents complained that City Park was overused, as what little remained of the Ogopogo Pool began falling apart. For a few years, an Aquatic Exhibition Park was created at the north end of town and though the demise of the Kelowna International Regatta was likely underway, few would have admitted it at the time.

The Ogopogo looked a little more benign when he greeted visiting beauty queens in 1969. | KELOWNA PUBLIC ARCHIVES 5186

KELOWNA: A FOUR SEASON PLAYGROUND

Kelowna's new logo with its "Four Season Playground" tagline was introduced to the Kelowna Chamber of Commerce at a dinner meeting in 1964. Most of those attending were mystified by the four blank quarters of the circle until springtime golfers filled one quarter, swimmers and boats on a blue-green lake another, grapes and a travelling car another, and finally skiers in the fourth. The logo was the symbol for the 1964 visitor promotion program and members were urged to add it to their stationery, bumper stickers and brochures, and have gas station attendants and waitresses wear it as part of their uniform. A small pocket-sized card was prepared so those who were asked about the logo would have the information handy. It was hoped that those wearing the logo would feel they were officially representing Kelowna and would reap the benefits that would naturally follow from being more polite. While the logo has been abandoned and the tagline has become "Kelowna—Ripe with Surprises," the city continues to portray itself as a vibrant and inviting four-seasons playground.

THE OKANAGAN'S VERY OWN

The *Courier* headline proclaimed "Kelowna opened a major door to the Electronic Age" when "The Okanagan's Very Own" CHBC-TV was launched in 1957, only five years after Canadian television was launched in Montreal. Its creation came about as the result of a unique collaboration between the owners of the valley's three radio stations—the Browne family from Kelowna's CKOV, Roy Chapman from Penticton's CKOK and Messrs. Pit and Peters from Vernon's CJIB. The colleagues put up a quarter of a million dollars and created the Okanagan Valley Television Company. Engineers came from RCA Montreal to scout the surrounding mountaintops for the best line-of-sight signal; the production studio, which needed to be near the main transmitter, was created out of the renovated Smith Garage in downtown Kelowna. Roy Chapman became the managing director and hired engineers, program directors, promotion managers and on-air personalities. Several pages of the *Courier* featured the station's launch, stating the channel would be the vehicle for a "great visual and aural exchange of ideas, both nationally and internationally and give Valley citizens new dimensions and stature." The schedule was guaranteed to entertain and educate viewers, connecting them to a bigger world. *Ed Sullivan, Douglas Fairbanks Presents, Dragnet, I Love*

Lucy, *Captain Kangaroo* and *The Lone Ranger* were regulars, and when all else failed the station's camera was trained on its fish tank—at least something was moving on the screen.

The *Courier* was full of stories about how those pictures got into that box, what style of cabinet would be most appropriate for a television—sophisticated modern would be jarring in the Victorian living room—and new buyers should not worry about keeping up with their neighbours. Stories also warned that the biggest set might not be the most suitable for your room, and you shouldn't stare at the screen for long periods of time. Most importantly, the correct viewing distance from the screen was calculated as ten times the width of your screen: fourteen feet away from a seventeen-inch screen and eighteen feet away from a twenty-one-inch screen. "Baby Sitter Problem? Get a TV." The newspaper was full of advice; advertising filled its pages as every store in town seemed to be selling TV sets and the *Courier*'s new TV program guide became a sought-after weekly feature.

Okanagan Lake Bridge's official opening provided the first opportunity for live TV coverage of a major outdoor event. With no mobile equipment, the studio, control room and microwave receiver had to be dismantled and reassembled at the east end of the bridge. When the hour and a half broadcast was over, the equipment was disassembled and returned to the main studio.

EVERYONE'S A "PACKER BACKER"

Everyone in town supported the Kelowna Packers during the hockey-mad years of the early 1950s. Cavalcades of fans followed the team to each game as they played the Kamloops Elks, the Vernon Canadians, and the Penticton Vees in the Okanagan Senior Hockey League. Rivalries were physical and noisy and there was rarely an empty seat at Memorial Arena: fans "literally hung from the rafters." The Penticton Vees won the national Allan Cup in 1954 and represented Canada in the World Amateur Hockey Championships in West Germany the following year. Their five-nothing defeat of the Russians vaulted them into legendary status.

The Kelowna Packers won their league championship in 1958 as well as the subsequent quarter-finals and semifinals on the way to the Allan Cup showdown with the Belleville (Ontario) Macs. Kelowna lost in a final "titanic seventh game struggle" but earned themselves a trip to

Sweden and Russia as a result. This was during the height of the Cold War and the Packers were the first Western sports team to be invited behind the Iron Curtain. The strength and speed of the Russian teams were legendary and no one gave the Packers a chance of winning even one game. When they lost the first game against Sweden, Kelowna fans sent a huge telegram wishing them well: they won the next two games and the fourth game was cancelled without explanation.

The team flew on to Moscow, arrived at the Sports Palace and faced a highly partisan crowd. Kelowna lost the first game against the Wings of Soviet, then tied the second. When they tied the third game against the Moscow Dynamos, Kelowna fans danced on Bernard Avenue. Then the Packers started to win: four-three in the next game and then they trounced the vaunted Russian team five-one in the final game. The Russian players were gracious and said, "the Canadians are magnificent hockey players." Kelowna held a giant civic reception and banquet for the Packers when they returned home.

A somewhat different picture emerged when the returning players told their stories. They had considerable apprehension about going behind the Iron Curtain and team members recalled being constantly afraid. Soldiers had silently boarded their plane when it arrived in Moscow, they were followed everywhere and they even felt compelled to leave the lights on in their hotel rooms at night. Some said that aside from winning, the best part of the trip was leaving—"we were only there nine days but it seemed like a month." There was no traffic on streets so wide you could have landed an airplane on them, there were no neon signs, everything was concrete, so bleak, so poor, and everyone dressed the same—in black. The only good food they ate was at the Canadian Embassy. No one was in a hurry to return to Russia, though all agreed it was an experience they would never forget.

The Kelowna Packers captured the league title again for the 1959–60 season but hockey's popularity had begun to wane by then and it wasn't long before the league disbanded. During the height of the team's popularity, Kelowna Memorial Arena was filled beyond capacity. | COURTESY OF RAY OTTENBREIT

KELOWNA MOVES ON

These were twenty transitional years for Kelowna. It was no longer a small town—it had become the fifth largest city in the province—but neither was it very big. The Hope–Princeton Highway brought people to the area from Vancouver and the new Okanagan Lake Bridge made it easier to move within the valley. The Rogers Pass became part of the Trans-Canada Highway in 1962 and access from the east was easier. It still wasn't a direct route to the Okanagan, but it was a vast improvement over the gravel Big Bend Highway that had previously been the only Canadian alternative.

The Kelowna Airport runway was extended and paved, navigation lights were added on the field and surrounding mountaintops and Canadian Pacific Airlines scheduled twice-daily service. The two-hour trip to Vancouver included a brief stopover in Penticton. With a one-way ticket costing eighteen dollars, businessmen were encouraged to fly to Vancouver and return home the same day.

New highways and bridges, more cars and trucks, and improved air service soon pushed train service to the margins. By 1961, the CN passenger train was replaced by a Railiner, a self-propelled diesel passenger car. This lasted for about two years until CN put their passenger train back into service in hopes of attracting more traffic. It took only a few months for them to realize that times had truly changed. In October 1963 the passenger train was replaced by a chartered bus, which left Kelowna at 8:30 p.m. and made various stops on its way to Kamloops, where passengers transferred to the transcontinental about midnight. Kelowna's love affair with passenger rail travel had lasted thirty-eight short years. CP ended their barge service on Okanagan Lake in May 1972 and CN followed a year later. Soon, their tracks were torn up, the wharf demolished and their tugs were sold. Trucks had become the carrier of choice and the storied era of lake travel was over.

The ALR, coupled with its expanded boundaries, profoundly impacted the way Kelowna evolved over the next few years, as pastures, orchards and vineyards became part of the community. Residents who otherwise had little to do with farming began looking forward to spring blossoms and fall harvests as they settled comfortably into their midst.

The neighbouring communities of Okanagan Mission, Rutland and Glenmore, and the smaller communities of East Kelowna, Ellison and Benvoulin, initially feared they would lose their unique identities when they became part of Kelowna. But it wasn't long before residents realized they could retain the character and feeling that defined them when the areas were first settled.

CHAPTER SEVEN

The Past Thirty-five Years—Kelowna Finds Its Heart, 1976 to the Present

Kelowna's iconic *Spirit of Sail* sculpture was suspended from a helicopter in October 1977, flown down the middle of the lake and gently lowered onto the fountain at the foot of Bernard Avenue. The artist, Robert Dow Reid, had created it in his Okanagan Mission studio, where he'd sculpted since arriving in Kelowna in 1964. Most of his works were much smaller in scale, and Kelowna's sculpture was the first of his monumental pieces to be installed. It was the second sculpture to be placed in the fountain; the first had been a series of cement half-circles arranged around a central plume that shot a great geyser of water forty feet into the air. It looked wonderful for the six warm months of the year but for the remaining months it simply sat as an inarticulate bunker at the end of the main street. The original designer also apparently didn't know about the Bear Creek winds that gusted across the lake most summer afternoons. It didn't take long before pedestrians and building owners complained to city hall about being drenched by the wind-whipped geyser.

The fountain was originally a tribute to Pasquale "Cap" Capozzi, who had arrived in Kelowna in 1920 and established a number of thriving businesses, including City Grocery, the Capri Shopping Centre and Hotel, and Calona Wines. The fountain was initially going to be built in the bay at the foot of Bernard Avenue until sailors and boaters complained it would be a navigation hazard. Then there was talk of putting it at the end of a pier before it was realized there was no money to build a pier. The grass at the foot of Bernard Avenue eventually became the fountain's default location. When it was decided the geyser had to go, city staff began looking for alternatives; the suggestion of a bronze likeness

R. Dow Reid's *Spirit of Sail* is referred to by most people as "the Sails." Located on the lakeshore at the foot of Bernard Avenue, the sculpture has become as much a symbol of Kelowna as its nearby companion, the Ogopogo. | STUART KERNAGHAN, XYPHOTOS.CA

of Premier W.A.C. Bennett in the middle of the fountain didn't gain much support.

It was finally an off-chance visit by a member of city staff to the Dow Reid Studio that revealed a three-foot-high version of the sails sculpture. City council was interested and when the small sculpture was displayed at the Capri Mall and comments were positive, the decision was made. The concrete half-circles and the geyser were removed and replaced with the creative and somewhat abstract *Spirit of Sail*.

Kelowna's Waterfront Park officially opened in 1995. | H. BRUST
COLLECTION Q9024

The arrival of the sculpture in downtown Kelowna seemed to change the community's focus. While city hall dealt with the implications and fallout from the recent boundary expansion, things began to happen downtown. When CN decided to sell its marshalling yards and wharfs in the north end in 1975, Kelowna had the wisdom to buy them. In anticipation of future development, sewer pipes were installed but those in charge were apparently unaware that most of the land had previously been swamp and bog. It wasn't long before the pipes had disappeared into the water-soaked soil among the sawdust and slabs that had been used to fill the swamps. The experience gave rise to the notion that Kelowna's downtown couldn't support high-rise development. The problem was overcome when new engineering methods were introduced, which usually involved preloading the proposed development site with mounds of soil for several months to force the residual water from the ground prior to construction.

It took several more years for the city to figure out what it wanted to do with the site. Left empty, the land was muddy and covered with weeds until a proposal call was sent out in 1988 soliciting plans to develop the property. The city talked about parkland, condos, a destination hotel and a convention centre. The submissions were fascinating, exotic, totally impractical, engaging and sometimes oblivious to the city's requirements. Though the decision to go ahead with a mid-market Calgary-based hotel developer was risky, the lagoon system and lakefront park that were part of the proposal had enormous appeal.

A large section of the old railway marshalling yards and wharf was transformed into Waterfront Park. Brandt's Creek had run through the area for years but had been neglected—and was an outlet for industrial waste. At one time, an unintended discharge from Calona Wines left

The Laurel Packinghouse underwent a further $2.7 million restoration in 2010, which removed the second floor offices, replaced the roof, opened the main floor, dealt with wood rot and brought the building up to current building code standards. The restorations have cost substantially more than the original building. The Laurel Packinghouse is now on the National Historic Register and has become one of the city's most picturesque and best used historic assets. | STUART KERNAGHAN, XYPHOTOS.CA

the neighbourhood ducks staggering in delight as they clamboured in and out of their wine-laced pond. The creek bed was also full of debris and overgrown with weeds. The area was restored as part of the project and is now known as Brandt's Creek and the Rotary Marsh. Osprey, mallards and tree-eating beavers have made the wetlands their home. The new park also included a swimming beach, created at Tugboat Bay, and the Island Stage, built in the lagoon. Simpson Walk, named for S.M. Simpson, circles the reclaimed land around the lagoon. Waterfront Park opened in 1995 as part of the transformation of the derelict railway yards; it also includes the Grand Okanagan Lakefront Resort and the Dolphins and Lagoon condo developments. The area has become one of the city's signature residential and hotel areas as other condos have been added, overlooking what is one of the community's best utilized and most beautiful parks.

The crumbling Laurel Packinghouse was set to be bulldozed out of existence in the early 1980s. Built of bricks made from Knox Mountain clay in 1917, the Laurel was the oldest, largest and last of BC's historic packinghouses and its demise would have obliterated the remaining vestiges of Kelowna's once vibrant fruit-packing industry. The city was reluctant to save the building, but after much persuasive lobbying it relented, restoring the packinghouse and recognizing it as

The gem of Kelowna's revitalized cultural district is the Kelowna branch of the Okanagan Regional Library. | H. BRUST COLLECTION Q3694

the city's first heritage building. When it opened in 1988, the main floor was used for displays and various public functions while the second floor office space was made available to various arts and commercial groups. To commemorate the hundredth anniversary of the founding of the British Columbia Fruit Growers' Association, the Orchard Industry Museum opened in the Laurel in 1989. The BC Wine Museum and a VQA wine shop opened in the building ten years later.

The Kelowna Art Gallery was created in 1977 and for a number of years shared display space in the Kelowna Museum. Plans were underway to build a stand-alone building on the parking lot in front of the museum until the board was encouraged to look farther afield. Amid some consternation, they chose instead to build their new gallery on the old industrial land across from the new hotel complex. The facility is home to a number of different galleries, all of which meet national standards for the storage and exhibition of artworks. Most of the gallery's collection has been created since 1940 and focusses on historical and contemporary visual arts, and particularly landscape images of the Okanagan.

The architectural gem of the area is the Kelowna branch of the Okanagan Regional Library. The building's design evolved when many stakeholders participated in a fractious day-long workshop. The various community members somehow managed to resolve all their issues and moved ahead, then celebrated the opening of the new library in 1996. It

The Rotary Centre for the Arts, in Kelowna's cultural corridor, was created when a cement-block building selling fertilizer and orchard tools was transformed into a facility providing performance and studio space for all branches of the arts.

was also built on what had previously been Kelowna Saw Mill property. The surrounding green space adds air and light to the increasingly dense neighbourhood though the open spaces may be slated for future development as the city attempts to recoup some of the costs of acquiring the land.

The latest addition to what has become known as Kelowna's cultural corridor is the Rotary Centre for the Arts. The new building was built over and around the old concrete-block Growers Supply building and came about after years of complaining, lobbying and fundraising by the local arts community, who were perpetually short of affordable performance, studio and storage space. The building, which opened in 2002, houses the 326-seat Mary Irwin Theatre, artists' studios, an art gallery, a dance studio, a bistro and rental space. Affordability continues to be a challenge for the arts groups who lobbied and worked so hard to create the building.

BILL BENNETT

Following in the footsteps of a popular, larger-than-life leader is challenging at best, but when that leader was your father, it's huge. From the start of his political involvement, Bill Bennett knew he wasn't the populist his father had been. Neither was he a showman, and initially he had the speaking ability of a wooden statue, though he improved with time. Bill also knew a high-visibility leader was a magnet for the media and decided he didn't need to be centre stage all the time. By the end of W.A.C.'s time in office, the Social Credit Party was in disarray. Members had drifted off, the organization had all but vanished and election readiness wasn't an issue—whenever Premier W.A.C. had called an election, he was ready and the party only needed to be marginally involved. When Bill declared he would seek the leadership, his first step had to be the revitalization of his own party. Most thought Social Credit was dead and began looking around for another party that could bring the Liberals and Conservatives back to life.

Bill had done his homework. "Build with Bill" became his slogan and when he ran for the leadership he was ready and handily defeated his opponents. Then he travelled the province rebuilding his party, enticing members of the other parties to get on board. Tina the elephant joined the last campaign rally before the 1975 election… apparently trumpeting the change in government that Bill and the Social Credit Party were sure was going to happen. Dave Barrett and the NDP had been in office for 1,200 days and his rationale for calling an election has never quite been understood; perhaps it was because his predecessor had called elections every three years. The NDP had been unprepared to govern: money was spent with little accountability, governance was sloppy and back-to-work legislation had alienated the Party's labour constituency. In contrast, the programs the NDP brought in, notably the ALR and the Insurance Corporation of BC (ICBC), were innovative and left intact when the party was defeated. However, the NDP had also amalgamated Kelowna with its neighbouring communities and brought in similar legislation for Kamloops and Prince George. Most voters in these communities weren't impressed.

Bennett campaigned on the NDP's lack of fiscal accountability and sloppy management, and won the election. The time between father and son Social Credit premiers was only three years. Bill lived in the Harbour Towers Hotel during the time he was in Victoria, took over Dave Barrett's old car and headed back to Kelowna every weekend he could. Not being

Premier W.R. Bennett. A very different kind of politician than his father, Bill nonetheless made a significant impact on BC. His legacies include Expo 86 and the Coquihalla Highway.

drawn to the cocktail circuit, he worked long hours and expected everyone else to do the same. Bill deferred to his cabinet ministers to introduce legislation, and also justify it and the costs involved. Most found the opportunity unique and fulfilling, though they knew Bill was keenly aware of whatever was going on.

There were a number of challenges during his three terms in office: the NDP had taken over several companies, which didn't sit well with the free enterprise mantra of the Socreds. BC Resources Investment Corporation, soon referred to as BCRIC, was created and everyone in the province could apply for five free shares of the company. Almost ninety percent of citizens took up the offer and the novel concept made for huge headlines in the newspapers, but when various scandals also hit the headlines BCRIC shares ended up as wallpaper. By the late 1970s and early 1980s, the worst recession ever hit the province, skyrocketing interest rates and collapsing resource revenues. Wage restraints were introduced after teachers won a twenty-one-percent wage hike. The government introduced the most drastic restraint program the province had ever seen.

Bill had already decided that this would be his last term in office and as protest marches blanketed the province, and his family received death threats, Bill made concessions, but on his own terms. Bennett wasn't the province's most popular politician though most people grudgingly respected his decisions. There were some major accomplishments during his term of office including Expo 86, the domed BC Place Stadium and Vancouver's Trade and Convention Centre. To balance out the perks to Vancouver, the Coquihalla Highway would tie the Lower Mainland to the Southern Interior, and the port at Prince Rupert and Tumbler Ridge coal would provide economic stimulus in the north.

Bill was a pragmatist who saw the big picture and looked for the best solutions with that in mind. He rewrote the province's financial accountability legislation, was a principled leader who did what he thought was best and saw the province through one of the most challenging times in its history. In contrast to W.A.C., the charismatic leader who built during the good times, Bill was seen as an aloof no-nonsense leader, one who also left a positive legacy to the province but did so during the toughest of times. He led the government through three elections over eleven years, and left office in the middle of Expo 86, having completed the list of things he wanted to accomplish before stepping down.

BC politics are often described as wacky, zany, weird and wonderful. The province hasn't always followed the more traditional political model and party leaders have often added their own colourful and unconventional take on their role, including Premiers W.A.C. Bennett and Bill (W.R.) Bennett. A Bennett from Kelowna had led the Social Credit Party as the premier for thirty-one of the previous thirty-four years. It was quite an amazing family commitment to public life, and an unquestioned commitment to the development and betterment of BC.

UNPRECEDENTED GROWTH

As the province worked its way out of the economic crisis of the 1980s, Kelowna began to thrive. Retirees arrived to settle, families from Alberta built holiday homes, and space that had previously been designated for agricultural use became available for residential development. A projected fifteen-year time period to build the area suddenly collapsed into a four- to five-year completion schedule. In the ten years between 1986 and 1996, Kelowna's population grew by over 28,000 people. The impact on schools, hospitals and recreation facilities was profound.

Kelowna General Hospital got its first emergency department, more long-term beds were added to Cottonwoods Extended Care facility and plans were made to add another acute care and diagnostic centre to the hospital. In 1985 the province announced that a new cancer treatment centre would be built somewhere in the province. Kelowna, Prince George and Kamloops each began intense lobbying campaigns to have the facility built in their community. In 1989, amid a fair amount of animosity, Kelowna was chosen as the location. Ten years later, the BC Cancer Agency Centre for the Southern Interior opened. The Southern Interior Rotary Lodge opened a thirty-five-bed facility the same year to provide support and accommodation for patients undergoing or being assessed for cancer treatment.

As the population moved outward from the original town centre, so too did many of the services: schools at all levels have abandoned their downtown locations and been replaced by modern or renovated buildings

The Okanagan Mission's sports facilities include the Capital News Centre (named for the city's second newspaper), with its indoor soccer field and arenas, and the H₂O Fitness Centre, with its wave and lap pools and children's swimming areas. Water has been drained from the low-lying area and now encircles the fields. The Thomson farm, which once covered the area, is above the facility to the south. The fields to the left once were prime celery- and lettuce-growing areas. A golf course is in the left corner. | H. BRUST COLLECTION Q1615

in the suburbs. The Parkinson Recreation Centre continues to provide pool and recreation services. On the outskirts of town when it was built, it now sits in the community's geographic centre. Rutland has had the benefit of Athans Pool since the 1980s, and with recent renovation and expansion it continues to offer a broad range of programs to its members. With Okanagan Mission's population growth and the city's need for more ice rinks and playing fields, a new recreation complex opened on what was a portion of the Thomson family's farm. It took more than one try and a few years before the city was able to convince the Agricultural Land Commission to release the often boggy, waterlogged land for its use. The Capital News Centre opened in 2004 offering indoor soccer and baseball fields, ice rinks and fitness space. The H₂O Fitness Centre opened five years later in what had once been an adjacent field, offering state of the art swimming and wave pools.

2,4-D IS NOT FOR ME

By the mid-1970s, environmental issues began creeping onto the public agenda as Okanagan newspapers talked of threats from an "alien invader." Eurasian milfoil is a nuisance aquatic plant that spreads quickly, crowds out native species and creates a dense mat of weeds, which is a menace for boaters and unpleasant for swimmers. New plants grow from stems broken off the main plant, which float and re-establish themselves quickly nearby. The initial fear was that the weed would keep reproducing and invade greater and greater areas of the lake, making it unusable. As milfoil spread throughout the Okanagan lake system, outraged citizens mobilized against the province's attempts to eradicate the weed by applying the "moderately toxic" herbicides diquat and 2,4-D. Washington state was using the chemical and the BC government declared complaints by local environmental groups were irrational, unscientific, and their mantra of "2,4-D is not for me" unhelpful.

Kelowna's medical health officer, Dr. David Clarke, was alarmed, and when the mayor of the day declared the city would only harvest the weeds mechanically and not use the herbicides, the province refused to pay. They insisted that both methods had to be used to tackle the weeds, that pesticide drift would be minimal and swimmers would not be affected, and that they would avoid all water intakes. When the province declared Vaseux Lake, at the south end of the valley, off-limits for the herbicide application because it wanted to protect migratory birds, the lapse in logic didn't seem to register.

The South Okanagan Environmental Coalition in Penticton commissioned reports, applied for injunctions and threatened to jump into the weed beds where the pesticides were applied. The RCMP was called in and those running in municipal elections sidestepped making decisions by lobbying for a referendum. The herbicides were applied to about thirty-five acres of test plots in various Okanagan lakes. Injunctions to stop protesters were appealed in the Supreme Court; ministry officials declared the weeds were dying and the test was a success. Environmental groups looked at the same test patches and saw no change. By early 1979, the public outcry had become so loud that the province declared 2,4-D to be too dangerous to use and announced that mechanical harvesting would replace the herbicides.

There was a gradual shift away from eradicating the weed to controlling the spread, though some efforts to get rid of it persisted: jets of water were used to dig plants up by the roots but this also reconfigured the lake bottom and was stopped. Then the tops of the weeds were cut off and piled on the beaches until sunbathers fiercely complained about the ghastly smell. At other times the valley's scuba divers were hired to vacuum the lake bottom and suck up the milfoil roots. When the vacuum inhaled an unexploded mortar shell near Vernon and bomb demolition experts had to be hastily dispatched from Ottawa, the project ended.

As mechanical harvesting became the most viable option, a number of creative inventors devised machines to do the job: the "Aquanautus Billygoatus" won the $10,000 design prize, but the machine was never built. The Okanagan Basin Water Board took over weed management in 1981 with a combined program of rototilling the weed beds during the winter and harvesting them in the summer. They built their own machinery, ingeniously adapted it when necessary, and then retrieved the machines when they sank. The board continues to manage Eurasian milfoil within the Okanagan Lake systems and has been successful enough that the weeds rarely show up on the public's radar today. Though most of the story of the environmentalist community's adamant stand against 2,4-D use in the valley's lakes has been lost to time, resident action was enormously significant in preserving the somewhat tenuous quality of the Okanagan's water supply.

EXPLODING DEVELOPMENT

When the northern part of Glenmore Valley was absorbed into greater Kelowna in the 1973 boundary expansion, it was recognized that the bottom lands were plagued with frost pockets and clay soil, which challenged even the most stalwart orchardists. Kelowna applied to the Agricultural Land Commission for the release of Glenmore's valley floor from the new Agricultural Land Reserve in 1977. This was the first large-scale application received by the commission, and by the time decisions were made BC had slid into economic turmoil. All the development in the area stopped and the growth that drove it ground to a halt. Between 1981 and 1986, Kelowna's population only grew by two thousand people and there was almost no demand for new housing.

By the end of the 1980s, the world had begun to change and developers suddenly converged on Glenmore landowners, wanting to buy their property. Large homes on small lots began to proliferate as walled retirement communities appeared amid discussions about whether this new kind of housing was a benefit to the community or not. The city carved out large slices of land for future roads, and the landscape was soon devoid of trees as the Glenmore Valley was transformed from its rural roots into an urban community in an astoundingly short time. The area grew by seven and eight percent per year. Kelowna's population, between 1991 and 1996, grew from 75,950 to 89,442. The majority of that development was in the Glenmore Valley. The clay soil created challenges for builders, more domestic water users tapped into the Irrigation District system and the social fabric of the community was challenged by the rapidity of the change.

IT'S A HIGH PRICE TO PAY

The turmoil that followed the creation of the Agriculture Land Reserve continued as the original plan to pay farmers for the development potential of their land was scrapped. A farm income stabilization program was created in its place and continued until 1991. At that time, there were about 26,000 acres of orchards in the valley, most of which were apples. As government support declined, growers found it increasingly difficult to maintain their orchards and respond to changing market preferences. The amount of fruit being produced also declined, as did the infrastructure supporting the

Farmers' markets and farm-gate sales divert increasing amounts of each year's crop. Many, including those who still support collective selling, now take advantage of the opportunity to sell independently as well. Most operate from spring to fall in communities throughout the Okanagan.
| SHARRON SIMPSON COLLECTION

orchardists. Between 1957 and 1972, the number of co-op societies and packinghouses had shrunk from thirty-six to fourteen. The number of independent shippers fell from twenty to four during the same period. In 1998, those fourteen packinghouses became four. In 2008, the four remaining co-ops—in Osoyoos, Oliver, Kelowna and Winfield—folded into one operating company, the Okanagan Tree Fruit Co-operative. It owns four packinghouses with BC Tree Fruits Ltd. as its marketing company. Three independents also remain in operation.

ALL THOSE APPLES

Events beyond the Okanagan have had a profound impact on the valley's orchards. Washington had no apple industry during the 1930s and 1940s, but when W.A.C. Bennett opened the province for business and built hydroelectric dams on the Columbia River as part of that plan, he signed on to cross-border water sharing agreements. Before long the Columbia River Irrigation Project was irrigating the Wenatchee Valley, and Washington's Red Delicious apples began taking over traditional Okanagan markets, often selling at a lower price. Then Wenatchee began calling itself the "Apple Capital of the World." For awhile, government support for orchard replanting programs in BC helped growers to change to more marketable varieties and meet the competition. Those programs, for the most part, have vanished.

AN OKANAGAN WITH NO APPLES?

Though apples are Canada's most popular fruit and the Okanagan's biggest cash crop, the industry is struggling to survive. Many orchardists wonder about the future as they deal with competition from low-cost imports, changing consumer preferences, bad weather, low prices, labour problems and increasing overhead. It's impossible for people to imagine the Okanagan without its orchards, though many orchardists are concerned about their survival. In better times, packinghouses were located at railroad sidings, dotted among the orchards and scattered up and down the Okanagan. Now there are only about eight hundred orchardists in the valley and, since the 2008 amalgamation, the single Okanagan Tree Fruit Co-op. This one organization receives, stores, grades and packs apples, pears, cherries, peaches, nectarines, apricots, crabapples, prunes, plums and table grapes. It also stores and warehouses the fruit and uses BC Tree Fruits Ltd. for sales and marketing.

The early favourites—the McIntosh, Yellow and Red Delicious, and Spartans—have lost some of their popularity and been replaced by the Galas. Growers of the Royal Gala and the Aurora Golden Gala now risk producing into an oversupplied market, and the Golden Gala is no longer commercially viable because its unpredictable markings have reduced its market appeal. The Ambrosia is the newest and most popular variety to be introduced. The variety seeded itself in Similkameen Valley in a new planting and when pickers kept devouring the apples from that particular tree, the orchardist knew he had something special. It's taken a few years for production to reach commercial levels but this new crisp arrival is now in demand.

The number of orchard acres is shrinking and production along with it. The drop from the maximum of 10 million boxes of apples produced in the late 1980s to 3 million boxes today is significant. With only about eight thousand acres now planted in apples and grapes at about nine thousand acres, the Okanagan Valley's agricultural landscape is in the midst of significant change. The injustice of the system rankles the orchardists: the cost of land is so high that new orchards are unlikely. Various levels of government promise to support programs like the Sterile Insect Release (SIR) program, which reduces the need for pesticides, and then renege on their commitment and the cost falls to orchardists. As houses cover the hillsides, wildlife are driven down onto the valley floor and into the orchards: deer are notorious for taking one bite out of a peach, a pear or an apple and then moving on to the next. Orchards that previously didn't need fencing must now be enclosed to save the crop.

Today, the Wenatchee area has over 170,000 acres of orchards and *is* likely the apple capital of the world. The Okanagan, its nearest competitor, is fast becoming the smallest producer in Canada. Washington dumps its apples into BC and the industry is too small to be able to fight back. Grocery chains undermine local growers for a cent or two a pound and consumers don't seem to notice—or care. The replant programs, which were a major factor in establishing the grape industry, have not been available to apple growers for some time. Orchardists who can no longer survive financially are pulling out their trees and returning their land to hay and pasture... and turning the clock back a century, to before the rangeland was divided into small acreages so it could be planted in orchards.

Kelowna and the northern part of the valley are prime apple-growing areas. Orchardists feel they are losing both government and community support to maintain what most residents see as an integral part of their community. Will we notice when we no long see or smell the apple blossoms? What will replace the apples if they are no longer a visible marker of the history and abundance of the Okanagan? It's a question worth pondering.

The apple by-products business is also changing. Sun-Rype Products Ltd. continues to buy industry culls though at today's price of between twenty and twenty-eight dollars a bin, it's a very thin return for the growers. The company is also diversifying its product line and has recently purchased Yakama Juice in Washington state. The company, previously owned by the Confederated Tribes and Bands of the Yakama Nation, has been a key supplier of Sun-Rype products for several years. The purchase also gives Sun-Rype processing and manufacturing facilities and expanded marketing opportunities in the US.

Orchards with even greater density have become commonplace and are more compact overall with the planting of dwarf trees. Only short ladders, if any, are needed to harvest the crop. | SHARRON SIMPSON COLLECTION

The Kelowna Story: An Okanagan History

The first apple trees planted in the Okanagan grew to enormous heights. Pickers moved and then climbed heavy wooden ladders, buckets in hand, to pick the crop. The ladders ranged from eight to twenty-four feet in height, which was measured by the number of rungs: eight rungs, eight feet. | KELOWNA PUBLIC ARCHIVES 2223

WINE TAKES OVER

The Okanagan's wine industry went through a remarkable transformation during these years. Vineyards of hybrid grapes had been part of the Kelowna landscape since the 1930s when most were shipped to the fresh fruit markets on the Prairies. Yet it wasn't a profitable venture and many growers grew tomatoes between the rows to sustain themselves. These grapes were also used to make the early Okay sparkling white wine and Calona's Royal Red when efforts to make apple wine weren't successful. Some Okanagan grapes were also sent to the Growers Winery in Victoria to replace the loganberries they had started out with. When apple prices dipped, many orchardists dug up their trees and planted grapes.

The Rittich brothers arrived in the Okanagan from Hungary in the 1930s with years of experience working in various European vineyards and wineries. They experimented with forty varieties of vinifera (the classic European wine grape) vines, chose the most promising, pruned them low to the ground and buried them to ensure they survived the cold valley winters. The practice was popular in some parts of Europe but it didn't offer much of an incentive for the valley's growers to replace their old hybrid vines. Though not one of their original favourites, the Rittichs' Okanagan Riesling grape was successful and continues to be grown in many parts of the valley today.

BC's wine industry began to thrive when "pop" wine appeared in the early 1960s: Baby Duck, Love-A-Duck and Fuddle Duck, among others. They were wild concoctions of fermented grapes, sugar and water, and resembled soft drinks. A group of local businessmen were convinced they could capitalize on the country's new enthusiasm for wine and founded Mission Hill Winery in 1967, across the lake from Kelowna. The winery was sold three years later to the colourful Ben Ginter, a road builder and brewer from Prince George. He changed the winery's name to Uncle Ben's Gourmet Wines. Other wineries struggled to keep up with exploding demand for pop-style wines and encouraged growers to plant more hardy hybrids: quantity mattered more than quality. When winemakers couldn't get enough local grapes, they imported California grapes and unfinished wines to cover the shortfall.

By the end of the 1970s, tastes became somewhat more sophisticated and wine lovers began searching for alternatives to Baby Duck and his friends. Some of the imported products became popular and benefitted from marketing campaigns designed to tap into the appeal of the newly popular European wines: a Marlene Dietrich sound-alike sang the merits of Hochtaler's light white wine while Calona's Schloss Laderheim, with European castles on its label, became Canada's bestselling white wine. Both remain on the market today.

The valley's wineries held promise and the grape industry was stable, though its future looked modest at best. Then Dr. Becker, a German wine expert, was invited by his former student, Walter Gehringer, an assistant winemaker at Andrés Wine, to tour the valley and recommend ways to improve the industry. The study took almost ten years to complete but he identified some vinifera grape varieties that could thrive in the valley's climate. Many of these varieties have gone on to become the base for the Okanagan's now-thriving wine industry. The grape industry began to move beyond quantity and focus on quality: it was a seismic transition for one of the valley's oldest businesses.

However, it was NAFTA—the North American Free Trade Agreement—in 1989 that propelled the industry into what it has become. BC wines at the time were marked up by 50 percent in the liquor stores while imported wines were marked up 110 to 120 percent. The new trade agreement levelled the marketplace and BC wineries lost their competitive advantage. The industry was plunged into more uncertainty than it had ever experienced. Then the federal government provided a one-time grant to help the wineries adjust to the NAFTA requirements. BC's grape growers chose to use the grant of eight thousand dollars per acre to pull out their hybrid vines and the additional thousand dollars to replant viniferas. When the program was announced, over 3,000 Okanagan acres were planted in hybrids. When it ended, less than 350 remained. Today, over 9,000 acres of vinifera vines are planted throughout the valley.

In 1985, there were ten wineries in the valley, two of which were in Kelowna: Calona, dating back to the 1930s, and Uniacke Estate, part apple orchard and part vineyard. Uniacke was a local curiosity: its slightly Mediterranean building was perched on a remote hillside at the edge of the wilderness, south of town. The only access was along a gravel road. It was one of BC's first estate wineries, founded by David Mitchell in 1980 and named after his Nova Scotia ancestors. The winery struggled to survive and its future was uncertain until Ross Fitzpatrick, whose family had historic agricultural roots in the south end of the valley, purchased it in 1986.

Ross was initially involved with the tree fruit industry when, after being awarded a UBC degree in commerce and business administration, he became research director to the Royal Commission into the Tree-fruit Industry of British Columbia in 1958. When his work with the Royal Commission was finished, Ross worked for BC Tree Fruits before moving on to create and operate a number of businesses in the aerospace, oil and gas, and mining industries in various parts of the world.

Having a strong focus on environmental protection, Ross returned to the Okanagan and to his agricultural roots. With a commitment to promote value-added agriculture, Ross founded CedarCreek Estate Winery, and was among the first growers in the valley to plant vinifera grapes with the goal of producing premium quality wines. Ross Fitzpatrick was subsequently appointed to the Senate of Canada, and from 1998 to 2008 he represented both Canada and the Okanagan-Similkameen in a number of high-profile initiatives.

The development of CedarCreek mirrors the dramatic changes in what has become one of the Okanagan's leading industries. There are about two hundred wineries in the Okanagan Valley and neighbouring Similkameen Valley. Several have been named "Best in Canada." The area has become a destination for wine connoisseurs from around the world and has provided other entrepreneurs with opportunities to start complementary businesses. The Vintners Quality Alliance (VQA) program regulates and sets high standards for the area's wines. An abundance of creative, quirky and unique labels and colourful destination wineries are now nestled among the valley's lakes and mountains. In the past ten years alone, wine sales have gone from just under $7 million to over $160 million and the average price per bottle has gone from under seven dollars to about twenty. Vineyards have altered the valley's landscape, and the wineries have changed the area's tourist focus and conferred a certain cachet and ambiance to the Okanagan that didn't exist before. The journey from table grapes to vineyards, wineries and "best in class" wines is a remarkable Okanagan success story.

During this same period, much of the southern Okanagan converted to grape production. With the VQA guaranteeing one hundred percent BC-grown grapes—and the market cachet that goes with that—the industry has developed a loyal following. The rapid expansion is now raising questions, however: is the market over-supplied, and might consumers be driven to less expensive imports and away from the costlier local wines in a recession-plagued marketplace?

Vineyards cover valley hillsides and share the beautiful views of Okanagan Lake with surrounding housing developments. Windmills dot the landscape to move the air and keep frost from settling on the vines. | SHARRON SIMPSON COLLECTION

TOURISM

Kelowna bills itself as an international, year-round tourist destination, and relies heavily on the industry for employment opportunities and its economic well-being. The projected 1.2 million annual visitors are tied to 6,900 direct jobs and $130 million in revenue: tourism is one of the largest economic generators in the city. Outdoor activities are the main draw and take advantage of the surrounding mountains, lakes, beaches, forests, orchards and vineyards. Two thirds of the revenue flows into the area in July and August, as water sports and boating remain the biggest draw. However, subtle changes are taking place—the area's rich cultural heritage is now being showcased by world-class wineries, restaurants, museums and galleries.

The Apple Triathlon, the Centre of Gravity beach festival and the Dragon Boat Festival currently fill the calendar during the warmer months while biking, hiking and wine festivals fill the valley's shoulder seasons. The city draws meetings, conventions and sporting events such as the BC Summer Games and International World Children's Winter Games, which attracts people of all ages. For many, the area's fifteen golf courses, open for play seven or eight months a year, are the biggest draw. Some courses wind around old orchards while others are nestled among the pines and rocks.

Big White and neighbouring Silver Star Mountain are both about an hour away and attract skiers from around the world. Several cross-country ski and snowmobile trails are nearby and a downtown outdoor skating rink is available to all. Kelowna is billed as a city with a progressive modern lifestyle and a wide variety of amenities for tourists. That is also why so many people have moved to Kelowna, or have chosen to have a holiday home in the area.

In a fiercely competitive marketplace, Kelowna works hard to both retain visitors and attract new ones from among those looking for a new and unique travel experience. However, tourism and resource-based businesses are no longer Kelowna's only major industries. Though still in its infancy, Kelowna's thriving technology sector has made an impact in the broader marketplace. A well-educated, well-paid workforce has begun to move to town as some of the more traditional industries have moved on: Western Star Trucks departed in 2002 and the call centres that took over some of their space departed a few years later. Various high-tech companies have their headquarters in the Landmark Technology Centre, and the Okanagan Science and Technology Council was formed as a resource and lobbying group.

OKANAGAN UNIVERSITY COLLEGE

Okanagan College gradually took on an air of permanence in 1978 when construction began on the new campus at the technical school's KLO Road site. Business and fine arts courses were added to the curriculum, though they had to be taught off-campus for two years until new buildings were ready. That fall, 2,230 full- and part-time students enrolled in vocational, career and university-transfer classes at the one site for the first time. Then came the recession and cutbacks, and the Vernon, Penticton and Salmon Arm campuses feared for their existence—delegations were sent to board meetings to argue against possible closures. Labour turmoil and protest rallies blanketed the province and swept the college up in the furor. The board locked the faculty out over a pay dispute and students occupied Premier Bennett's constituency office in protest.

Once the turmoil passed, it wasn't long before both faculty and students wanted more than just the two-year academic program offered. Access to higher education, closer to home and at a reasonable cost, was becoming a priority for everyone in spite of the government's 1987 declaration that a university in the Interior wasn't part of its plans. The bumper sticker "Getting there by Degrees" began showing up in the community; the Kelowna Chamber of Commerce created the "Friends of Okanagan College" organization and circulated petitions, sold T-shirts, raised money and lobbied the government. Statistics were on their side: only six percent of Okanagan students received a post-secondary education, versus eighteen percent in the Lower Mainland. An interim solution appeared in 1989 when the college began offering third- and fourth-year courses leading to a University of British Columbia Bachelor of Arts or Bachelor of Science degree, as well as a University of Victoria Bachelor of Science degree in nursing and a Bachelor of Education degree. It was a complicated way to achieve the desired end but applications for admission skyrocketed.

The existing facilities weren't adequate and space on the KLO site was limited, but plans went ahead to extend labs and build more classrooms. When the college president was driving a deputy minister to the airport and happened to mention his concerns about the college's confined space, the search for a new site was soon underway. A minimum of 300 acres was needed, hopefully nearby, and on land not within the ALR. The first choice was in Okanagan Mission but it was in the ALR and the application to remove the designation was refused. The search continued until a property near the airport was chosen to become the college's North Kelowna campus. It was farther from town than was hoped for, but highway access was good. The original KLO site was also "out of town" when the technical school began but development soon followed, and filled the spaces in between.

It was two years before buildings appeared on the north campus. The government was still operating on the college model and scrutinized every minute decision. Others were thinking of it as a university. College faculty offices were to be 80 square feet while university faculty offices were entitled to one hundred square feet. How many square feet should be planned per student? How many volumes should be planned for the library? And the list went on and on. The arts building, science building, library and student services building, along with two residences, were opened in January 1993. The official opening five months later drew nine thousand people—it was a great community celebration.

In 1995, Okanagan College officially became Okanagan University College (OUC) and the change in legislation finally enabled it to confer its own bachelor degrees in a number of fields as well as honorary doctorates in law, letters and technology. Degrees were offered at OUC's Kelowna campus while Salmon Arm, Vernon, and Penticton became more secure with new campuses as well, offering two-year academic courses and developing their own unique identities. Achieving academic autonomy had been a convoluted and contentious process, complicated by historic valley animosities, but the multi-campus college had finally become a reality.

FROM OUC TO UBCO

The creation of OUC didn't end the debate about its being a college or a university. Some felt the dream of a full-status university was fading and their institution was becoming a "glorified community college." Vocal advocates lined up on both sides of the issue. A tuition freeze imposed in 1996 by the NDP government had limited funding, enrolments were declining and course offerings were limited. These were challenging times but no one was ready to eliminate the college's technology, trades, vocational and adult education programs. The problem became one of maintaining these programs while trying to create a university. A Liberal government ousted the NDP in 2001, fired the college board and improved funding to build a gymnasium at the north campus. It was, more or less, the gymnasium that had originally been promised by Premier W.A.C. Bennett when he opened Kelowna's BCIT campus in 1961. The fine arts, health and social work programs moved to the north campus and improvements were made to the KLO campus.

The solution came when an announcement was made in Victoria in March 2004 that OUC would be divided: the north campus would become the new University of British Columbia Okanagan (UBCO) and the Vernon, Salmon Arm, Penticton and Kelowna campuses would become Okanagan College… again.

Though some where initially skeptical, the two institutions have established their own identities and flourished. UBCO has added economic, social and academic value to both Kelowna and the region. The

Early morning on the University of BC Okanagan campus. Robert Lake and part of the adjacent Glenmore Valley were recently acquired by the university. | COURTESY OF UBCO

campus almost tripled in size in its first five years, enrolments grew from 3,500 to over 7,000, and research funding increased as UBCO focussed on issues relevant to the Okanagan: water, biodiversity, urban sprawl, indigenous rights and traditional knowledge. Value-added agriculture and organic farming was also on its agenda. UBCO was identified as the site of BC's fourth medical school a year later. A new clinical teaching building opened at Kelowna General Hospital in January 2010 in conjunction with a new health sciences building at the UBCO campus.

In June 2010, UBCO added 104 hectares (256 acres) of adjacent farmland to its campus. The land doubled the size of UBCO and was added to UBC's endowment lands, which the institution holds in perpetuity. The land is in the ALR and includes Robert Lake, an environmentally sensitive wildlife refuge. Though a land use plan has yet to be worked out, the new acquisition is expected to enhance the university's research and teaching opportunities and serve as a living laboratory for future students.

In spite of some misgivings about the future of a reconfigured Okanagan College, shedding the north campus and refocussing its mandate has paid enormous dividends. The four main campuses have expanded both their physical plants and the number of programs offered. Full-time equivalent enrolment exceeds 8,500, while over 12,000 students are enrolled in continuing education courses. Learning centres offer courses in Revelstoke, Princeton, Keremeos, Oliver and Osoyoos. Trades courses that were originally only offered in Kelowna are now offered throughout the Okanagan Valley. Two-year academic programs continue to be offered and allow students to transfer to the university. Clarity of purpose and drive has clearly paid dividends.

ARRIVING AND DEPARTING

In the 1970s, driving to Kelowna from anywhere still took a long time. The Hope–Princeton Highway remained the main route from Vancouver as it was quicker and easier to drive than the Trans-Canada route through the Fraser Canyon. However, it still didn't bring travellers directly to Kelowna. To the east, the Trans-Canada Highway opened over the Rogers Pass in 1962, which officially completed the highway (though Newfoundland Premier Joey Smallwood refused to attend in the ceremony, calling the "completion" a sham as the route had not been extended to his province). But as important as the route was to Canada, the closest travellers got to the Okanagan was Sicamous, which was even farther from Kelowna than the end of the Hope–Princeton Highway.

By the late 1970s, the BC government decided it was time to improve access to the Interior and began planning the Coquihalla Highway. It would be a toll highway through the mountains and sections of the new route would be built near the original Kettle Valley Railway line: the Shakespearean place names Romeo, Juliet, Lear, Iago, Shylock, Jessica and Portia along the highway still locate the train stations chosen by Andrew McCulloch, the engineer who built the remarkable railway. The new highway would be built in three phases: the first connected Hope and Merritt, while the second connected Merritt and Kamloops; passenger cars would pay a toll of eight dollars. Most importantly, the highway had to be open in time for travellers to visit Vancouver's Expo 86.

Though the fair opened amid considerable skepticism, it signalled the end of the gloom and confrontational mindset that had engulfed the province during the recent recession. As 22 million people from across the province and around the world flocked to Vancouver for the five-month party, it was hard not to get caught up in the enthusiasm and excitement. Newspaper headlines were full of accusations about over-budget construction costs because of the rush to complete the highway before Expo opened. A much publicized inquiry followed, though it made little difference.

The new highway cut an hour off the drive between Hope and Kamloops and provided another route into the BC Interior. It was still a long way from Kelowna and it wasn't until phase three, the Coquihalla Connector, was built that Kelowna finally felt some benefit. On October 1, 1990, large crowds gathered at the lookout near the end of the highway where Okanagan Lake first came into view. Bumper stickers encouraged motorists to "Discover the Missing Link" as Mayor George Waldo of Peachland, the closest community to the highway, told visitors to keep their sticky fingers off his pristine valley. Either they didn't hear him or ignored his cautionary words as the highway not only shortened the travel time between Kelowna and Vancouver, but turned visitors into residents and added to Kelowna's 1990s economic and construction boom.

A SECOND BRIDGE

The first Okanagan Lake Bridge was meant to solve the problem of crossing the lake for all time. By the turn of the century, it was already over capacity. With added traffic and growth, the old floating bridge was a bottleneck—its original two lanes had become three and there was talk of reconfiguring it to four. Perhaps it was cheaper to build a new bridge, one that was elevated over City Park and downtown to avoid the traffic lights? Then a four-lane tunnel was suggested. Though it was an interesting made-in-Kelowna solution, it was too expensive, too innovative and never given serious consideration.

Another bridge was built alongside the original in 2008; the five-lane W.R. Bennett Bridge was opened by Premier Gordon Campbell. Its namesake, former premier Bill Bennett, joined hundreds of people following the Kelowna Pipe Band to the mid-span ribbon cutting ceremony. Okanagan Lake presents unique engineering challenges for

The W.R. Bennett Bridge was completed in 2008 to replace the fifty-year-old Okanagan Lake Bridge. | STUART KERNAGHAN, XYPHOTOS.CA

bridge builders as its bottom is unstable and changing: the W.R. Bennett Bridge is the only floating bridge in Canada and one of only eight in the world.

The new bridge was designed to accommodate traffic well into the future, though early morning reports already suggest congestion. City Park was again reconfigured, to accommodate the re-engineered approaches, and a new interchange on the west side along with a second a short way along the highway keep traffic moving on that side of the lake. In spite of attempts to streamline traffic flow through the city, Highway 97—sometimes called Harvey Avenue from pre-bridge times—is lined with a succession of traffic lights that are synchronized better some days than others. There are occasional conversations about designing another bridge and a route around the city, but it isn't likely to happen anytime soon.

The Kelowna Story: An Okanagan History

When the new bridge was built a few options were considered for the disposal of the old bridge: reusing the pontoons that were still reasonably intact, then sinking ones that were too decrepit to reuse or breaking them up for disposal. Kelowna City Council expressed interest in transforming some of the pontoons into a pier or a breakwater, but studies showed the cost of hauling them to the site and rehabilitating them would be several million dollars. The idea came to a controversial end.

It soon became apparent that no one was interested in reusing either the pontoons or the causeways at either end of the old bridge, and plans were made to sink them in the deepest part of the lake. That would have been the most cost-effective disposal method and had the least overall environmental impact. Studies revealed that nothing was growing or alive at the bottom of the lake: it was a layer of loose grey silt or clay overlain with a layer of black material, likely ash from forest fires. The biggest risk of dropping the pontoons into the lake would come from the plume of sediment that would rise as the concrete hit the bottom. Concern about polluting nearby water intakes was dismissed as residents would be notified and could take the necessary precautions. Then the public got involved, discussing unsafe levels of arsenic, chromium and nickel, and whose measurement was accurate, and whether enough samples had been taken. Eventually, the piers and pontoons were hauled to the graving dock near Bear Creek Provincial Park, where the new bridge had been assembled. They were demolished and trucked to a landfill. A few small iron girders are all that remain of the old bridge: they have been made into a curious orange sculpture that sits on the grass at the eastern end of the new bridge.

BETTER AIR AND THE REMNANTS OF RAIL

Improved air service has also changed travel patterns in and out of the city: more airlines, carrying more passengers, travel to more destinations, and more frequently. Kelowna International Airport has clearly eclipsed its neighbours and has become one of the city's most vital economic engines. It is also the tenth busiest airport in the country. Fifteen years ago about 300,000 passengers arrived and departed from the terminal each year; today, that number is closer to 1.4 million passengers. Penticton's airport, which offered the first scheduled air service out of the valley, now serves about 70,000 passengers a year. Vernon's airport offers charter services only.

Kelowna's runway has been extended to handle long-haul flights from Europe and Australia, and seasonal charters offer regular service to Mexico and Las Vegas. Plans are underway to double the size of the existing terminal, add a new customs hall to facilitate international flights and improve baggage handling. A cluster of significant aviation-related businesses has also grown up around the airport. It's a remarkable transformation from the early 1950s, when propeller-driven planes landed on a grass runway and got their instructions from the "control tower" perched on the flat deck of a truck. Kelowna's once-struggling airport became one of the fastest-growing in North America.

The railways have all but gone except for the Kelowna Pacific Railway Ltd. which continues to provide service to the city, handling about sixteen thousand carloads of forest, grain, and industrial products a year. Only about 170 kilometres (106 miles) of mainline track remain. There are occasional quiet rumblings about restoring some form of passenger service along that line—to UBCO, or to Vernon, or to the CPR mainline in Sicamous. The comments aren't loud but as long as the track remains, the opportunity also remains. Kelowna's historic ties to Okanagan Lake also resonate among a few who wonder if some form of passenger travel might return to the lake in the future. As air quality deteriorates, traffic congestion worsens and gas becomes more expensive and less available, Kelowna might look to its past for solutions.

A TROUBLING END TO THE KELOWNA REGATTA

As Kelowna muddled through the recession of the 1980s, the legendary Kelowna International Regatta became increasingly irrelevant, and the opening of Expo 86 in Vancouver underscored just how much the entertainment world had changed. The Regatta's bathtub races, logging shows, beer gardens and bikini parade no longer attracted families, and the event's entire atmosphere changed. Kelowna's first riot broke out on a hot August night in 1986. Though everyone said that Regatta wasn't at fault and young people had been gathering downtown and drinking openly for years, the unrest broke out on the Saturday night of Regatta. People had been driven out of City Park when the carnival rides and the beer garden closed, and began gathering on Bernard Avenue. Those leaving a rock concert at Memorial Arena added to the crowd, and police stepped up enforcement as its size grew. By nine p.m. there was a very palpable sense on the street that something was going to happen. Bernard Avenue was closed to traffic so everyone abandoned their cars and congregated around the Sails. Beer bottles started flying, police reinforcements were called in from Penticton and Vernon, and the Kelowna Fire Department began using their hoses as water cannons. As tear gas began spreading through the area, windows were smashed, stores were looted and the mayor read the Riot Act. The next day, the town was in shock. Downtown store owners were furious and 105 people had been arrested. The police chief said it was "the usual crowd of idiots," while the mayor said those involved "were just insane, like little animals… mostly punky kids too young to drink" and who should be shipped off for military training.

A new police chief and a new mayor had taken over by the following year and plans were in place to avoid a repeat of the previous year's events. Word of Kelowna's Regatta party had spread far and wide. Roadblocks set up outside town didn't make much difference. Beer flowed freely as crowds gathered on Bernard Avenue and chanted, "Let's riot, let's riot!" Others climbed onto rooftops and threw the rocks and sticks they'd imported in the trunks of their cars. Windows were broken, stores looted, trash cans upturned and nearby residents terrified. The mayor read the Riot Act, and the crowds eventually drifted away. The police chief said the army couldn't have stopped the destruction, and store owners were even more furious.

The rest of the 1987 Regatta carried on as planned and the event was considered a success with thirty-three thousand attending. Everyone acknowledged that the Regatta hadn't caused the riot, but it *had* become a beacon for those looking for trouble, and it was subsequently noted that nothing had been planned for the fourteen- to twenty-two-year-olds, the primary age of the rioters. But no one seemed to know what to do about it. The Regatta had lost much of its community support by this time, though some thought the decline had started when the Regatta grandstand was destroyed by fire eighteen years earlier. Times had changed, and when city council cancelled future Regattas, some were outraged, some were relieved and most didn't care.

A hardy few tried to keep the Regatta tradition alive… they called their event "the Regretta." A parade of sorts and a breakfast were all that remained, and that only lasted for a couple of years. After eighty-two years, Kelowna had outgrown what had been its signature event, its International Regatta.

Today's Ogopogo is a friendly cute monster who sits at the end of Bernard Avenue, and his green fluffy likeness is found in local tourist shops. This is quite a transformation from the early days when settlers patrolled the shores of Okanagan Lake to protect their families from the monster's attacks. The MV *Fintry Queen* is docked behind the Ogopogo statue. | STUART KERNAGHAN, XYPHOTOS.CA

The Kelowna Story: An Okanagan History

OGOPOGO'S STILL AROUND

Though the Regatta didn't survive, the Ogopogo did. In 1983, the Okanagan Similkameen Tourist Association posted a $1 million reward for proof of the Ogopogo's existence: acceptable proof would be a photograph or the actual monster. Greenpeace became concerned about zealous bounty hunters. When a group of young men fired their rifles at the monster from shore, the Attorney General declared the Ogopogo an endangered species under the Fisheries Act and proclaimed hunting the legendary monster illegal. In the years since, scientific and film crews from the US, Japan, Germany and Switzerland have come to the Okanagan, armed with sophisticated sonar devices and cameras, and searched around the lake monster's reputed home near Rattlesnake Island, at Squally Point. They have occasionally seen "something" but their findings have never been conclusive. Many books have been written, many television programs have aired and the mystery remains. However, both those who believe and those who don't agree that there is something mysterious in Okanagan Lake. Curious holes have appeared in the bottom of boats and many of those who have drowned in the lake have never been recovered. Is Ogopogo... or N´ha-a-itk... an explanation?

MISSION CREEK GREENWAY

Mission Creek begins in the Greystoke Mountains, about forty-three kilometres (twenty-seven miles) east of Kelowna, and contains almost a quarter of all the water that flows into Okanagan Lake. It was named for the mission Father Pandosy built nearby in 1859. Cottonwoods frame its shoreline, kokanee—the land-locked salmon once the diet staple of local Native communities—are slowly returning and there is hope that the meanders removed during the flood control work of the 1950s might eventually be restored. The creek has always been central part of valley life, and in 1996 a group of residents decided something had to be done to preserve it. Access to the creek channel was being encroached upon and its pristine natural surroundings were at risk of being destroyed.

The Friends of Mission Creek joined a number of user groups, including the Westbank First Nation, and began an audacious plan to create a pathway along the banks of the creek—soon to be called the Mission Creek Greenway. What started as the dream of a few mushroomed into a community-wide campaign to sell the idea, and to raise funds to buy the land and build the trails. Over six and a half hectares (sixteen acres) of land was donated, as well as almost half a million dollars: many signed on and bought a metre of trail for fifty dollars; schoolchildren took field trips, painted pictures and cleaned up the creek. Kelowna was blanketed with the preservation message as shopping centres hosted displays, raffles were held, signs appeared in buses and local businesses displayed posters in their windows. It was a remarkable campaign.

The initial seven-kilometre (four and a half mile) trail opened in October 1997, the same year Mission Creek was given BC Heritage River status. The Greenway provides a quiet, natural retreat for legions of walkers, bikers, runners and horses who use the trail throughout the changing seasons. The songs of red-winged blackbirds filter through the trees as the sound of nearby traffic gradually disappears behind the screen of pines, cottonwoods and Saskatoon bushes. The area is an easily accessible and peaceful retreat for those wanting to escape the pavement and bustle of the city.

The Mission Creek Greenway has become one of Kelowna's most popular urban trails. It is easily accessible, open to all and offers an unparalleled opportunity for residents to enjoy each of nature's seasons on their doorstep. | H. BRUST COLLECTION Q6924

Phase two of the popular Greenway project opened in 2005. At just less than ten kilometres (six miles) in length, this new trail is more rugged, narrower and more challenging that the first phase of the project. It features a wetland boardwalk, three pedestrian bridges and stairs below the Gallagher's Canyon Golf Course. The views of some of the area's most unique geological features are spectacular as the trail winds through Scenic Canyon Regional Park and past Layer Cake Mountain, a 200-metre (650-foot) layered rock face formed millions of years ago by cooling lava. It continues on past Pinnacle Rock and the Hoodoos, the glacial deposits that line the canyon escarpment. Cave-like openings at the bottom of the high rock wall are the only evidence of the Chinese fortune-seekers who panned the sand and gravel deposits for gold over a century ago. Interpretive kiosks tell of the area's rich history and unusual features while a viewing platform and trail guides add to the amenities.

Phase three of the Greenway is now being planned, and will stretch from KLO Creek to the beautiful and currently inaccessible Mission Creek Falls. The Greenway is a remarkable achievement for a dedicated group of volunteers whose efforts transformed the dikes of Mission Creek into a unique community asset.

THE OKANAGAN MOUNTAIN FIRE

In 2003, an epic wildfire raged along the east side of Okanagan Lake and into the forest and residential neighbourhoods south of Kelowna, an area known as the South Slopes. Fire had ravaged the community before and residents had long been familiar with smoky air during the summer forest fire and orchard-burning seasons. But this was different. People watched in fascination as a small fire ignited by an early morning lightning strike spread across the dry mountainside. When it started across from Peachland at Squally Point, in Okanagan Mountain Park on the east side of the lake, the fire seemed a long way away. Everyone expected it to be contained. Over 240 wildfires were burning in the Southern Interior at the time and the Forest Service felt their crews and equipment were needed elsewhere. People took their lawn chairs to the beach and watched the smoke billow and glow in the setting sun. Record-breaking heat had blanketed the valley for weeks and the forests were already parched from the lack of rain: the result was almost inevitable. When the wind picked up, the layers of dry needles and leaves sucked in the flames, and then flared up all along the mountainside.

Over 1,000 hectares (2,400 acres) were burning within a day. The fire grew from 2,000 to 11,000 hectares (5,000 to 27,000 acres) in another day and raced along the dry rocky hillside. A fire break seventeen kilometres (ten and a half miles) long was built along Kelowna's southern boundary, but the flames flared up the trees and leapt across. Trees candled as their sap boiled and they too exploded into flame. Everyone expected it would stop: the sun shone as residents raked the needles under their pines, put sprinklers on their roofs and carried on with their usual summer activities. Bard on the Hill was performing Shakespeare's *A Midsummer Night's Dream* in the amphitheatre of Mission Hill Winery on the west side. The actors had to compete with the smoke and the audience's fascination with the flames advancing along the hill—they were across the lake but seemed so close. The smoke swirled and engulfed the performers and the audience.

A huge plume of smoke heads toward Kelowna in the setting sun. In the early days of the Okanagan Mountain Fire, residents were certain the flames would be contained and took their chairs to the beach for a better view. It wasn't long before heavy smoke and flying ash obliterated the sun. | SHARRON SIMPSON COLLECTION

"Awesome" barely describes the magnitude of the 2003 Okanagan Mountain Park fire. | H. BRUST COLLECTION Q9000

The wind had split at Squally Point and carried the flames northward toward Kelowna and southward to Naramata. The fire kept advancing and the first of what would become a series of evacuations was ordered for both communities. Many had little warning: the question everyone was asking was, "If you had to evacuate, what would you take?" In the panic some chose lamps and mattresses while others grabbed their animals, leapt into their cars and left their front doors open in the rush. Kelowna's fire department was familiar with structural fires but this was a whole new experience: smoke often screened the flames and obscured escape routes. Against advice, some lakeshore owners stayed behind to do what they could to save their homes, though most kept their boats nearby in case they needed to leave in a hurry.

People were drawn to the beaches to watch a succession of water bombers fly over Okanagan Lake Bridge, one after the other, dipping to skim along the lake's surface, fill their tanks and head back to drop their loads just minutes away. More evacuations were ordered and those fleeing often ended up stuck in traffic; horses, cows and chickens were rescued and moved to secure farms; people stayed with friends and used binoculars to see if their homes were burning. At one point, thirty thousand people were ordered to leave their homes: some returned only to be told to leave again.

Wildfires are so unpredictable, and sound like a jet revving up to take off. They create their own wind patterns and change direction with a turn in the road, a clump of trees or a gully: this house survives while the one next door doesn't. The Okanagan Mountain Fire was no different. The plastic garden furniture on one patio survived while the house right next to it was gone. Stones shattered; a boat stored in a garage became a puddle of fibreglass; flames would encircle and then miraculously retreat. The fire was so intense in other places that a mound of fine dust might be all that remained of a house and its contents.

The army arrived. Firefighters converged from across Canada and the US. Evacuation centres were set up as chunks of still-hot ash floated over the city. Fire Chief Gerry Zimmerman held regular media briefings to keep evacuees, the media and everyone else up to date. When asked if there was anything he needed, he jokingly said a cold beer would be nice... and it wasn't long before a refrigerated truck loaded with beer arrived at the fire hall. CedarCreek Winery built a firebreak, while St. Hubertus burned to the ground: smoke permeated both wineries' ripening grapes and they couldn't be used. In one night, 223 houses vanished.

When the wind died down, firefighters went looking for hotspots in tree roots and deep in the debris-covered forest floor. Then the wind returned and blew the fire up the hillsides into Myra Canyon and the surrounding area. In all, the fire took just over two weeks to destroy more than 25,000 hectares (62,000 acres) of forest and parkland and 239 homes. An inquiry followed, and when wildfires are spotted now, the response is immediate: water bombers, fire retardant and firefighters are on the scene in minutes.

THE KETTLE VALLEY TRESTLES

Although the Kettle Valley Railway (KVR) was never intended to be Kelowna's railway, the city has claimed the stretch of roadbed, trestles and tunnels above Okanagan Mission as its own. Now part of the Trans Canada Trail, the KVR not only draws local hikers and mountain bikers, but also tourists who arrive from all over the world to travel the awe-inspiring historical remnant. Myra Station, which is named for the daughter of a track-laying foreman (it's the first of the "daughter" stations), is Kelowna's access to the most scenic part of the old railway. Ruth and Lorna Stations—named for the daughters of Andrew McCulloch, the railway's chief engineer, and James Warren, president of the KVR system—follow, but no station buildings remain at any of the sites.

Myra Canyon is rocky and has numerous steep gorges along its sides, carved by creeks. The line's highest elevation, 1,260 metres (4,133 feet) above sea level, is just before the first tunnel while the lowest, 349 metres (1,145 feet), is at the Penticton terminus. It was challenging terrain to build a railway as it was essential to keep the grade under two percent to ensure efficient operation of the railway. Andrew McCulloch referred to Myra

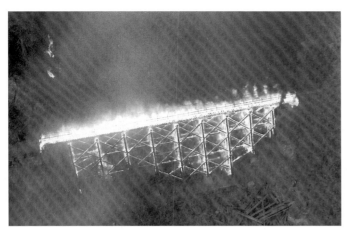

The Kettle Valley Railway

The photo on the far left shows the original wooden trestle over the west fork of Canyon Creek in 1915. The Okanagan Mountain Park fire of 2003 destroyed the Kettle Valley trestles (near left photo) and was a devastating blow to Kelowna as well as to the thousands of people who regularly biked or hiked the rail line. The trestles were fortunately restored to look very much like the originals (below photo). The platform across the ties, with railings on either side, ensures safe usage.

as that "damn bad canyon," increased the grade slightly and built a track that doubled back on itself not once, but twice, by adding a curved tunnel through a rock face, plus another tunnel, and building twenty wooden trestles. The Myra Canyon stretch of the KVR remains an engineering marvel in the annals of railway construction. It also makes for a relatively easy hike or bike ride through the wilderness, with spectacular views of Okanagan Lake.

Many changes have been made over the life of the rail line. The original trestles and tunnel supports had a life expectancy of about fifteen years. By the time the last train crossed the tracks in 1972, two trestles had been replaced by steel bridges while the remaining trestles were fourth-generation wooden ones. The last replacements had been built in the mid-1950s and treated with creosote in hopes of doubling their lifespan.

The BC government acquired the track right-of-way and lifted the rails in 1980. The trestles remained in place but the ties deteriorated: some were missing and others were vandalized. The adventurous were undeterred and continued to drive cars across the trestles and carry their own boards to lay across in place of the missing ties. Others hiked or biked across and around the increasingly hazardous trestles and made their way through the rock-filled tunnels. A death and several serious injuries soon had the government calling for the area to be closed to the public.

An enthusiastic group of volunteers formed the Myra Canyon Trestle Restoration Society in 1992 to repair the trestles and make them both more accessible and safer. Two years later, a boardwalk crossed each trestle with guardrails along each side, all as a result of volunteer labour, scrounged materials, borrowed equipment and a few donated dollars. The group went on to repair the trail bed and the tunnel portal, and then removed some of the collapsed rock from inside the tunnel. Over fifty thousand visitors flocked to the area by the late 1990s, which soon became one of the top fifty biking destinations in the world. It took a few years, but the canyon eventually became part of a new Myra–Bellevue Provincial Park. The trestles were added to the National Historic Sites register in 2003 and the route became an important link in the Trans Canada Trail.

Seven months later, twelve of the sixteen wooden trestles were destroyed by the Okanagan Mountain fire. Even water bombers dropping fire retardant on the trestles couldn't stop the devastation. The winds changed and towering flames could be seen along the hillside as the succession of the old creosote trestles were engulfed in flames. It was a demoralizing blow, even for those who had never been near the old rail line.

Because of its provincial and national importance, disaster relief funds became available and a number of those who worked on the original restoration became part of the Myra Canyon Reconstruction Project. Their goal was to rebuild the trestles to resemble the originals as closely as possible. Bridge builders gathered from around the province, large Douglas firs were brought from the Lower Mainland and by a year after the blaze, the first trestle had been rebuilt. A few more were restored during each of the next four years, and in 2008 the area was again accessible to the public. At the opening celebration, bagpipes led "Andrew McCulloch" and a joyous and unexpectedly enormous crowd along the restored railbed and through the tunnels. The rebuilding of the trestles became symbolic of the area's recovery after the devastating fire, and the Kettle Valley Railway finally, after many years, truly became Kelowna's railway, and one of the city's most popular tourist attractions.

A HOCKEY REVIVAL

Organized hockey has been the centrepiece of Kelowna's sports scene since the early 1950s. The original Kelowna Packers were followed by the Buckaroos, the Wings, another Packers team, and the Spartans. Memorial Arena was home ice for all of them, but it became harder over the years to sustain the franchise and entice fans to fill the arena's 2,600 hard seats. The promise of a new arena enticed the Rockets of the Western Hockey League to leave Tacoma, Washington, and relocate to Kelowna. The only trouble was that the referendum to build the rink was defeated and the team had to play in the old Memorial Arena, until a partnership with a private developer resulted in the building of the six-thousand-seat Skyreach (now Prospera) Place. Built on what had earlier been part of the CNR marshalling yards, the arena opened in 1999 as the home of the Kelowna Rockets.

The Rockets drew Kelowna residents back to the hockey rink when for three straight years (2003, 2004 and 2005) they qualified to play in Memorial Cup tournaments. The cup is awarded annually to the Canadian Hockey League (CHL) junior ice hockey club that wins the round robin tournament between the host team and the champions of the CHL's three member leagues. The Rockets won the Memorial Cup for the first time in franchise history in 2004, the same year they were selected to host the event. Every game in the tournament was sold out and the whole city celebrated their team's victory. In 2009, and for the fourth time in seven years, the Kelowna Rockets qualified again to play in the Memorial Cup. Though the team was defeated by the Windsor Spitfires in a tournament held in Rimouski, Quebec, a loyal hometown fan base continues to fill Prospera Place throughout the season.

The multipurpose building is also used for various community events including monster truck shows, roller derbies, craft shows and figure skating performances. Cirque du Soleil, Elton John, Harry Belafonte and Sarah McLachlan are among the various artists who perform in the venue. Though limited to eight thousand concert seats, Kelowna's Prospera Place is a popular choice for many artists travelling between larger venues in Calgary and Vancouver.

THE SIMPSON COVENANT

In the early summer of 2008, Tom Smithwick, legal counsel for the Save the Heritage Simpson Covenant Society, prefaced his final argument in the BC Supreme Court with the words: "Your Worship, we should not be here today."

The story began in the mid-1940s when the City of Kelowna was looking for property large enough to build a city hall and house other civic services. Stanley M. Simpson had purchased the old Kelowna Saw Mill from David Lloyd-Jones in 1942, and continued to run the mill until it was destroyed by fire in 1944. The sawmill had had sheds and wharves along the lakeshore north of Bernard Avenue since the late 1800s, while old buildings and piles of lumber and sawdust were scattered across another 16 or so acres that extended eastward to Ellis Street and northward to near today's courthouse. The city approached Simpson to see if he would sell them the land.

Though he had postwar plans to locate a new type of building supply store at the foot of Pendozi Street (the present location of the Bennett Fountain), S.M. agreed to sell the land to the city, under specific conditions, which he attached as a covenant on the land. The initial agreement was for seven-plus acres, but it wasn't long before the lakeshore portion, across the street from the original parcel, was also included.

The covenant specified that the land could only be used for civic purposes, for the use and enjoyment of the citizens of the city, not commercial or industrial use, and that it could never be sold. The sale was conditional upon the city accepting the terms of the covenant. Council held a referendum to approve the expenditure of $55,000 to purchase the roughly eleven and a half acres of land, a price that was acknowledged at the time to be well below the market value of the property. The citizens approved the expenditure, and the terms of the covenant had also been well publicized. There was both an implicit and explicit awareness of the terms of the Simpson Covenant during a succession of municipal administrations.

The covenant was never questioned until 2002, when a developer proposed the construction of a cluster of high-rise condos on the waterfront, at the foot of Queensway Avenue. The plan encroached on approximately one third of the city's lakeshore property. City staff approached Stanley Simpson's descendants, who continue to live in Kelowna, in an effort to get their agreement to change the boundaries of covenanted land. Many meetings, over several years, ensued with various Simpson family members. The family would not, nor did they feel they had the right to agree to any changes to the original agreement.

In an unexpected move and at an open council meeting in April 2004, Kelowna City Council unanimously voted to remove the historic Simpson Covenant, which had been attached to the civic centre properties for the previous fifty-eight years. Council determined the covenant was no longer valid and the City of Kelowna was no longer legally bound nor restricted by it. The response from both the public and the Simpson family was swift. The public were outraged, and the family immediately filed a notice of intended legal action. The Save the Heritage Simpson Covenant Society formed to reflect the broad community support and to challenge the city's decision. Most felt it was an attempt to rewrite history, and seen as disrespectful of both Stanley Simpson and the citizens and council that had made the original agreement.

In 2007, the society filed a petition in the Supreme Court of BC to bring an end to the legal questions surrounding the Simpson Covenant. After a two-day hearing the following year, the Supreme Court ruled that the "Simpson Covenants are a valid and subsisting charitable trust" and as such, the terms of the original covenant, namely "that the land shall be maintained and used for the enjoyment of Kelowna citizens, that there shall be no commercial or industrial use of the land, and that the land shall not be sold," remain in force.

The judgement affirmed that the civic centre lands belong to the citizens of Kelowna and that they are held, in trust, by the City of Kelowna. The judgement also awarded the society costs. Mr. Smithwick's legal services were provided pro bono, but there were still significant legal costs incurred which were paid by donations to the society by outraged citizens. The City of Kelowna appealed the court's decision; however, facing an upcoming civic election and an angry electorate, it withdrew the appeal.

Today, the civic centre lands provide a unique core to the sprawling city. The Memorial Arena was the first building on the property. The city hall followed, as did a curling rink, a public health centre, a library, an art gallery and a museum. The arena (with the Okanagan Military Museum as an addition), the Kelowna Historical Museum and city hall, with many renovations and additions, remain today. Stuart Park is now on the lakeshore portion of the original properties. The vision of Kelowna's early citizens that their city needed a civic centre for the use and enjoyment of future residents has been reaffirmed, and the legal documents that supported the society's position have now been lodged in the Kelowna Public Archives, in case they should ever be needed again.

THESE WERE TRANSFORMATIVE YEARS

As the last century drew to a close, a pent-up demand for jobs and housing exploded, and by 2002 Kelowna's population exceeded the 100,000 mark. The surrounding trading area mushroomed to about 450,000 people and the city became the primary hub for commercial, retail, business and health care services between Vancouver and Calgary. A significant niche market developed in vacation homes and housing prices became among the most expensive in the country.

Kelowna booms when real estate booms, and the economic slump that hit the world in 2008 also hit the city. Most development abruptly ground to a halt, plans for significant projects were shelved and a bold proposal to transform a four-block slice of downtown into several high-rise towers met with such opposition that it too was set aside for reconsideration. In the past decade or so, condo towers have begun filling open spaces in what had previously been the industrial part of town and people moved into the city's cultural district. The area is rich with art galleries, sculpture, parks and walkways edging the lake. Information kiosks tell of the area's industrial past, and unique signage, lighting and benches have created a showpiece for the community. It has been a remarkable makeover.

The few remaining industries left in the north end are gradually moving to the edges of town. The sawmill remains, though production has slowed, and a single rail line still hauls lumber and wood chips out of the valley and delivers tank cars to Sun-Rype in the process. The most significant recent residential development has been in Okanagan

Mission, and while Rutland has been able to hang onto its rural origins longer than other areas, it too has seen an increase in house construction. Development in Glenmore continues on the hillsides and in areas once covered by orchards.

Kelowna still has a substantial agricultural land base within its boundaries, with orchards, vineyards, pastures and hayfields scattered throughout the city. Gordon Drive, Valley Road, Byrns Road and Benvoulin Road, along with a few others, have become identifiable dividing lines between rural and residential.

OF LEADERS AND CHARACTERS

Community leaders and community characters are sometimes best determined in hindsight rather than by current newspaper headlines—or having a park, a street or a building named after them. Lord and Lady Aberdeen served as leaders when they made the Okanagan Valley a desirable place to live by having homes here and encouraging others to join them. Lequime, Boyce and Sutherland all left their mark on early Kelowna by creating the town or making it a better place to live.

"Turkey" Turner was a character who, though apparently educated at Oxford, lived in a shack with his turkeys in the north end of town. They sat on his table and on his bed, and were, by all accounts, his favourite companions. When he ran low on funds, the reservoir on the hillside above him somehow sprung a leak, and when the resulting flood wiped out his house and did in some of his turkeys, the compensation was enough for him to live on until his money ran out and the same thing happened again. And again.

Then there was Dr. Campbell who, during the later years of the Depression, built a preventorium and collected underprivileged children from around the region. He made sure they were fed fresh milk and vegetables daily, slept outdoors in screened-in porches, and then got plenty of exercise, fresh air and sunshine. He may have saved them all from getting tuberculosis.

And there was Maggie Smith, a long, lanky lady who was always seen around town with her glassy-eyed fox stole over her shoulders and a stylish hat at a jaunty angle. She had the mouth of a stevedore. When she got into her cups, she would terrify every shopkeeper into shaving cents off a dozen eggs or a bar of soap, or talk any housewife she called on for tea into parting with her favourite elegant hat. They all added colour to small-town Kelowna, which tolerated their quirkiness.

If there was a poll today to ask about Kelowna's most influential or most colourful characters, it's unlikely there would be much unanimity. It would be challenging to come up with a politician who garnered widespread admiration. Even identifying someone as quietly influential behind the scenes would likely be a problem. Perhaps it was Reverend Albert Baldeo, who passed away in May 2011. He was a unique combination of both colourful character and influential leader, and was much admired by many in the community. Albert, as he was most commonly known, and his wife, Beryl, arrived in Kelowna in 1981; he was the new minister for St. Paul's United Church, and she was his devoted sidekick. The church, conservative Kelowna and Albert were an unlikely match: he was, according to his obituary, "part passionate prophet and part stand-up comedian." He was born in Trinidad and, being a short cherubic figure, he didn't take up much room at centre stage. He did, however, have a great sense of humour and an enthusiastic singing voice, which he never hesitated to use, even when it might not have been in tune. Though the early years may have been challenging, he welcomed everyone and filled his pews.

Albert was a leader and a character. Over the years he rallied the community behind the RCMP when the tide of public opinion was against them, he prayed for and sustained the victims of the 2003 wildfire, and he cared for and protected the family of a young murder victim. He wrote poems for everyone and for every occasion, for people he knew and those he didn't. He visited patients in the hospital when he was sick enough to be in a hospital bed himself. "He was Kelowna's Chaplain, its Spiritual Concierge." He was the most ecumenical of ministers and never hesitated to remind those of other denominations or other faiths that once they all arrived in heaven, they would all be united—or perhaps, for Albert, it was United. Hundreds attended his funeral, and left the service with smiles on their faces.

WHERE WE ARE TODAY...

The Okanagan has been transformed since Father Pandosy walked over the mountains and into the valley. The landscape changed as cattle ranges were subdivided into orchards and then, in more recent years, transplanted with vineyards. Sparse settlements grew to become villages, and those that survived became towns. In recent years, many have grown into more substantial communities. A continuous string of lights now defines a shoreline of Okanagan Lake, which was once unoccupied wilderness. And as Kelowna has grown and changed, so have its neighbours.

The District of Lake Country

Early residents travelled the wagon roads from Father Pandosy's Mission northward through the Postill Ranch and past Duck, Wood and Kalamalka Lakes, on their way to Vernon, the largest and most prosperous of the valley's early communities. The settlements of Winfield and Oyama grew as orchards flourished and it wasn't long before schools, churches and stores were providing for local residents. On the other side of the hills, Okanagan Centre took advantage of its setting on Okanagan Lake and became a bustling community with its own wharf, two packinghouses, a cannery and hotel. Nearby Carr's Landing remained rural as settlers planted orchards and formed a tight-knit community.

The area was growing so rapidly and changing so substantially by 1995 that the District of Lake Country was incorporated to provide better local control of future development. While all four communities preserve their own identity, a town centre is emerging below the intervening highway and the area focusses on its agricultural heritage and the arts. Lake Country is in the midst of creating a unique Okanagan niche for itself.

West Kelowna

Westbank had its historic roots in the fur brigades that travelled through the area in the mid-1800s. When settlers arrived, their wharves and packinghouse were located in Gellatly Bay and then along the lakeshore, including at Siwash Point, Bear Creek and Wilson's Landing. Before it was easy to get across Okanagan Lake, settlers on the west side of it loosely formed their own communities.

Westbank, however, came to embody the rampant growth taking place in the Central Okanagan: with almost thirty thousand residents by 2007, it was the largest unincorporated area in the province. It was a challenging transition, but that year the District of West Kelowna was incorporated. The district includes the communities of Westbank and Lakeview Heights, which had been the agricultural land originally settled by World War II veterans as well as the area overlooking Okanagan Lake previously known as West Kelowna Estates and the small settlements along Westside Road. Challenging traffic patterns, defining a town centre, containing the sprawling community and creating its own identity are among West Kelowna's challenges today.

The Westbank First Nation

The most substantial changes in the Central Okanagan have taken place within the Westbank First Nation and on Tsinstikeptum Indian Reserves Nos. 9 and 10. Big box stores and shopping centres now line Highway 97, and new residential developments house about eight thousand non-Native residents on the reserve. The area has been transformed, and major highway upgrades and interchanges have reconfigured the landscape. The Westbank First Nation, in partnership with the province, also managed the construction of the new west side accesses to the William R. Bennett Bridge. Two tall steel sculptures featuring the band's logo—which incorporates a full moon, a bear's paw and a howling wolf—tower over the roadway. A second interchange project near the band's office, also managed by the Westbank First Nation, is currently underway. It will incorporate significant commercial development.

The Westbank First Nation has been developing and updating land-use plans for its reserve lands since 1973. The band membership is currently about 650, half of whom live on the reserve. In recent years the band's council has created a number of new opportunities for its members, built solid relationships with developers and attracted high-profile tenants to the commercial ventures on the reserve's property. By encouraging economic growth and creating a community in which its members can both flourish and lead, the Westbank First Nation has carved a unique place for itself within both the Okanagan and Canada.

Kelowna

Even though the city is more than one hundred years old, Kelowna still finds it challenging to figure out what it wants to look like when it grows up. Despite recent moves to ensure Kelowna preserves its heritage, the realities of the decision made in the 1950s to route the major highway though the centre of town leaves a legacy of strip malls, big box stores and shopping centres. Newcomers driving through town along Highway 97 soon realize they could be in any sprawling city, anywhere.

Kelowna City Council's intent to cluster residential and commercial development in certain neighbourhoods is paying dividends, though some areas are still trying to find their way. Others, such as South Pandosy, have creatively adapted. The troublesome area remains the downtown core. Despite some wonderful restorations of the old one- and two-storey buildings constructed of Knox Mountain brick, the community's cultural life flourishes on one side of Bernard Avenue while on the other side

Kelowna celebrated its one hundredth anniversary in 2005. Stuart Park, which was to commemorate the event, opened in 2010 with a modern whimsical grizzly bear sculpture as its centrepiece. It's a tribute to "Kelowna," which translates as "grizzly bear" in the Sylix language. The whimsical sculpture was created by artist Brower Hatcher and features "objects which represent the city's inner landscape," including colourful apples and pears, flowers, and fish nestled inside the body of the creature. | STUART KERNAGHAN, XYPHOTOS.CA

buildings are boarded up, land is vacant and people who are struggling to manage their lives congregate. Some advocate that the space be filled with high-rises; others are adamant that scale and history matter and need to be respected. Low-rise, high-density developments that respect and enhance the scale of what remains of Kelowna's main street could create a vibrant, healthy downtown. Kelowna today reaps the benefits of decisions made in the past. In time, today's choices will also become part of Kelowna's history. Let's hope they are wise and respectful of the decisions made by our predecessors.

A TIMELINE FOR KELOWNA

The S-Ookanhkchinx, the Interior Salish peoples, lived in the Okanagan before the arrival of the first Europeans. They travelled the valley according to the season—hunting and gathering, and fishing for the kokanee that spawned in Mission Creek—and then settled in family communities for the winter. They were small, independent bands who peacefully traded with other indigenous people living along the lakes and rivers of the Okanagan.

Our recorded history begins with the arrival of the first Europeans, whose explorations brought them to the Okanagan Valley in 1811. There are several milestones that mark the settlement of the area and the creation of Kelowna. Some dates are pivotal to the development of the community and are easily remembered. Others get lost to time. When no one makes note of a significant community event, or the opening of a major park, or when a new building appears or disappears from the civic centre site, it may not matter in the day-to-day scheme of things. However, these details do matter when one is telling stories of how and why and in what ways Kelowna has changed. As a result, I've compiled a more exhaustive timeline than might otherwise be indicated. I hope it will be a useful framework for those in the future who will build on to the stories in this volume.

1811 – David Stuart of the Pacific Fur Company arrives in Astoria (now Oregon) and joins David Thompson as he retraces his paddle strokes up the Columbia River. Stuart left the explorer at the confluence of the Okanogan River and continued through the Okanagan Valley en route to Fort Cumloops (Kamloops). He discovered a route to connect the Fraser River to the Columbia River and a port on the Pacific Ocean. This route became known as the Okanagan Fur Brigade Trail.

1811 to 1826 – Intermittent use of the Okanagan Fur Brigade Trail.

1826 to 1846 – Regular use of the Okanagan Fur Brigade Trail.

1846 – The international boundary is established at the forty-ninth parallel. The fur brigades are now diverted to Fort Langley, BC.

1848 to 1855 – California gold rush: as discoveries diminish, miners gradually move northward to BC, following the promise of gold.

1858 – Gold is discovered at Rock Creek, BC. The BC gold rush begins, including along creeks near what will become Kelowna.

– Mainland BC becomes a British colony.

– Palmer and Miller wagon train passes through the Okanagan, bringing cattle, miners and supplies from the Oregon Territory.

1859 – Father Pandosy establishes Okanagan Mission, which he calls L'Anse au Sable.

1861 – Eli Lequime and family arrive at Father Pandosy's Mission.

1862 – Cariboo gold rush begins; miners and cattle travel through the Okanagan en route to the Central Interior.

– Auguste Gillard pre-empts land that will become the Kelowna townsite.

1871 – Fredrick Brent establishes the first grist mill in the valley.

– BC enters Confederation.

1875 – First wagon road is built between Priest's Landing (near Vernon) and Okanagan Mission.

1883 – Rancher A.B. Knox arrives in Kelowna and ranches on land to the north and east of what will become the Kelowna townsite.

1885 – Canadian Pacific Railway company completes the transcontinental railway.

1888 – Eli Lequime leaves the Okanagan for San Francisco.

1890 – Bernard Lequime buys the future Kelowna townsite property from Auguste Gillard.

– G.G. MacKay buys land in the Mission Valley.

– Lord and Lady Aberdeen buy the Guisachan property, sight unseen, from MacKay.

1891 – Father Pandosy dies.

– Bernard Lequime moves his sawmill and builds a general store on the lakeshore of what will become the Kelowna townsite.

1892 – City of Vernon incorporated.

– Benvoulin townsite registered by MacKay.

– Kelowna townsite registered by Bernard Lequime.

– Shuswap & Okanagan Railway is completed, linking the CPR mainline at Sicamous, through Vernon, to Okanagan Landing.

– SS *Aberdeen* launched—the first of the CPR's fleet of sternwheelers on Okanagan Lake.

– Lake View Hotel is built in Kelowna.

A Timeline for Kelowna

1893 – Lord Aberdeen becomes Governor General of Canada.

– First Kelowna post office opens.

1894 – Louis Holman plants the first tobacco in Okanagan Mission.

– Dr. Boyce, the town's first doctor, arrives in Kelowna.

1895 – Father Pandosy's Oblates of Mary Immaculate move their headquarters from Okanagan Mission to Kamloops.

1902 – Father Pandosy's church at Okanagan Mission is closed.

1902 to 1903 – J.H. Rutland arrives from Australia, and irrigates and plants new orchards in the area soon to be called Rutland.

1904 – Bank of Montreal opens in Kelowna.

– *Kelowna Clarion*, Kelowna's first newspaper, is established.

– Kelowna Land and Orchard Company is formed and buys 6,743 acres from the Lequime family.

– A four-room school house is built in Kelowna.

1905 – Kelowna is incorporated as a city on May 5, with a population of about six hundred people.

– The Palace Hotel becomes Kelowna's second hotel; it later becomes the Royal Anne Hotel.

1906 – First Kelowna Regatta is held.

1907 – SS *Okanagan* is launched—the second CPR sternwheeler.

1908 – Kelowna hospital opens.

1909 – City pays thirty thousand dollars for the land that will soon become City Park.

– First Kelowna High School opens.

1911 – Kelowna Volunteer Fire Brigade is officially formed.

– Cornerstone laid for St. Michael and All Angels Anglican Church.

– Cornerstone laid for the second Immaculate Conception Catholic Church on Sutherland Avenue.

1912 – Maternity wing added to Kelowna hospital.

1913 – Kelowna Public School (now called Central School) opens on Richter Street.

1914 – SS *Sicamous* launched—the last and grandest CPR sternwheeler.

1922 – Glenmore incorporated as a municipality.

1925 – Canadian National Railway arrives in Kelowna.

1926 – Countess Bubna, owner of the Eldorado Ranch, builds the Eldorado Arms Hotel.

– Air charter services become available from Rutland airfield.

1927 – MV *Kelowna–Westbank* (aka MV *Hold-up*) begins scheduled ferry service between Kelowna and Westbank.

1929 – Original Kelowna Junior High School is built on Richter Street.

1930 – Oil wells are drilled at Mission and Canyon Creeks, in Okanagan Mission.

– Stanley M. Simpson purchases Manhattan Beach property and soon builds a sawmill, a veneer plant and a box factory.

1931 – Kelowna's first commercial radio station, CKOV, begins broadcasting.

– First Regatta queen contest.

1933 – Domestic Winery and By-products becomes Calona Wines.

1937 – New art deco Kelowna Post Office is built.

1939 – Kelowna Senior High School is built at the north end of the Kelowna Junior High School.

– MV *Pendozi* ferry is launched to provide service between Kelowna and Westbank.

– Dr. Boyce sells the 190-acre Okanagan Mountain Park to Kelowna for one dollar.

1940 – New fireproof wing is added to the Kelowna Hospital.

1945 – Kelowna Yacht Club established.

1946 – Kelowna purchases Ellison Field for an airport.

– BC Fruit Processors start up a juice plant in Kelowna, using the brand name Sun-Rype.

– Kelowna ratepayers approve purchase of property from S.M. Simpson and the Kelowna Saw Mill for use as a civic centre.

1947 – MV *Lequime* becomes the second Okanagan Lake ferry.

1948 – Province inundated by floods, including the Okanagan Valley.

– Kelowna Memorial Arena is dedicated.

1949 – Hope–Princeton Highway opens.

1950 – MV *Lloyd-Jones* launched—it is the third and last Okanagan Lake ferry.

1951 – Kelowna's new city hall opens.

1952 – W.A.C. Bennett of Kelowna becomes first Social Credit premier of BC.

1955 – Kelowna celebrates fiftieth anniversary of its incorporation.

– Jubilee Bowl opens in City Park.

– New provincial court house opens across from Kelowna City Hall

1957 – "The Okanagan's Very Own CHBC-TV" goes to air.

1958 – Okanagan Lake Bridge is opened by Princess Margaret and Premier Bennett.

– Kelowna Packers are the first Western hockey team to play behind the Iron Curtain.

1959 – Capri Mall opens.

1962 – Kelowna Community Theatre opens.

1963 – BC Vocational School opens on KLO Road.

1967 – Mission Hill Winery opens.

1968 – Okanagan College begins classes.

1969 – Kelowna Aquatic Club destroyed by fire.

1971 – Kelowna's art deco post office is demolished and replaced by the federal building on Queensway.

– BC Vocational School and Okanagan College amalgamate.

1973 – Okanagan Mission, Rutland and Glenmore are amalgamated into a greater Kelowna.

– Agricultural Land Reserve legislation is passed. About half of Kelowna's land base is designated agricultural.

1975 – W.R. (Bill) Bennett, son of W.A.C. Bennett, is elected Social Credit MLA and premier.

1977 – The *Spirit of Sail* sculpture is installed at the foot of Bernard Avenue.

– Kelowna Art Gallery is created.

1978 – Construction of new Okanagan College buildings begins on the KLO site.

1980 – Uniacke Winery founded (becomes CedarCreek Estate Winery in 1986).

1981 – Bennett Clock is installed at the foot of Pandosy Street, to commemorate W.A.C. Bennett.

1986 – Coquihalla Highway opens.

1986 – First Kelowna Regatta riot.

1987 – Second Kelowna Regatta riot. After eighty-one years, the Kelowna International Regatta is cancelled.

1988 – Laurel Packinghouse restored and named Kelowna's first heritage building.

1989 – Okanagan College begins conferring University of British Columbia and University of Victoria degrees.

1990 – Okanagan College purchases a new site near Kelowna Airport (opens there in 1993).

1991 – Coquihalla Connector opens: the shortest, most direct route to the Lower Mainland.

1993 – R. Dow Reid's *Rhapsody* sculpture is added to the Waterfront Park fountain.

1994 – New BC Supreme Court building opens.

1995 – Kelowna's Waterfront Park officially opens.

– Okanagan College officially becomes Okanagan University College.

1996 – Kelowna Art Gallery opens in its new home in the Cultural District.

– New downtown Kelowna branch of Okanagan Regional Library opens.

– First phase of the Mission Creek Greenway is announced.

1999 – Prospera Place opens.

– Laurel Packinghouse receives National Historic Site designation.

– BC Cancer Agency for the Southern Interior opens.

2001 – The original BC Court House, across from city hall, is torn down.

2002 – Rotary Centre for the Arts opens, including the Mary Irwin Theatre.

2003 – Okanagan Mountain Fire sweeps across the mountainside south of Kelowna.

– North campus of Okanagan University College becomes UBC Okanagan.

2005 – Kelowna quietly celebrates its hundredth anniversary (Stuart Park, celebrating the landmark date, opens five years later).

– UBCO officially opens.

– Second phase of Mission Creek Greenway opens.

2008 – W.R. Bennett Bridge opens—Kelowna's second bridge across Okanagan Lake.

2010 – Grizzly bear statue unveiled at Stuart Park.

SOURCES

Aberdeen and Temair, Ishbel Gordon. *Through Canada with a Kodak*. Toronto, ON: University of Toronto Press, 1994.

Anderson, Kyle, and Jo Ann Reynolds, compilers. *The Century in Review, 1900–1999: An Okanagan Perspective*. Kelowna, BC: Okanagan Valley Newspaper Group, 1999.

Battye, Clement. *Okanagan Valley (Edenholme) 1900–1966*. Penticton, BC: Penticton Writers and Publishers (PWAP), 1966.

Bealby, J.T. *Fruit Ranching in British Columbia*. London, UK: Adam and Charles Black, 1909.

Boyko, John. *Last Steps to Freedom: The Evolution of Canadian Racism*. Revised ed. Winnipeg, MB: J. Gordon Shillingford Publishing, 1998.

Buckland, F.M. *Ogopogo's Vigil: A History of Kelowna and the Okanagan*. Kelowna, BC: Okanagan Historical Society, 1966, reprinted 1979.

Dendy, David, and Kathleen M. Kyle. *A Fruitful Century: The British Columbia Fruit Growers' Association, 1889–1989*. Kelowna, BC: British Columbia Fruit Growers' Association, 1990.

Freake, Ross, and Don Plant, eds. *Firestorm: The Summer BC Burned*. Toronto, ON: McClelland & Stewart, 2003.

Freake, Ross. *OUC Memoirs*. Kelowna, BC: Okanagan University College, 2005.

From Slates to Blackboards to Computers: A History of Public Schools in the Central Okanagan. Kelowna, BC: The Educational Heritage Committee of the Central Okanagan Retired Teachers Association, 1999.

Gaal, Arlene. *In Search of Ogopogo: Sacred Creature of the Okanagan Waters*. Surrey, BC: Hancock House, 2001.

Gillespie, T.L. *History of the KLO Benches: Their Tragedies and Comedies*. Introduced and edited by Wayne Wilson. Kelowna, BC: Kelowna Museums Society, 2009

Glenmore Centennial Committee. *Glenmore: The Apple Valley*. Kelowna, BC: Glenmore Centennial Committee, 1958.

Gray, Art. *Kelowna: Tales of Bygone Days*. Reprinted from articles in the *Kelowna Daily Courier*, 1962–63. Kelowna, BC: Kelowna Printing, 1968.

Hayman, Len. *Captain Len's Ferry Tales of the Okanagan*. Collected by his son, Bob Hayman. Kelowna, BC: self-published, 1988.

Holliday, C.W. *The Valley of Youth*. Caldwell, ID: Caxton Printers, 1948.

Holt, Simma. *Terror in the Name of God: The Story of the Sons of Freedom Doukhobors*. Toronto, ON: McClelland & Stewart, 1964.

Jones, Jo Fraser, ed. *Hobnobbing with a Countess and Other Okanagan Adventures: The Diaries of Alice Barrett Parke, 1891–1900*. Vancouver, BC: UBC Press, 2001.

Kelowna Museum. *Kelowna: One Hundred Years of History, 1905–2005*. Kelowna, BC: Kelowna Museum, 2005.

Kelowna Street Names: Their Origins—A Brief History. Second ed. Kelowna, BC: Okanagan Historical Society, 2010.

Kelowna: One Hundred Years of History, 1905–2005. Kelowna, BC: Kelowna Publishers, 2005.

Metke, Evelyn R. *Ninety Years of Golf: A Chronology of Golf in Kelowna*. Kelowna, BC: self-published, 1992.

Middleton, R.M., ed. *The Journal of Lady Aberdeen: The Okanagan Valley in the Nineties*. Victoria, BC: Morriss Publishing, 1986.

Plecas, Bob. *Bill Bennett: A Mandarin's View*. Vancouver, BC: Douglas & McIntyre, 2006.

Rutland Centennial Committee. *History of the District of Rutland, British Columbia, 1858–1958*. Kelowna, BC: Rutland Centennial Committee, 1958.

Sanford, Barrie. *McCulloch's Wonder: The Story of the Kettle Valley Railway*. Vancouver, BC: Whitecap Books, 1978.

Schreiner, John. *A Wine Journal: CedarCreek Estate Winery*. Kelowna, BC: CedarCreek Estate Winery, 2003.

Schreiner, John. *John Schreiner's Okanagan Wine Tour Guide*. Third ed. North Vancouver, BC: Whitecap Books, 2010.

Simpson, Sharron J. *Boards, Boxes, and Bins: Stanley M. Simpson and the Okanagan Lumber Industry*. Kelowna, BC: Manhattan Beach Publishing, 2003.

Simpson, Sharron J. *Kelowna General Hospital: The First 100 Years*. Kelowna, BC: Manhattan Beach Publishing, 2008.

Staff of the Vernon Museum. *Steamboats of the Okanagan*. Vernon, BC: Vernon Museum, 1978.

Surtees, Ursula. *Kelowna: The Orchard City*. Burlington, ON: Windsor Publications, 1989.

Surtees, Ursula. *Sunshine and Butterflies: A Short History of Early Fruit Ranching in Kelowna*. Kelowna, BC: Kelowna Centennial Museum/ Regatta City Press, 1979.

Vielvoye, Evelyn, and Elaine Senger. *Down Memory Lane: Rutland 1908–2008*. Kelowna, BC: self-published by the authors, 2008.

Williams, Maurice. *Myra's Men: Building the Kettle Valley Railway, Myra Canyon to Penticton*. Kelowna, BC: Myra Canyon Trestle Restoration Society, 2008.

OTHER RESOURCES

The Okanagan Historical Society's annual reports have been published almost every year since the 1930s. Together, these reports are an astounding collection of stories that are often the only record of the changing life and times in the Okanagan Valley. They are a remarkable, much treasured and invaluable source of information.

The *Kelowna Daily Courier* often includes stories about the town's early days, in addition to reporting on current happenings. I've often referred to their articles for stories about Kelowna's history.

Internet resources have revolutionized the way we learn about our history. I delved often, and with relief that so much information is available so readily. Most of it supported information I was researching from other sources. I'm grateful to those whose material is online for all to use.

ACKNOWLEDGEMENTS

I am delighted to have the opportunity to work with Harbour Publishing, the publisher of this history of Kelowna. As I've written the stories, chosen the photographs and commissioned the maps to ensure this book is worthy of its topic, I've realized that publishing is akin to handing over your small child, expecting it to be returned to you well formed and looking good. It's a daunting leap of faith, and I've taken comfort in Harbour's standing as one of BC's finest publishers.

An unexpected bonus of this connection with Harbour has been working with Pam Robertson, editor of this book. Pam's familiarity with the area has bridged a gap that might have otherwise required more explaining. I am in awe of her skill and ability in finding the errors in pages I've read many times and am certain are perfect. Her perspective and her suggestions about reordering and reorganizing have made this a much more readable and entertaining story. I am grateful for her support and the insight she has brought to all the various stages of this project. It has been my great pleasure to have been able to work with her. There are so many people who have been interested in this book and involved in its preparation. The risk in mentioning any of them is that some will inevitably be left out. I apologize to them and thank them for sharing their recollections, books, photos and memorabilia. Many are local historians in their own right. Some, such as Dorothy Zoellner and Alice Lundy, are both wonderful repositories of information and friends. They have generously answered my questions and happily shared their recollections. I am indebted to them.

Connie and Mark W. Smith shared photos and documents about Kelowna's Mr. Regatta, Mayor Dick Parkinson. Diane Knowles and Sylvia Knowles shared photos passed on to them by their father, Bill. Jerry Vansom shared his interesting collection of local files, photos and memorabilia. Jennifer Hindle remembered the Eldorado Arms with affection and great stories. Linda Brena-Ghezzi Ben-Hamida shared her father's files about the early days at Calona Wines.

Bob and Bernice DeMara had stories and photos of the Willow Inn Hotel and Lodge from when they were among Kelowna's finest facilities. Ruby Poonian shared photos and information about the Rutland School Legacy project. As I scouted locations for taking photos to showcase the seasonal beauty of our orchards, I encountered Ed Hoffman and his picking crew in Glenmore, who generously allowed photos to be taken of their apple harvesting.

Kathy Butler at Okanagan College provided *OC Memories*, which was a great and previously undiscovered source of information. Penny Gambell shared her remarkable recollection, her perspective and her experience in the valley's apple industry. I appreciated Penny's willingness to share her knowledge and her concerns about the future of the troubled industry. Senator Ross Fitzpartick has been involved in the valley's wine industry from its early days and willingly shared his knowledge and views of the future. Harald Hall, a colleague from my city hall days, recalled the changes in Kelowna during the 1990s and agreed that these were the years when Kelowna built its heart: we had a wonderful time reminiscing. Brenda Fournier eased the way to finding photos of UBCO, while Judy Ohs and Kaye Benzer, who have encyclopedic knowledge of the Glenmore Valley, ensured I had both photos and stories to incorporate into Kelowna's history. The staff of the Glenmore–Ellison Improvement District generously loaned photos and seemed unfazed when I took pictures off their walls.

Choosing, taking, scanning and placing the photos that are such an integral part of Kelowna's story, and this book, has been a challenging task. I am grateful to those who helped make this happen. Peter at Kettle Valley Graphics, who took old photos and restored them so they could be used. The always affable and superbly organized Harry Brust at Quest for Success looked after photos from the Kelowna Public Archives and then generously made some of his own fine photographs available to me. Donna Johnson and Tara Hurley, the archivists at the Kelowna Heritage Museum, helped me find photos and made sure they were sent onward. Their assistance was invaluable and I am immensely grateful to them both. The Kelowna Public Archives are a rich and undervalued resource, and Kelowna's story would be so much less without them. Kelowna artist Neil Thacker created the funky maps that make my recounting of the early communities come to life. I am grateful he agreed to add his talents to this book.

The support of my family over the life of this project has been crucial to its form, its character and its completion. My daughter, Catherine, has been interested and supportive and ensured I have had the space and time to write and to put this book together. My son, Stuart, has willingly shared his considerable knowledge about writing and editing, and then reminded me to back up the backup. Stuart has also organized and refined my photos so they can be included, and added his own—he is a superb and published photographer in his own right. He took most of the current photos found throughout this volume. I am grateful to them both for their support and encouragement. I'm also grateful to Payton and James, who have been patiently waiting for me to come out to play.